Before Our
Very Eyes

Fake Wars and Big Lies

From 9/11 to Donald Trump

by

Thierry Meyssan

ProgRESSive

2019

Before Our Very Eyes

Fake Wars and Big Lies

From 9/11 to Donald Trump

by Thierry Meyssan © Progressivepress.com, 2018

First Edition, Published Feb. 22, 2019

Length: 105,000 words on 285 pages

ISBN 1-61577-012-7, EAN 9781615770120

Translated by Pete Kimberley from the original French edition entitled
Sous Nos Yeux, de 9 septembre à Donald Trump,
from Collection Résistances, Editions Demi Lune

Library of Congress Subject Headings

Terrorism, ISIS: HV6433.I722   Muslim Brotherhood: BP10.I385
Syrian Civil War 2011- : DS 98.6   Libyan Civil War 2011- : DT 236
Imperialism: E713   Conspiracies: HV6275

BISAC Subject Area Codes

POL037000 Political Science / Terrorism
POL061000 Political Science / Genocide & War Crimes
POL045000 Political Science / Colonialism & Post-Colonialism
HIS027170 History / Military / Iraq War (2003-2011)
SOC058000 / POL506000 Conspiracy Investigations

Cover photo: the inverted reality of the war on Syria, turned upside down by the controlled media: Massive *pro-government* demonstrations took place in Damascus, rather than "Arab Spring protests."

"Syrian media showed demonstrations of millions of people against US intervention – practically the whole able-bodied population was out on the streets waving the real Syrian flag. Western media ignored that, and made a big show over tiny anti-Assad protests, numbering a few knots of people, at most a couple hundred, many of them likely hired, hungry beggars. The media with their fakery are absolutely guilty of enabling these war crimes, which could never occur without their "coverage" (or rather, coverups.)" – *ISIS IS U.S.*, p. 144

By the same author:

• La Protection des homosexuels dans le droit européen, with Thierry Montchâtre and Antoine Ulma, Projet Ornicar (Paris), 1993 (ISBN 2-910209-00-8)
• L'Intégration des transsexuels (2 volumes), with Thierry Montchâtre and Antoine Ulma, Projet Ornicar (Paris), 1993 (ISBN 2-910209-01-6)
• Charles Millon, le porte-glaive, Collectif, Golias (Lyon), 1998 (ISBN 2911453395)
• L'Énigme Pasqua, Golias (Lyon), 2000 (ISBN 2911453883)
• Terrorisme en soutane: Jean-Paul II contre l'IVG by the Voltaire Network for the freedom of expression, L'Esprit frappeur (Paris), 2000 (ISBN 2844051413)
• L'Effroyable imposture, Carnot (Paris), 2002 (ISBN 291236244X); The Big Lie (English edition) 2002 (ISBN 1592090265)
• Le Pentagate, Carnot (Paris), 2002 (ISBN 2912362776), Pentagate (English Edition) 2002 (ISBN 2912362768)
• Os Senhores da Guerra, Frenesi (Lisbonne), 2002 (ISBN 972-8351-67-4)
• Préface (with Jean Ziegler) du Cartel Bush by James Hatfield, Timéli (Genève), 2004 (ISBN 2-940342-05-9)
• Politicamente Incorrecto, Collective, postface by Fidel Castro, Ciencias sociales (La Havane), 2004 (ISBN 959-06-0640-7)
• Préface (with José Saramago) de El Neron del siglo XXI, Apostrofe (Madrid), 2004 (ISBN 844550258-1)
• L'Effroyable imposture 1 et Le Pentagate, new annotated edition, éditions Demi-Lune, 2007 (ISBN 978-2-952557-16-0)
• Resistere alla menzogna in Zero, Perché la versione ufficiale sull'11/9 è un falso (with Giulietto Chiesa), Piemme (Milan), 2007 (ISBN 978-88-384-6838-4)
• L'Effroyable Imposture 2. Manipulations et désinformation, éditions Alphée-Jean-Paul Bertrand (Paris), 2007 (ISBN 9782753802391)
• Postface and annexes (with Tariq Ramadan) for Yasser Arafat, intime d'Isabel Pisano, éditions Demi-lune, 2009 (ISBN 9782917112069)

Documentary:

• Syria, 10 years of Resistance (6 programmes), Syrian National Television, 2014.

"Every State has the duty to refrain from organizing, instigating, assisting or participating in acts of civil strife or terrorist acts in another State, or acquiescing in organized activities within its territory directed towards the commission of such acts, when the acts referred to in the present paragraph involve a threat or use of force."

Resolution 2625 of the General Assembly of the United Nations

Contents

Contents

Introduction

Knowledge is never definitive. History, like any other science, questions what we is believed to be true but which, in the light of new factors, must be modified, even refuted.

I reject the choice we are given between the dogmas and intellectual orthodoxy of the ivory towers and think tanks on one hand, and the "post-truth" era of manipulating emotional messages on the other. I am working on another level – I seek to distinguish facts from appearances, and truth from propaganda. Above all, as long as some people continue to exploit others, I do not believe that international relations can be completely democratic or truly transparent. Consequently, it is by nature impossible to see through all the tricks in real time and interpret international events with certainty as they are occurring. Truth can only come to light with the passage of time. I must accept the risk of inaccuracy in the first moment, but I never give up reviewing my first impressions and seeking to get at the truth. This is all the more difficult since the world is now plagued with wars which demand that we take sides immediately.

For my part, I have sided with the innocent people who watch strangers enter their cities and impose their alien laws there, innocent people who hear international television echoing the mantra that their leaders are tyrants and must relinquish their place to Westerners, innocent people who rebel and are quickly smashed under the bombs of NATO. I claim the role of an analyst who is attempting to see things objectively, and that of a man offering as much help as he can to those who suffer.

In writing this book, I will try to go further than current documents and witness statements. However, unlike the authors who have preceded me, I am not trying to justify my country's policies, but to understand the chain of events in which I myself have been involved, both as actor and observer.

Some will object that, contrary to my profession of good faith, I am actually trying to justify my actions, and that consciously or unconsciously, I am revealing my bias. I hope that they will participate in the search for truth and publish any documents of which I am unaware.

It so happens that my role in these events enabled me to learn and verify a number of things which are as yet unknown to the general public, and often to many of the other participants. I learned these things empirically, by direct experience. It is only over time that I have come to understand the logic behind these events.

In order to allow the reader to follow my line of enquiry, I have not written a "General History of the Arab Springs", but three partial histories, from three different points of view – that of consecutive French governments, the Muslim Brotherhood, and the authorities of the United States.

Pursuing their own objectives, the French leaders made no attempt to understand the logic of the Muslim Brotherhood, nor that of their US overlord, but sought only to win back the advantages of colonisation, and pocket as much wealth as possible. Seeking power, the Muslim Brotherhood placed themselves in the service of the United Kingdom and the United States, all the while speculating about how they could rally France to their campaign to dominate the peoples of the Middle East. Only Washington and London had a complete picture of what was happening, and what they themselves were preparing.

It is something like an onion or a Russian Matryoshka doll – it is only one layer at a time that we may uncover the organisation of events that appear spontaneous, as the origins and outcomes of certain decisions.

My own story is so different from what readers will have heard on the subject that some may become afraid of the implications of what I am writing. Others, on the contrary, will examine and understand this gigantic manipulation and begin thinking about how to put an end to it.

It is probable that this book, which exposes hundreds of facts, will contain a few errors which I shall be obliged to correct later on. It is possible that one or other of the correlations I bring to light may be due only to chance, but this will not be the case when the accumulation of facts is overwhelming.

There is no doubt that the partisans of imperialism will miss no opportunity to accuse me of spinning "conspiracy theories", to use their pet expression. It's a cheap insult which they roll out constantly. They have used it extensively ever since I contested the official version of the attacks of 11 September 2001. They persist in their denials and their lies, yet betray themselves when they publicly support al-Qaeda in Libya and Syria, while accusing it of the massacres in the United States, in France, in Belgium, etc.

Finally, once the minor errors are corrected, it is to this preponderance of the facts that all sincere readers will have to respond by proposing their own logical and coherent explanation.

Part One: The "Arab Spring" as seen from Paris

France's foreign policy, once guided by the strategic vision of Charles de Gaulle, progressively gave way to a hunt by certain people for easy money. Jacques Chirac resisted US imperialism at first, but then surrendered and mixed the affairs of state with his own personal interests. Nicolas Sarkozy served U.S. interests while negotiating, for his own benefit, anything he could get his hands on. François Hollande went even further, placing the Republic at the service of a few private interests which formed the new colonialist party. Always greedy for more money, France's venal leaders hired her out successively to Turkey, Qatar, and then Saudi Arabia.

Jacques Chirac, "the Arab"

Jacques Chirac held Hafez al-Assad in very high esteem. He saw in him an exceptional personality with a vision for his country and his region.

France had fought Al-Assad during certain phases of the Lebanese civil war, and publicly accused him of responsibility for the assassination of its ambassador in Beirut, Louis Delamare (1981). The riposte followed immediately, in the form of the terrorist attack ordered by President François Mitterrand against the National Bureau for Military Conscription in Damascus, killing 175.

After Syria's defeat by Israel in 1967, Hafez al-Assad took power, relying on support from the Ba'ath party as well as a number of adventurers, including his own brother Rifaat, who became a regular golf partner of François Mitterrand and the friend of Abdallah, the future King of Saudi Arabia. In 1982, when Rifaat was living between France and Syria, he organised an attack, on the rue Marbeuf in Paris, against the newspaper Al-Watan Al-Arab, which had criticised him. His friendship with President Mitterrand smothered the police enquiry, however, and his country was accused of the crime in his place. France expelled two Syrian diplomats, including the head of the Intelligence services, Michel Kassouha. But in the end, the affair did not weigh on the relations between the two states.

Jacques Chirac was the only foreign head of state present at the funeral of Hafez al-Assad (2000). While a wave of political opposition spread across Syria, France, which had banked on Assad being succeeded by Vice-President Abdel Halim Khaddam, finally recognised the Ba'ath party's choice of Bashar al-Assad as the next President.

Playing the mentor, Jacques Chirac – nicknamed "The Arab" because his authority was so highly considered by the regional heads of state – tried to introduce Bashar to the international stage. But the young man had no intention of allowing himself to be led. Chirac negotiated with the new President in order to gain permission for Total, France's major oil company, to exploit several of the Syrian oil fields. At the moment of the official call for tender, however, Total's proposal proved to be outrageously unfavourable. It was nonetheless backed by certain Syrian senior civil servants, including the President's economic advisor, Nibras el-Fadel, who was quickly revealed as a double agent working for Total and the Syrian-British head of Petrofac, Ayman Asfari. Learning of this corruption, Assad sanctioned Total by excluding it from the call for tender, provoking a furious reaction by Chirac.

Jacques Chirac experienced a similar disappointment in Lebanon. In the name of the French Republic, he had negotiated with his personal friend, Prime Minister Rafic Hariri, for the right to explore Lebanese territorial waters for oil. The operation was under the protection of two leaders of the Syrian Peace Force, which occupied Lebanon at the time -- the head of the Intelligence services, Ghazi Kanaan, and Vice-President Abdel Halim Khaddam. Chirac sent a French naval vessel to begin prospecting, but when Lebanese President Emile Lahoud heard about it, he summoned the French ambassador, telling him that Mr. Hariri's personal arrangements did not engage his country. The French warship was asked to leave the area.

Reacting to these calls to order, Chirac avoided speaking to the Syrian and Lebanese Presidents.

Jacques Chirac had voiced his support of the United States in the attacks of 11 September 2001, but became concerned that he had been deceived after reading my book "L'Effroyable imposture"

("The Big Lie"). He ordered the DGSE (Direction Générale de la Sécurité Extérieure, the French equivalent of the CIA) to verify my thesis. After having mobilised several hundreds of civil servants and numerous embassies, the security services replied that they were not in a position to approve the book, but that all the elements that had been available for verification – except for one quote – were exact. Chirac, who knew Saddam Hussein very well, found confirmation in the book that France should not support the Anglo-Saxon attack in the Near East.

The French Minister for Foreign Affairs, Dominique de Villepin, took his stance against Secretary of State Colin Powell. He had flown in haste to New York, leaving the dossier that the DGSE had prepared for him on the desk of his Paris office. No matter, his improvised speech on February 14, 2003 sparked unprecedented applause from the members of the United Nations Security Council, and anger from Washington. De Villepin refrained from criticising Powell's gargantuan lies – concerning President Hussein's alleged support for al-Qaeda and his programme of weapons of mass destruction – but emphasized that nothing justified the war.

At the G8 summit in Evian, France, President George W. Bush honoured the meeting with his presence for no more than a few hours. A campaign of "France-bashing" was building in the United States, and the Pentagon advisor who inspired the coup d'état of September 11, Edward Luttwak, publicly threatened President Chirac on 9 December, on the France2 TVnews programme. He declared unambiguously – "Chirac has a bill to pay in Washington! He has an expensive bill to pay in Washington. And here in Washington, obviously, we are determined to make him pay that bill. Chirac expected to wine and dine on the diplomatic stage at the expense of the United States, and obviously, he's going to pay".

Panicked, Jacques Chirac changed sides, and fell into line with all US initiatives, going as far as to let his ambassador in Tbilisi, Salome Zourabichvili, serve as Georgia's Minister for Foreign Affairs during the "Rose Revolution" (December 2003); or participating in the kidnapping of the President of Haiti, Jean-Bertrand Aristide, and having him jailed in the Central African Republic (March 2004).

Following the same line, Jacques Chirac and his friend, billionaire Rafic Hariri, wrote UN Resolution 1559, demanding the withdrawal from Lebanon of the Syrian Peace Force and the disarmament of all

Lebanese militias, including Hezbollah and the Palestinian groups. Unlike other militias, which serve a feudal warlord, or are mercenaries sponsored by a foreign state, Hezbollah is a network of resistance to Israeli colonialism, inspired by the Iranian Revolution, and was at that time armed by Syria. If applied, the resolution would result in turning Lebanon over to the Israeli army. Moreover, President Chirac decided to boycott his Lebanese counterpart, Emile Lahoud, who was not even invited to the *Sommet de la Francophonie* (Summit of French-speaking Nations).

On February 14, Rafic Hariri – who was no longer Prime Minister – was assassinated, allegedly by an explosive charge hidden in a van.

Jacques Chirac hurried to Beirut, not to take part in the funeral service, nor even to meet with Lebanese officials, but to spend an entire day with the dead man's lawyers signing private commercial documents. He then returned to Paris, while the "Cedar Revolution" was at its height in Lebanon, under the discreet supervision of Gene Sharp's crew, Washington's Serbian agitators.

Easily influenced, Jacques Chirac followed the line that Bashar al-Assad and Emile Lahoud had together plotted the murder of his friend and private business partner, Rafic Hariri. He therefore supported the United Nations Commission charged with investigating the crime, instead of the Lebanese Ministry of Justice. Over a period of several years, there followed a number of accusations levelled by the UN, global ostracism of Bashar al-Assad, and the arrest of the four generals closest to President Emile Lahoud. An international "Tribunal" was created, under the auspices of the Secretary General of the UN, Ban Ki-moon, but without the approval of the Lebanese parliament, to try the two Presidents alleged to be responsible for the assassination.

However, Jacques Chirac's obsessions did not alter Franco-Syrian cooperation. From 2003 until the suspension of diplomatic relations in 2012, Syrian intelligence kept their counterparts informed about young French citizens who wanted to go to Iraq, or who were already fighting there against the US occupation. If by chance some of them transited by Syria, they were arrested and discreetly repatriated to France by military aircraft. This cooperation allowed France to maintain public order and prevent a number of terrorist attacks on its territory. Among the jihadists extradited by Syria was Boubaker al-Hakim (the assassin of Tunisian leader Cokri Belaid) and Sabri Essid (the half-brother of Mohamed Merah, who was to become an executioner for Daesh[1]). However, not only did France interrupt this relationship during the "Arab Spring", but it also freed the accused, thanks to its alliance with the Muslim Brotherhood.

In any case, after September 2, 2005, Jacques Chirac ceased to govern. He suffered a serious stroke, and was no longer able to execute his functions, even though he would conserve them in appearance. For two years, his government was divided between the Gaullists led by Prime Minister Dominique de Villepin, and the Atlantists led by the Minister of the Interior, Nicolas Sarkozy.

During the Israeli attack on Lebanon in the summer of 2006, Villepin supported Hezbollah, whose disarmament Chirac had demanded. Once his mandate was over, Chirac no longer made any secret of his corruption, and settled into a luxurious apartment made available to him by the Hariri family for his retirement. Supported by Madame Chirac, Sarkozy took over.

Nicolas Sarkozy, American agent[2]

Nicolas Sarkozy was elected President of the French Republic in May 2007, not for his programme, but for his force of will. The French people saw in him the man who would be capable of reviving a dormant, ham-strung country. However, they were unaware that Sarkozy had been raised as an adolescent in New York by his mother Christine de Ganay, who was his father's third wife. She had remarried the diplomat Frank Wisner Jr., son of the founder of the CIA/NATO secret services, the Gladio network. This is why Sarkozy was sponsored by Washington to become the President of France.

Unlike Jacques Chirac, who had proved to be a brave Gaullist in 2003 before mutating into an unscrupulous wheeler-dealer, Nicolas Sarkozy was considered by Washington to be their man. He was immediately associated with the projects of the United States.

---

[1] Daesh, al-Dawla al-Islamiya fi al-Iraq wa al-Sham, is an Arabic acronym for ISIS, Islamic State in Iraq and Syria. Islamic extremists reportedly dislike the label "Daesh."

[2] Sarkozy, an American of Greek, Hungarian and Jewish extraction. "Bernard Kouchner... the previous foreign minister of France ... whose own father was Jewish... said that former president Nicolas Sarkozy was widely disliked because of his Jewish origins." *The Times of Israel,* Oct. 15, 2014

While he was still Minister of the Interior, Nicolas Sarkozy initiated contact with Abdullah Senussi, the head of Libyan interior secret services, and brother-in-law of Muammar Gaddafi. Senussi had been found guilty *in absentia* in France for his role in the 1989 attack on flight 772 of the French airline UTA, which caused 170 deaths. Libya proposed to finance Sarkozy's electoral campaign in exchange for a promise of amnesty or a legal decision of *nolle prosequi* (dismissal). One of Sarkozy's trusted collaborators, Brice Hortefeux, a ministerial delegate, negotiated the amount with Colonel Gaddafi. Finally, according to the senior Libyan official who had supervised the transaction, a Franco-Lebanese businessman, Ziad Takieddine, transported 57 million Euros to Paris.

During the electoral campaign, Libya noticed that the Socialist candidate, Ségolène Royal, also had a chance of winning. Senussi then made contact with the Socialist ex-Minister for Foreign Affairs, Roland Dumas, who – still according to the same source – went to Tripoli to collect 25 million Euros, about half the sum that had been offered to Mme. Royal's competitor.

French law forbids the financing of electoral campaigns by foreign states. Moreover, the cost of a political campaign is not allowed to attain these sums. Sarkozy and Royal could not promise to fabricate a legal dismissal without overriding the law and the independence of the Justice system. They could, however, pronounce an amnesty, but were not allowed to negotiate it for the benefit of their own personal affairs. Roland Dumas knew this, particularly since he was also the President of the Constitutional Council (1995-2000) charged with verifying the honesty of the election process. Accordingly, the French legal system investigated Sarkozy's indiscretions, but not those of Mme. Royal.

Business between Gaddafi and Sarkozy continued until after he had taken possession of the Elysée (the French "White House" or presidential palace). The "first lady" (*sic*), Cécilia Sarkozy,[3] was tasked with obtaining the release of five Bulgarian nurses and a Palestinian doctor, who had been imprisoned in Libya for eight years.

In 1999, more than 400 children had been contaminated by the AIDS retrovirus in Benghazi hospital. The Islamists accused Muammar

---

[3] Née Ciganer-Albeniz, of Russian-Jewish and Gypsy origins.

Gaddafi of neglecting the city of Benghazi, and of having plotted to kill their children. The local public prosecutor preferred to accuse the foreign hospital staff, in order to exonerate The Guide. He had them brutally tortured to extort their confessions.

Bulgaria, which had just joined the European Union, asked the European Commission to negotiate with Tripoli for the liberation of its citizens. Libya thus found itself face to face with the same officials who had accused it of the 1988 attack on PanAm flight 103, which exploded over Lockerbie (Scotland), causing 270 deaths. Although Muammar Gaddafi had always denied any involvement in the attack, Libya agreed to compensate the families involved for a total sum of $2.7 billion, as a means of settling the last dispute which opposed him to the Western powers.

Aware that he would have to deal with the fantasies of the Islamists, the Guide decided to use the infection in the Benghazi hospital to recover what he had been unjustly forced to pay for Lockerbie. He then demanded that this money be given back in exchange for his withdrawal from certain African states and the freedom of the nurses and the doctor. Finally, the United States paid the sum to Qatar, who in turn paid Libya, under the control of the European Union. Minister for Justice Moustafa Abdul Jalil, a member of the Muslim Brotherhood who had covered up the tortures when he was President of the Court of Appeal in Tripoli, thus came to meet President Sarkozy's emissaries. As for Cécilia – still according to the same senior Libyan official – she received a proportional gratuity from Libya ($2.7 million). Nicolas Sarkozy, who was then in the middle of his divorce proceedings, gave it to her as a present. She could now afford to open a public relations bureau, first in Qatar, later in New York, with her new husband, Richard Attias.[4] Bulgaria celebrated the liberation of its citizens, while also frowning on the way the agreement had been reached.

Now that he was "respectable" again, Muammar Gaddafi undertook a European tour, including a five-day visit to France. He caused a scandal by pitching his tent in the gardens of the Hôtel Marigny, the residence of guests of state. Above all, he declared on France 24 that

---

[4] According to her Linked-in page, she founded the Cecilia Attias Foundation for Women in 2008, and since 2016 has been a VP in Richard Attias's PR firm doing "work with governments to increase their global influence and create platforms to brand and position nations."

Libya was more democratic than France. The provocation is not as crazy as his listeners thought, as we shall see as this story unwinds – in reality, France is not a democracy, as neither the people nor their representatives are really consulted about any number of decisions, particularly those concerning foreign policy and defence. On the other hand, France was a Republic under Jacques Chirac, who made decisions based on his perception of the general interest. We shall see that this did not hold true for very long.

As for Libya, it was a direct democracy inspired by the experiences of the French utopians of the 19th century. However, this system is also a trap. In fact, Libyan society is founded on tribal ethnicity, so that personal opinions have little significance. It is in fact this social reality which allowed Gaddafi to exercise the function of head of state, while officially, this post does not even exist. The major difference between the two countries lies elsewhere – in negotiating with the United States, Libya ceased all intervention in the affairs of its neighbours, while France cheerfully violated the Charter of the United Nations, particularly in Africa, and soon also in the Levant. Above all, Gaddafi proclaimed the emancipation of all human beings and ended slavery, while France – which has not practised slavery on its own territory since 1848 – has no problem allying itself with slave states like Saudi Arabia and Qatar.

President Sarkozy's first act concerning Syria, in March 2008, was to organise the flight of the most important false witness in the Hariri affair, Mohammed Zuhair al-Siddiq, who was given a fake Czech passport. Certainly, the accusations of murder against Emile Lahoud and Bashar al-Assad collapsed, but the identity of the real organiser of this masquerade remained a mystery. As if he was so cool that butter wouldn't melt in his mouth, Sarkozy made an official visit to Damascus to reboot the relations between the two countries, and to ensure that Syria would no longer intervene in the political affairs of Lebanon.

In May 2008, the Prime Minister of Lebanon (and agent of the Jordanian secret services), Fouad Siniora, opened hostilities with Hezbollah. He attempted to neutralise the air bridge between Iran and the Resistance as well as Hezbollah's own internal communications system, so that the United States and Saudi Arabia could take control of the country and attack Syria. But Hezbollah attacked first. Within a few hours, Siniora's security system collapsed, and he was obliged to retreat.

Peace negotiations opened in the Qatari capital of Doha. Qatar and France imposed a new President in Lebanon, which had not had one since the end of Emile Lahoud's mandate six months earlier. Paris chose the Chief of Staff, General Michel Suleiman, because he could be easily manipulated. Suleiman had forged documents in an attempt to obtain double French nationality for himself and his family, and the affair was ongoing in the courts. His designation as President of Lebanon left this problem hanging over his head like the sword of Damocles. Worried about Syria's possible reaction to this affair, Qatar offered President Assad – who had not asked for anything – a plane and a fleet of official vehicles.

The Emir of Qatar, Atari Hamad bin Khalifa Al Thani came to inaugurate "President" Suleiman as the replacement for his predecessor Emile Lahoud, who was not even invited. During the ceremony at the Lebanese National Assembly, French Minister for Foreign Affairs Bernard Kouchner was seated not on the public benches, but on the benches of the Lebanese government. He expressed his irritation when the ex-President of the Assembly observed that article 49 of the Constitution forbade a Chief of Staff to become President less than two months after he had left military service. No one took the time to modify the law, and the deputies elected Michel Suleiman in violation of the Constitution.

In July 2008, Nicolas Sarkozy launched the *Union pour la Méditerranée* (UPM, or Union for the Mediterranean), a vast operation intended to compete with France's European partners, and also to reinstate Israel in the concert of regional nations. For the occasion, Lebanon and Syria finally reactivated diplomatic relations (which had been entirely absent since their separation by the French in 1943), while Sarkozy invited both Bashar al-Assad and his Israeli counterpart, Shimon Peres, to take part in the 14th July parade on the Champs-Elysées. The former carefully avoided the latter.

The UPM failed for the same reasons as the Barcelona Process initiated by the European Union – it is impossible to bring all the actors of the region together as long as the Israeli conflict remains unresolved.

Sarkozy made a second official visit to Syria in January 2009. Contacted by the Obama administration, the French President abstained from deciding anything at all. It was simply a scouting trip.

The preparation for the invasions of Libya and Syria

Even before she had been confirmed by the Senate, future Secretary of State Hillary Clinton contacted London and Paris with a view to launching a double military operation in the "Greater Middle East". Washington was of the opinion that after the Iraq fiasco, it was impossible to use its own troops for this sort of adventure. From the US point of view, the moment had come to remodel the region, in other words, to redesign the states whose frontiers had been fixed in 1916 by the British, French, and Russian empires (the "Triple entente"), and to impose new boundaries which would favour US interests. The "Triple entente" agreement is known by the names of the British and French delegates, Sykes and Picot (the name of Russian ambassador Sazonov being forgotten because of the Russian Revolution). But how could London and Paris be persuaded to dismember their own heritage, except by promising to allow them to recolonise the region? This question gave birth to the "leading from behind" theory. The strategy was confirmed by the ex-Minister for Foreign Affairs under Mitterand, Roland Dumas, who admitted on television that he had been contacted by Britain and the United States in 2009, to determine if the French opposition parties would support a new colonial project.

In November 2010, that is to say before the beginning of the so-called "Arab Spring", David Cameron and Nicolas Sarkozy signed the Lancaster House Treaties in London. Officially, these documents were an agreement to share elements of defence, including nuclear weapons, in order to realise economies of scale. Although this was a stupid idea because of the differing interests of the two countries, public opinion did not understand what was really going on. One of the Treaties merged the "projection forces" (read "colonialist forces") of the two nations.

One appendix of these Treaties stipulated that between 21 and 25 March 2011, the Franco-British Expeditionary Force was to realise one of the most important joint military manœuvres in the history of the two countries, under the codename "Southern Mistral". The internet site of the French Ministry for Defence specified that the war game scenario was to be a very long distance bombing campaign mounted in order to come to the aid of populations threatened by "two Mediterranean dictators".

The date chosen by US AfriCom and US CentCom – the regional commands of United States forces – was precisely 21 March, the day on which France and the United Kingdom were to attack both Libya and Syria at once. Fortunately, it just so happened that the Franco-British Forces had no other engagements on those dates. They were available. But things never turn out the way they are planned, and the war on Syria was postponed until a later date. Nicolas Sarkozy, who wanted to strike the first blow, ordered his army to attack Libya on its own, on 19 March, during operation "Harmattan" (the French translation of Southern Mistral).

France believed it disposed of a master card – the head of Libyan protocol, Nouri Massoud El-Mesmari, had defected and asked for asylum in Paris. Sarkozy was persuaded that this man was a confidant of Colonel Gaddafi, and would be able to help them identify men who would be willing to betray him. Unfortunately, although this smooth talker organised the Guide's schedule, he was never present at the meetings.

A few days after the signature of the Lancaster House Treaties, a French trade delegation went to the Benghazi Fair with a number of civil servants from the Ministry of Agriculture, the directors of France Export Céréales and France Agrimer, and the managers of Soufflet, Louis Dreyfus, Glencore, Cani Céréales, Cargill, and Conagra. On site, the agents of the DGSE who accompanied them met secretly with Libyan military personnel to prepare a coup d'état.

Alerted by the United States, Tripoli arrested the traitors on 22 January 2011. The Libyans imagined that they were protected by their new alliance with Washington, while Washington was in fact preparing to kill them all. As for the French, they were obliged to step back into the shadow of their US Big Brother.

While the French were busy preparing the invasion of Libya, the United States launched their own operation, far more wide-ranging than they had told their agent Sarkozy. It was not simply designed to overthrow Muammar el-Gaddafi and Bashar al-Assad, but to destroy all Arab secular governments, and replace them with the Muslim Brotherhood. They began with the friendly states (Tunisia and

Egypt), leaving the British and French to deal with the enemies (Libya and Syria).

The first shots were fired in Tunisia. In response to the attempted suicide of a street merchant, Mohamed el-Bouzazi, on 17 December 2010, demonstrations were held to protest against police violence, and then against the government. France, who believed these uprisings to be spontaneous, offered to equip the Tunisian police with anti-riot gear. Nicolas Sarkozy and his Minister for the Interior, Michèle Alliot-Marie, had complete trust in Ben Ali, with whom they did personal "business". After having themselves a fully-equipped Airbus A330 custom-built as a Presidential super-plane, they sold the two old planes which had been used for official travel. One of the A319CJ's was discreetly erased from inventory and ceded to the Tunisian company Karthago Airlines, owned by Aziz Miled and Belhassen Trabelsi, the brother of Mrs. Ben Ali. No one seemed to know who the fortunate beneficiary of this transaction might be. Once President Ben Ali had fled, the aircraft was recovered and sold to a gaming company in Singapore, then to Turkey.

Occupied with protecting their "business partner", Nicolas Sarkozy and Michèle Alliot-Marie were staggered when President Ben Ali asked to land in Paris and seek refuge there. The Elysée presidential palace had just enough time to cancel the mission of a cargo plane transporting the promised peace-keeping equipment – the plane was sitting waiting on the tarmac because of delays in the customs formalities – and direct the fallen President's plane out of French airspace.

Meanwhile, in Egypt, computer engineer Ahmed Mather and Islamist blogger Israa Abdel Fattah called for a demonstration against President Hosni Mubarak, on 25 January 2011, the "Day of Anger". Immediately supported by the Qatari television channel Al-Jazeera and the Muslim Brotherhood, and with the help of CIA-run "NGOs," they launched a movement which, destabilised the régime. The demonstrations took place every Friday from 28 January, as soon as the faithful left the mosques, and were supervised by Serbs trained by the creator of the "colour revolutions", Gene Sharp. Nicolas Sarkozy learned about all this on 11 February by a telephone call from his father-in-law, US ambassador Frank Wisner Jr. who, on instructions from the White House, had convinced General Mubarak to step down.

The CIA then organised a secret meeting in Cairo, to which President Sarkozy sent a delegation including the lobbyist Bernard-Henri Levy,[5] an ex-lover of Carla Bruni and Ségolène Royal. Muslim Brother Mahmud Jibril el-Warfally was the number two of the Libyan government when he walked into the room. He was the leader of the "opposition to the tyrant" by the time he walked back out. Among the Syrians present were, notably, Malik al-Abdeh (ex-collaborator of the BBC and creator of BaradaTV, with funding from the CIA and the State Department) and Ammar Qurabi (member of a whole string of associations for the defence of Human Rights and creator of OrientTV).

The wars against Libya and Syria had just begun.

---

[5] Levy is a staunchly pro-Israeli, anti-Muslim, Jewish supremacist writer who agitates for the neo-con agenda in world politics, behind the mask of a man of culture and literature.

The beginning of the war against Libya

The Western Press alleged that the Libyan police had dispersed a demonstration in Benghazi on 16 February 2011 by shooting into the crowd. Since then, the country was in uproar, they wrote, and the authorities were shooting anything that moved. Fearing a possible return to slavery, two hundred thousand immigrant workers attempted to flee the country, and international TV channels showed them waiting at frontier posts. Muammar Gaddafi appeared on screen three times. He denounced the demonstrations as an operation organised by al-Qaeda, and declared that he was ready to die as a martyr. Next he announced the distribution of arms to the population in order to spring "rivers of blood", exterminate these "rats", and protect the country. These phrases from the Guide were taken out of context and broadcast by the Western TV channels, who interpreted them as announcing not a struggle against terrorism, but the suppression of a hypothetical revolution.

In Geneva, on 25 February, the UN Human Rights Council listened in horror to the testimony of the Libyan League for Human Rights, which claimed that the dictator had gone mad, and was "massacring his own people". The ambassador of Pakistan denounced the abuse of force. Suddenly, the official Libyan delegation entered the room, validated the testimonies that had been heard, and declared solidarity with its fellow countrymen against the dictator. A resolution was adopted and transmitted to the Security Council, which immediately adopted Resolution 1970 under Chapter VII of the Charter, which authorises the use of force. This Resolution, oddly enough, had been ready and waiting for several days. The Council referred the matter to the International Criminal Court, and placed Libya under embargo. This last measure was immediately adopted and extended by the European Union. Going further than the other Western powers, President Sarkozy declared – "Gaddafi must go!"

On 27 February, the Benghazi insurgents founded the Libyan National Transitional Council, while Minister for Justice Mustafa Abdul Jalil inaugurated a provisional government as he was leaving Tripoli. These two instances, controlled by the Muslim Brotherhood, then united, giving the impression of national unity. Immediately, the flags of ex-King Idris flowered over Benghazi. From London, Idris's son, his Highness Mohamed Senussi, declared that he was ready to rule.

Since Abdul Jalil was unable to convince all the members of the Transitional Council to call on the Western powers, he initiated the nomination of a Crisis Committee with full powers, presided over by the ex-number 2 of Gaddafi's government, Mahmud Jibril, now back from Cairo.

Paris admired the way in which Washington managed these events. However, contradicting the information from Benghazi and the United Nations, the diplomats and journalists present in Tripoli assured that nothing they had seen looked like a revolution. But the truth matters little as long as appearances are on your side. Thus, "philosopher" Bernard-Henri Levy persuaded the French population that the cause was just by declaring that he himself had convinced the President of the Republic to stand up for freedom, after having met with the Libyan "revolutionaries".

The French army came to collect Mahmud Jibril and took him to Strasbourg, where, before the European Parliament, he pleaded for a Western "humanitarian" intervention. On 10 March, Nicolas Sarkozy and British Prime Minister David Cameron wrote to the President of the European Union requesting that he recognise the Transitional Council instead of the "régime", and also define a no-fly zone. On the same day, in perfect coordination, French Ecologist deputy Daniel Cohn-Bendit (the agent of influence for May '68) and Belgian liberal Guy Verhofstadt, forced the adoption by the European Parliament of a resolution denouncing the Gaddafi "régime", and calling for the control of Libyan airspace in order to protect the civilian population from dictatorial repression. Again, on the same day, the Secretary General of NATO, Anders Fogh Rasmussen, announced that he was working on the technical infrastructure for setting up the no-fly zone.

On 12 March, the Arab League voted in favour of the no-fly zone, despite opposition from Algeria and Syria.

The only discordant notes in this symphony of unanimity came from Bulgaria – which had not forgotten that Abdul Jalil had covered up the torture of the Bulgarian nurses and the Palestinian doctor. Bulgaria refused to recognise the Transitional Council, as did the African Union, strongly opposed to any foreign military intervention.

The Libyan Arab Jamahiriya was organised according to the principles of the Green Book by Muammar Gaddafi. He was an admirer of the 19th century French libertarian socialists, Charles Fourier and Pierre-Joseph Proudhon. He therefore imagined a minimal state, which unfortunately proved incapable of defending its people against imperialist armies. Furthermore, he tasked the state with the mission of responding to the aspirations of the Bedouins – freedom of transportation, shelter, and water. Everyone therefore possessed their own car, meaning that public transport was *de facto* reserved for immigrants. Everyone received an apartment on their wedding day, although there was often a three-year wait for the house to be built before the marriage could take place. Gigantic works were undertaken to drill for water in the thousand year old water tables deep beneath the desert. The country prospered. Its standard of living was the highest on the entire African continent. But little was done in terms of education.

Although the universities were free, most young people gave up their studies before they had finished their courses. Muammar Gaddafi had underestimated the weight of tribal traditions. Three million Libyans lived in peace, while two million African and Asian immigrants lived to serve them.

On 19 March, 18 states (Germany, Belgium, Canada, Denmark, the United Arab Emirates, Spain, the United States, France, Greece, Italy, Iraq, Jordan, Morocco, Norway, Holland, Poland, Qatar and the United Kingdom) plus 3 international organisations (the Arab League, the European Union, and the UN) met in Paris to announce the imminence of their military intervention. A few hours later, France double-crossed its partners and attacked first.

Meanwhile, the situation in Syria was taking a long time to crystallise. The calls for demonstrations on 4, 11, 18 and 25 February, and 4 and 11 March in Damascus came to nothing. However, in Yemen and Bahrain, the people took to the streets without having been invited to do so.

In Yemen, the Muslim Brotherhood – including young Tawakkol Karman, who was to receive the Nobel Peace Prize – launched a "revolution". But like Libya, this country is organised in tribal form, and consequently it is not possible to make an exclusively political reading of the events.

On request by the Bahraini sovereign, the Saudi army came to "restore order" in this tiny Kingdom, which sheltered the 5th fleet of the US Navy. The United Kingdom sent its torturer Ian Anderson, who had done a fine job of directing the repression during the colonial era (in other words, before 1971). And in order to reorganise the police force, France sent Alain Bauer, security advisor to President Sarkozy, ex-head of the United States NSA for Europe, and ex-Grand Master of the Grand Orient de France.

Disorder spread like a disease. It now only remained to convince the world that it had been initiated by the people, and that it was aimed at establishing democracies.

The start of the war against Syria

While Al-Jazeera finished all its reports in Tunisia, Libya and Egypt by asking when the chaos would spread to Syria, we had to wait until Friday, 18 March, 2011 to witness the start of the operation – a demonstration in Daraa turned ugly, causing four deaths. In a few days the protests had spread, and the city was placed under military control. The clashes caused more than a hundred deaths, and the city centre was devastated. Al-Jazeera claimed that the police had arrested some children for making anti-government graffiti and tortured them by tearing out their finger-nails.[6]

The city of Homs, in its turn, became the theatre of a huge demonstration which also degenerated. Homs was placed under military control.

On 10 May, Germany, France, Holland, the United Kingdom and Sweden forced the adoption of sanctions by the European Union – a ban on the export of equipment destined for the police, and personal sanctions against thirteen officials, including Maher al-Assad (commander of the Republican Guard and younger brother of the President).

On 25 May, Germany, France, Portugal and the United Kingdom attempted to force the Security Council to pass a resolution placing Syria in the same position as Libya. But they failed. South Africa, Brazil, China, India and Russia all rejected the idea that the international community should dictate the behaviour of the Syrian Arab Republic.

---

[6] For a critique of this dubious scenario see *ISIS IS US: the Shocking Truth about the Army of Terror*, 2014, Progressive Press.

It was at this moment that BaradaTV broadcast photographs of the corpse of 13-year old Hamza Ali Al-Khateeb. He had allegedly been tortured and castrated by the secret services of the Syrian Air Force. According to Al-Jazeera, the régime tortured and killed children.

On 31 May and 16 July 2011, France, Qatar and Turkey sponsored the organisation of two conferences for the political opposition – the first in Antalya, the second in Istanbul. The second conference was entitled "National Security Conference," in reference to the "National Security Front" created by the Muslim Brotherhood in 2007.

The Istanbul conference gave birth, in September, to the Syrian National Council, modelled on the Libyan National Transitional Council, which the Western powers had presented as a credible alternative to the Libyan Arab Jamahiriya. The Libyan and Syrian organisations were composed by France, placing personalities who had been selected by the CIA over the preceding years. Like the Libyans, the Syrian members immediately received a salary. The majority of them were also affiliated with the Muslim Brotherhood, but they almost never sat at the assembly under this affiliation, so the two organisations were presented as secular. The Syrian Council was presided over by Burhan Ghalioun, professor of sociology at the university of Paris Pantheon-Sorbonne, and collaborator with the National Endowment for Democracy (NED). The Press refrained from mentioning that this "great secular layman" was in reality an ex-advisor to Abassi Madani, the President of the Algerian Islamic Salvation Front (FIS) during his exile in Qatar.

On 7 June, the leading TV news channel France 24, which is under the authority of the French Ministry for Foreign Affairs, broadcast a moving "live" telephone report by the Syrian Ambassador to France, Lamia Shakkour, announcing her resignation in protest against the massacres in her country. Although Renée Kaplan, assistant director of the editorial office of France 24, swore that the voice was truly that of the ambassador, whom she knew well, it was actually the voice of the wife of journalist Fahad Al-Argha-Al-Masri, speaking from another of the channel's own studios. Coordinating with France 24, the French Ministry for Foreign Affairs contacted all Syrian ambassadors throughout the world, announcing the live "resignation" of their colleague Lamia Shakkour, and demanding their resignation under the threat of being brought before the International Criminal

Court. The real ambassador protested immediately, and demanded a correction from France 24, which of course refused. When BFM TV finally gave the real Lamia Shakkour some air time, the masquerade collapsed – and not one Syrian ambassador had folded under pressure. At no time did the French Superior Council of Audiovisual Content – nominated by the President of the Republic, the President of the National Assembly, and the President of the Senate – ever investigate this affair.

On 4 July, lobbyist Bernard Henry Levy organised a meeting at a cinema in Saint Germain-des-Près to support the Syrian democratic opposition and the deposing of the tyrant Bashar al-Assad. He presided at the meeting with Sarkozy's ex-Minister for Foreign Affairs, Bernard Kouchner, and his future counterpart from the Hollande government, Laurent Fabius. The three men invited the right and left wing members of the ruling class to participate in their initiative. Personalities from the right, the left and the greens all willingly signed up. No one noticed the Israeli leaders in the room, nor the leaders of the Muslim Brotherhood. All of the people invited believed that they were doing the right thing, and none of them considered the consequences of what had just occurred.

On 8 July, the ambassadors of the United States and France in Damascus, Robert Ford and Eric Chevallier, participated in a demonstration in Hama. The Syrian government summoned the diplomats and accused them of supporting the opposition and disturbing public order. Partisans of the Republic demonstrated before the US and French embassies. Ironically, Robert Ford accused the Ba'athists of having attacked his diplomatic representation, while in Hama, the opposition had demonstrated without violence. Secretary of State Hillary Clinton stated that Assad "is not indispensable". In a Presidential declaration, the Security Council condemned the attacks on the embassies.

On 29 July, Colonel Riad al-Assad announced that he had defected and created the Free Syrian Army. He called on military personnel to join him and overthrow the "régime". The operation was led by the DGSE. Colonel Assad (or Asa'ad) had been chosen because his name was similar to that of President Bashar al-Assad. Unfortunately, while their family names are sometimes written the same in the Latin alphabet, they are quite distinct when written in Arabic.

The FSA was provided with a "flag of independence". In reality, it was the flag of French colonisation, which had remained in force at the moment of independence. It features the four pan-Arab colours – red for Mohammed, black for the Abbassids, green for the Fatimids, and white for the Omeyyads. The three stars represent the governments of Damascus, Aleppo, and the territory of the Nusairis (another name for the Alawites). The flag is well known to Syrians, since it has appeared since 2006 in the most famous of local television series, Bab el-Hara, the story of a village during the French occupation. The sinister commander of the gendarmerie decorates his office with the flag of the French occupier and the future flag of the FSA.

The "democratisation" of the Greater Middle East was under way. At least in appearance. Although it didn't understand much about what was going on, France, the "homeland of Human Rights", which had already covered itself with ridicule in Tunisia, imagined that it was obliged to follow the movement.

The common points between the operations in Libya and in Syria

The fact that the Free Syrian Army received the flag of the French mandate, and that the Libyan National Transitional Council received the flag of King Idris, bore witness to the planned distribution of roles. Libya was destined to come under British influence and Syria under French influence.

At first, Western propaganda was handled by France. On 5 July 2011, France 24, the TV channel of the French Minister for Foreign Affairs, received an order from the as the Libyan National Transitional Council, which did not have the necessary capabilities on its own. The agreement was signed with great pomp by Alain Duplessis de Pouzilhac, in his capacity as CEO of Audiovisuel Extérieur de la France (AEF), and Mahmud Shammam, Minister of Information for the Libyan National Transitional Council. The French Press unions protested this official bias, which violated professional ethics. Yet a similar agreement was made nonetheless – more discreetly – in October, with the Syrian National Council.

At the end of March 2011, a controversy arose, opposing French Minister of the Interior Claude Guéant and Turkish Prime Minister Recep Tayyip Erdoğan, concerning the nature of the war against

Libya, which Guéant had likened to a "crusade". This was the moment for the French Minister for Foreign Affairs, Alain Juppé, to negotiate a rapprochement with his Turkish counterpart, Ahmet Davutoğlu.

Since the time of King François I, there has existed a long and shameful tradition of alliance between France and the Ottomans. In the 16th century, Paris, ignoring religious cleavages, allowed herself to be seduced by "gifts" from the Muslim Suleiman the Magnificent. Corrupt to the core, François I accepted an alliance with his "adoptive father" against the Holy Roman Empire of the German Habsburgs. In his correspondence, Suleiman humiliated François, calling him his "French wali" (provincial governor). The Ottoman armies settled in the south of France, and François temporarily transformed the cathedral of Toulon into a mosque to welcome them.

The Juppé-Davutoğlu Treaty remains secret, although French law has forbidden secret diplomacy since the end of the First World War. It has therefore never been ratified by Parliament, and has no legal standing.

Nicolas Sarkozy and Alain Juppé could not publish this document without risking immediate removal by the High Court for the former and condemnation by the Law Court of the Republic for the latter. In effect, it planned for Turkish participation in the war that had just begun in Libya, and the war that had not yet begun in Syria. Turkey agreed to mobilise the inhabitants of the Libyan city of Misrata to help the Coalition overthrow the Libyan Arab Jamahiriya. These people are linked to Turkey as they are mostly descendants of the Adghams, Jewish soldiers of the Ottoman Empire, and the Muntasirs, nomads who traded in black slaves, and who had supported the Young Turks. It was also planned to mobilise the Turkmen populations of Northern Syria to overthrow the Syrian Arab Republic. In exchange, France agreed to support Turkey's entry into the European Union, despite the fact that President Sarkozy had promised just the opposite to the French people during his electoral campaign. Above all, the two countries agreed to solve the Kurdish question without prejudice to the territorial integrity of Turkey. In other words, they intended to create an independent state in Syria to be called "Kurdistan", to which it was planned to expel some of the Turkish Kurds. This project defies understanding, because historically, Kurdistan was located exclusively in Turkey. The Treaty was neither more nor less than a plan for the conquest of Libya and Syria, and for ethnic cleansing in Turkey.

For the record, Alain Juppé has never backed away from helping the practitioners of genocide when it seemed like a useful move. In 1995, during the massacres in Rwanda, he organised Operation Turquoise with François Mitterrand. There is no doubt that the operation was intended to create a "safe humanitarian zone" for the populations in danger, but also, and above all, to use the DGSE to get their friends out safely under cover of this initiative, and unknown to the armies concerned.

Combining business with pleasure, the Erdoğan government arranged for Turkish company leaders to offer "gifts" to Alain Juppé.

In parallel to his agreement with Turkey, Alain Juppé entrusted Gaullist senator Adrien Gouteyron with a mission concerning the situation of the Christian communities of the Orient. Gouteyron spent a long time visiting the communities of the Near East, with the exception of those in Syria, and concluded unsurprisingly that these Christians needed to be helped to stay where they were, and that they also needed to be welcomed more graciously if and when they emigrated to France. The parliamentarian did not understand that he was thus paving the way for the transfer of the Maronites.

During the whole of his mandate, President Sarkozy usually aligned himself with Qatari interests. The Emir of Qatar managed the greatest quantity of liquid assets in the world, and attempted to gain the status of world leader by buying people and functions. In this way, he had managed to bring peace to Sudan and nominate the unconstitutional "President" of Lebanon. Taking into account the fact that the French President is obliged to turn over all gifts of assets to the state, the Emir offered the Sarkozys all sorts of intangible personal advantages, in particular luxury holidays and the permanent use of one of his private planes.

Nicolas Sarkozy modified the Franco-Qatari tax treaty so that the embassy's tax exemption was extended to all the investments of the Emir and his family. In this way, over the space of a few years, the al-Thanis bought 5 billion Euros worth of real estate. They acquired several grand hotels and casinos. They acquired stakes in prestigious companies like Total, EADS and Areva. They bought a football club, the Paris-Saint-Germain, and created several TV sports channels.

The self-interested generosity of the Emir touched all sectors of French society. He greased the palms of about fifty parliamentarians from all political parties, and tried, but failed, to take control of the Muslim suburbs. Finally, one by one, he bought the majority of the country's political and economic leaders, so that the tiny emirate now disposed of its own French spokesperson at the Security Council, and could requisition the French army whenever it felt like it.

The fall of the Libyan Arab Jamahiriya

Returning to the war on Libya. Early on, France was the country most heavily involved in military operations against Libya, accounting for one third of them, while even the United States handled only a fifth, and the United Kingdom a tenth.

At first, the allied armies simply worked together. However, as of 31 March 2011, Washington imposed itself as the unique commander of NATO. The French army came under the orders of US Admiral James G. Stavridis and his assistants, Canadian General Charles Bouchard, US General Ralph J. Jodice II and Italian Vice-Admiral Rinaldo Veri. Some other states outside of NATO were also involved in this new "à la carte" Coalition.

As a result, the only thing the French staff knew about the general strategy of the war was what it was ordered to do and whatever NATO deigned to reveal. Besides which, the French forces engaged in the war were seriously under-equipped and uncoordinated, which made them extremely dependent on NATO.

At the beginning of the war, France participated in the slaughter of the 40,000 men of the Libyan army grouped near Benghazi, perhaps believing that the army was preparing to massacre the population. Over the next five months, the French military settled for bombing the targets assigned to them. However, it also had a few troops on the ground tasked with coordinating with the insurgents. It was therefore obliged to face the facts and admit the real reasons for the confusion of the initial orders – the armed insurgents were very few, and mostly from the Libyan Islamic Fighting Group (LIFG), in other words, al-Qaeda.

The Minister for Defence, Gérard Longuet, was informed specifically about the gigantic anti-NATO demonstrations organised by Muammar Gaddafi in Tripolitania and Fezzan. Consequently, in a private conversation with President Sarkozy, he voiced his opposition to the war. He was joined, notably, by the Minister of the Interior and ex-General Secretary of the Elysée, Claude Guéant, who knew a lot more about it than he did. A third man, Central Director of Internal Security Bernard Squarcini, gave them his support.

On 29 March, the United Kingdom and France organised a meeting in London with their principal allies. It was agreed that the salaries of the members of the Libyan National Transitional Council would be paid from frozen Libyan assets, via the Libyan Information Exchange Mechanism (LIEM). This decision was a double infringement of international law. Indeed, the law forbids interference in national conflicts via the payment of salaries to the adversaries – who would then be considered as their spies – and it is of course forbidden to divert frozen funds for personal profit.

It was only at this juncture that Nicolas Sarkozy learned for the first time about the Libyan treasure – $150 billion, including 143 metric tonnes of gold and almost as many tonnes of silver. Claude Guéant was authorised to send the ex-director of the National Police, Prefect Edouard Lacroix, to negotiate with Gaddafi for a withdrawal of French forces in return for a part of this treasure.

The situation became more complicated on 14 May, when the Director General of the International Monetary Fund, Frenchman Dominique Strauss-Kahn, was arrested in New York on sex charges. While the neutralisation of his Socialist rival was good news for Nicolas Sarkozy, what he learned on this occasion reinforced his determination to make the maximum possible profit from the Libyan war. Strauss-Kahn was arrested while he was travelling via Berlin to Tripoli, where he was supposed to meet Muammar Gaddafi with one of Angela Merkel's collaborators. The interview was intended to focus on Libya's monetary experience – how to live without the US dollar and the CFA Franc? It was planned to be the object of a report at the G8 conference in Deauville, a few days later. Quite obviously, Strauss-Kahn had fallen into a trap laid by people who were familiar with his promiscuous past. His lawyers flew to Tel-Aviv to seek help, but nothing could be done. Once again, the partisans of the military-industrial complex had won against the partisans of stateless money.

While the secret Franco-Libyan negotiations were ongoing, Assistant Secretary of State Jeffrey Feltman intervened from Washington, ordering Paris to break off the talks immediately.

Nicolas Sarkozy, David Cameron and Emir Al-Thani created a new Libyan Central Bank and a new oil company which would work with the French and British oil companies, Total and BP. The Libyan National Transitional Council (LNTC) was authorised to sell Libyan oil on the international market, under the control of Qatar, and to keep the profits. Greed was too strong, and no one had the self-control to wait for the end of the conflict. In a letter addressed to the Emir, the LNTC promised to allocate 35% of the crude oil to France – a quota corresponding to France's share of the bombing raids of the Coalition.

Once Cyrenaica had been separated from the rest of Libya, and its oil was being exploited once again, nothing of any importance happened on the battlefield. Since the inhabitants of Benghazi had recovered their independence, and the oil, they were no longer concerned about the future of Tripolitania and Fezzan.

During the five months that followed, several French personalities visited Libya. Particularly notable were the visits by lawyers Roland Dumas and Jacques Vergès. The two men proposed to defend the interests of the Libyans, and to lift the illegal freeze of 400 million Euros of their assets in France. They demanded to be paid in proportion to the sums concerned, and left Tripoli with 4 million Euros as a cash advance. Thereafter they sent a hand-written fax to Alain Juppé asking him to specify the legal reasons for the asset freeze. Since the Jamahiriya collapsed in August, they never finished the work for which they had already been so richly rewarded.

Another lawyer, Marcel Ceccaldi, agreed to defend Khaled Al-Hamedi – the son of Gaddafi's brother-in-arms – after his wife and his children had been targeted and killed by NATO in order to pressure him. Ceccaldi initiated several legal procedures before the African international courts in order to furnish himself with favourable jurisprudence to present to the UN. After the defeat, he became the advisor to the Guide's Chief of Staff, and negotiated the suspension of legal proceedings against him, in exchange for the non-publication of recordings of his conversations with Ziad Takieddine during the negotiation and funding of Nicolas Sarkozy's electoral campaign. Although Ceccaldi was also an adventurer, he scrupulously respected his engagements, including after the fall of the Jamahiriya.

Ex-Prime Minister Dominique de Villepin travelled to Djerba in Tunisia and demanded an audience in the Libyan capital of Tripoli. He had returned to his work as a lawyer, and represented the Emir of Qatar. He was accompanied by a friend of President Sarkozy, Alexandre Djouhri, who had already served as an intermediary with Libya. He came bearing a proposition for surrender in exchange for a safe-conduct for Gaddafi and his family. They met with emissaries who came to enquire as to the purpose of their visit, but finally were not allowed to enter Libya.

As for myself, I was invited by the Guide's daughter, Ayesha Gaddafi, to come and see what was happening on the ground. Ever since Fidel Castro had spoken to me with admiration about Muammar Gaddafi, I had suspected that we were being manipulated about Libya – I knew the "Commandante" did not speak lightly. I saw that the neighbourhoods of Tripoli that the UN Human Rights Council claimed had been destroyed by the Libyan aviation had never been bombed at all. I observed that international law is favourable to the Jamahiriya, and so I drew up a plan to re-establish the truth and save the country at the diplomatic level. However, the head of the secret services, Abdullah Senussi, was convinced that I was a spy. I was put on hold for the time it took him to verify my curriculum vitæ. France then sent a pseudo-delegation for the support of Libya, composed of "militants" who were all working for France's Special Branch. They submitted a file attesting to my opposition to the agreement between Libya and the Bush administration – these were authentic declarations which I had never hidden, and which had led to my invitation by Ayesha Gaddafi to come and check the facts in person.

This approach had the opposite effect to that expected – while the Minister for Foreign Affairs, Moussa Koussa, had defected and joined the British, Muammar Gaddafi made me a part of his government, and asked me to negotiate various alliances in preparation for the UN General Assembly in September in New York. However, I would only enjoy relative power, because Muammar Gaddafi would continue to negotiate through another channel with Israel, France, and the United States. Since I did not want to accept money for political action, it was agreed that if I was able to have NATO's intervention declared illegal by the UN, I would go on to direct the editorial staff of an English-language TV channel, for which the studios had already been bought in Malta, under the presidency of Khaled Bazelya.

Most of the government had fled. There were only six Ministers left in place, two of whom were incapable. However, despite appearances, their positions remained vague. Some of them, like the Minister for Oil, Shukri Ghanem, pretended to defect in order to regain the right to circulate freely in Europe and unblock Libyan assets. Everyone was suspicious of everyone else. Suspected of having gone over to the enemy, Minister Abdul Ati al-Obeidi was arrested and tortured for an entire day by Abdullah Senussi. It was a mistake. Conscious that he might still be able to save his people, the Minister heroically continued his work, limping, but saying nothing.

Like its Guide, the Libyan Arab Jamahiriya had no policy of alliances. As soon as the war began, it was bereft of friends, apart from a few African states, including South Africa, plus Cuba, Syria and Venezuela. Dmitry Medevedev's Russia betrayed the Jamahiriya, which provoked a marked reaction from ambassador Vladimir Chamov, who was relieved of his functions, and from Prime Minister Vladimir Putin, who was biding his time. China, with whom Libya was weathering a complicated dispute in the Horn of Africa, refused to take position. Worse, swept along with the tide, some of Libya's allies turned their backs. This was notably the case of President Abdoulaye Wade of Senegal. After having been especially favoured for years by Gaddafi, he was the first to condemn him and make the betrayal public.

I was afraid that the affair concerning Imam Musa Al-Sader,[7] who had disappeared in Libya or Italy in 1978, would make rapprochement with the Shiites more difficult. That was not the case. It seems that despite the public declarations of the Lebanese leaders, there were doubts about Sader's real personality. He had founded Amal, the Movement of the Disinherited (today headed by billionaire Nabih Berri) and freed the Lebanese Shiites from their condition. But for some people, he was a spy for the Shah, which may have played a part in the split between Hezbollah and his own party.

---

[7] Lebanese-Iranian Shiite philosopher who disappeared after a trip to Libya in 1978.

I gave great importance to the renewal of relations with Iran, which agreed to receive a top-level delegation, and also with the Lebanese Resistance. Among the journalists present in Tripoli, I recognised US photographer Tara Todras-Whitehill – I was aware of the role she had played for the Mossad during the assassination of Rafic Hariri. As a sign of good will, I therefore proposed, to hold her in Tripoli, inform Lebanon, and prepare her extradition. This was an error on my part – Muammar Gaddafi pursued his contacts with the Israelis, and sent one of his children to negotiate in Tel-Aviv. Abdallah Senussi once again thought about having me arrested. Todras-Whitehill challenged me when we next met.

The Guide began to behave irrationally. He took in a Bedouin woman who entered into a trance. The angels spoke to him using her voice. She persuaded him that everything would end well. The United States would suddenly withdraw, just as suddenly as they had triggered the conflict, without explanation. This woman and her family carried with them a great weight of obscurantism. No discussion was possible. When I asked her simple questions, her father replied that he "agreed to talk to the infidel" – that was me – and that it "did not bother him".

On 27 June, the French army bombed the broadcasting antenna for Libyan television at the precise moment that Yusuf Shakir, star journalist and ex-member of al-Qaeda, asked me to speak.

Believing that they could rely on public opinion as their witness, the Jamahiriya authorised the foreign Press to cover the conflict. Hundreds of journalists flooded in from all over the world to see the results of the NATO bombings. It happened that some of these bombs had missed their targets, hitting another building instead. It also happened that in each of these cases, a second strike immediately followed the passage of the journalists. Evidently, the journalists were spies in disguise. Since he was unable which of them was in contact with NATO, Muammar Gaddafi decided to gather all the journalists in the Hotel Rixos, and to allow them to leave only when accompanied by police.

The offices of government spokesman Moussa Ibrahim were also installed in the hotel. While his entire team was busy working, all of their computers were suddenly hacked. Data spooled across the screens at incredible speed, and the keyboards no longer functioned. They had to unplug the power in order to interrupt the hacking. Once again, it was impossible to tell which "journalists" had organised this operation. Abdullah Senussi then decided to use a software programme that he had bought from a French company. This software enables the hacking of all the emails in an account from its very beginning, by getting into the memory of the server which stores them. The results were staggering. With the exception of the Russians, the South Americans and the AFP correspondent, almost all the journalists, including the French contingent, were revealed to be spies, working mainly for the CIA and MI6. Before leaving for Libya, from computers which they did not bring with them, they had exchanged emails with their central command, containing their resumés and mission orders.

Generally speaking, television teams are composed of three or four people. The war correspondent who appears on screen is a correspondent for the company which supplies him or her with the information about all theatres of operation. Most of the journalists present had covered the wars in Afghanistan and Iraq before coming to Libya – despite appearances, there are not that many of these people. Two technicians handled the image and the audio input. In general they were embedded, under-cover members of the Special Forces. Finally, the US teams also included a producer, who was in fact an active operations agent.

The daily bombings, although they were usually on target, nonetheless wounded or killed their quota of "collateral victims". Besides which, certain targets were chosen in an exclusively criminal manner, the way racketeers operate, to break the people's spirit and force submission.

The political activity took place in three hotels – all the political leaders, except the Guide, were gathered together for their security at the hotel Radisson Blue. Foreign guests were billeted at the Hotel Corinthia, which would also be home for the provisional government. The journalists were under surveillance at the Hotel Rixos, which was later partially destroyed.

A secret meeting was organised by NATO at the Joint Force Command in Naples. France was represented by its Minister for Foreign Affairs, Alain Juppé, and not the Minister for Defence, Gérard Longuet, who was opposed to the war. In 2004, the Appeals Court of Nanterre had given Juppé, an ex-Prime Minister, a suspended sentence of 14 months imprisonment and 1 year of ineligibility for political office, as punish for a corruption offence. This extremely light sentence – he had at first been condemned to 10 years of ineligibility – led to his leaving France and living for a year in Quebec. In reality, he spent long weeks in Washington, where ambition led him to become a neo-conservative. Asked about his role at the meeting in Naples, Alain Juppé's office evasively replied that he had been unable to attend since he was on holiday at the time.

To create the National Liberation Army, France chose Generals Abdelfattah Younès and Khalifa Haftar. Until February, Younès had been one of Gaddafi's companions. We do not know how the DGSE managed to turn him. Nonetheless, he kept up relations with the Guide's son, Saif el-Islam Gaddafi. Haftar had betrayed his country during the war with Chad. He worked with France and the United States before being forced to flee and settle in Langley Virginia, near the CIA headquarters. However, Younès was arrested, tortured, mutilated and assassinated at the end of July. His corpse was partially burned and eaten. Although everyone pretended to be unaware of what had happened: he fell in a trap laid by Mustafa Abdul-Jalil and was executed by the soldiers of Abdelhakim Belhaj[8] in the headquarters of the February 17th Martyrs Brigade, an Islamist militia founded by France and Qatar.

Just before the start of the meeting in Naples, a negotiator who had been sent secretly by Nicolas Sarkozy left Tripoli in a motor dinghy. The decision had already been taken to render the *coup de grâce*. The trap closed. From then on, it became impossible to enter or leave Tripoli by air, by land, or by sea. During this time, the Assemblée Nationale, the French Parliament authorised the attack on Libya. No one there knew what was happening behind the scenes, and the leader of the Sarkozy clique, Christian Jacob, paid hypocritical homage to the soldiers on mission. "These soldiers are often very young, and yet they have signed up to defend our country and our values, at the risk of their lives. We know what we owe them, and the entire nation is aware of the value of their sacrifice". Revealing that these soldiers were sent on a mission of purely colonial conquest, far removed from Republican values, he screamed over the applause of his colleagues, "The French flag is flying over Benghazi, and for us, this is a source of immense pride".

---

[8] Emir of the infamous terrorist gang LIFG, the Libyan Islamist Fighting Group, which brought the insurgency from Libya to Syria in 2011.

While I was explaining to my friends that the North Atlantic Council would never authorise NATO to ignore the decision of the United Nations Security Council and bomb Tripoli, Washington stomped all over the statutes of the Alliance and gathered a group of conspirators, a secret "Committee of Defense" in Naples. Only the most intimate or interested allies were invited (France, Italy, the United Kingdom, Turkey), and a few friends from the region (Saudi Arabia, Israel, Qatar). Together, they defined the way they would use the power of NATO and place the North Atlantic Council before the *fait accompli.*

The minutes of the decisions of this meeting specified the targets assigned to each unit. One mission assigned to the French Special Forces was the order to eliminate me. Wanted posters featuring some fifteen Libyans and myself were actually posted around Tripoli the day after it fell. I nonetheless managed to escape with my companions, thanks to certain states and certain people – including Walter E. Fauntroy, an ex-member of the United States Congress and ex-assistant of Martin Luther King Jr. – and also the French and Russian television teams, who had just arrived. Once back in his own country, Fauntroy recounted that he himself had witnessed French and Danish regular soldiers decapitating Libyans alongside al-Qaeda.

The taking of Tripoli was a deluge of fire which lasted for three days. About 40,000 people were killed, without any way of distinguishing between soldiers and civilians – a repeat of the massacre committed by Italian troops in 1911. All the barricades situated at the main crossroads of the city were bombed, and then British helicopters dropped into the streets to machine-gun indiscriminately anyone who was still there. The city was not properly defended, because its military governor had been corrupted by NATO, and had sent his soldiers home just before the attack.

During the battle, Muammar Gaddafi took refuge in a bunker situated under the Hotel Rixos, where the foreign "journalists" had previously been grouped. Their presence prevented the Coalition from using the air force. The site was therefore surrounded by the al-Qaeda brigade commanded by Irishman Mahdi al-Harati – the CIA agent who had taken part in the Turkish operation "Freedom Flotilla for Gaza" – and supervised by the French Special Forces. The hotel was defended by Khamis Gaddafi and his men.

Once defeat was certain, the Gaddafis fled to Sirte. As for myself, I first found the Guardians of the Revolution, whom the Islamic

Republic of Iran had sent to save me, then I fled to Malta on board a small boat which had been chartered by the Czech Republic for the International Organisation for Migration. Before we left, my companions and myself were searched successively by NATO, the Senussis, the Muslim Brotherhood and al-Qaeda. The passengers had been selected in an agreement between NATO – who had changed their minds about me – and the Gaddafists, so that both groups would allow us to cross the combat lines. On board, I discovered I was travelling with the ex-mistress of Saif el-Islam, as well as the Italian Special Forces snipers, who had provoked the war by shooting from the rooftops into the crowds of demonstrators and police in Benghazi on 16 February 2011.

Finally in Sirte, the Guide negotiated with some Israelis for his own escape to Chad. It was a trap. He was arrested by the French forces and al-Qaeda, then raped, tortured and assassinated on 20 October. Far from hanging up their weapons, the Libyan "revolutionaries", that is to say al-Qaeda, found themselves in a similar position to the one they had enjoyed in Afghanistan, then in Yugoslavia. They were on a roll.

The transfer of Libyan combatants to Syria

Even before Tripoli had completely fallen, the United States gathered their employees from the Libyan National Transitional Council and from al-Qaeda headquarters at the Hotel Corinthia. The hotel was placed under the protection of the British services, while fighting continued in the city and the empty streets were littered with corpses. The world ex-number 3 of al-Qaeda, Abdelhakim Belhaj, was nominated military governor of the capital.

Alain Juppé declared to *Le Parisien* on 26 August – "When I am asked about the cost of the operation – the Ministry of Defence speaks of 1 million Euros per day – I tell them that it's also an investment for the future. The country's resources have been stolen by Gaddafi, who has accumulated stockpiles of gold. This money should serve for the development of Libya – a prosperous Libya will be a factor of stability in the region".

On 1 September, a lightning international conference in Paris formally acknowledged the "regime change". Less than one tenth of Libya's frozen $50 billion was liberated. Nobody knows what happened to the other $100 billion.

On 15 September, Nicolas Sarkozy, Alain Juppé and Bernard-Henri Levy travelled with British Prime Minister David Cameron to Benghazi, escorted by hundreds of French and British police and soldiers. They were triumphantly acclaimed by a group of 1,500 carefully-chosen "well-wishers". They had come to take possession of the oil they had won. In a short speech, President Sarkozy announced that France would stand by the side not only of Libya, but also of "all the Arab peoples who want to free themselves from their leaders". He was already eager to attack Syria and grab her colossal reserves of gas.

Emir al-Thani might well have been rubbing his hands. The international Press was praising him as a defender of democracy, this man who practised slavery in his own country, the infamous *kafala* system of forced labor. The conquest of Libya had cost him no more than 20,000 tonnes of weapons and $400 million.

Once the Libyan Arab Jamahiriya had been overthrown in Tripoli, the inhabitants of Benghazi arrested the black-skinned people who had been unable to escape. They were put into cages and exhibited as if they were animals. The ancient slaving tradition of the nomad Bedouin populations over the sedentary black people had resurfaced.

In November 2011, the special representative of Ban Ki-moon and ex-secretary general of Amnesty International, Ian Martin, organised the transfer by boat of 1,500 al-Qaeda jihadists from Libya to Turkey. Officially, these unmarried armed men were described as "refugees". They were placed under the authority of Abdelhakim Belhaj – who had nonetheless retained his functions in Tripoli – and Mahdi al-Harati. Disembarked in Turkey, they were taken by buses chartered by the MIT (Turkish secret services) to Jabal al-Zawiya in Syria. They constituted the primary unit of the Free Syrian Army (FSA) under French command. Belhaj returned to Libya at Christmas, after having been recognised in Syria by a Spanish journalist from ABC. Mahdi al-Harati then created another group, Liwaa al-Umma (the Brigade of the Islamic Nation), in order to train Syrian combatants. In September 2012, this group joined the FSA.

Syria – the 4th generation war

On 5 September 2011, President Sarkozy received the Maronite Christian patriarch, S. B. Bechara Rai, at the Elysée Palace. He explained to the prelate quite frankly that the Allies were going to place the Muslim Brotherhood in power in Damascus. The Catholics and Maronites of Syria, and probably those of Lebanon also, would soon be welcomed in France. Senateur Adrien Gouteyron was in the process of examining the conditions for their reception. The Orthodox Christian civilians would be massacred. His Beatitude argued at first, but then made the best he could of a bad deal.

In Syria, the United States were testing a new strategy. They were going to reverse the roles and use the same methods against the Syrian Republic that the Resistance usually uses against the Empire. But they would also be playing their master card – the power of their media. This is the very principle of "4th generation warfare" (4GW) – to give the impression that they are everywhere, whereas in reality, they intervene very little.

In these conditions, the Allies would rely on a few extremely mobile groups of Special Forces, who would operate with the Syrians to create confusion. Three types of operations were planned:

➤ Attacks on symbols of the state, for example against the statues of Hafez al-Assad, the founder of modern Syria and father of the current President;

➤ Sabotage, for example derailing trains, destroying electric power stations or water lines;

➤ Random murders, in order to give the impression of generalised conflict.

Since the French army had "reservations" about these methods, President Sarkozy handed over the direction of operations to his personal Chief of Staff, General Benoît Puga. The General had been successively the Commander of Special Operations (COS) and of Military Intelligence. He was born into an extreme right-wing military family (his father participated in the putsch of Algiers), and was a Lefebvrist Catholic and partisan of colonisation (Mgr. Lefebvre was the bishop of Dakar). An officer of the Parachute Brigade, he participated in numerous colonial operations in Africa and Lebanon. He was the military advisor to ex-Prime Minister of Sweden, Carl Bildt, who had been tasked with the administration of Kosovo at the end of the war, and then again when Bildt became the administrator for Bosnia-Herzegovina. Puga supervised the construction of the extension of the wall separating Israel and Egypt. His undeniable courage gave him a natural authority over the political leaders he served. He took soldiers from the French Foreign Legion and the COS in order to send them into the field under his command.

It is impossible to establish the positions of the French Forces during the war. The most we know is that 19 French soldiers were taken prisoner by the Syrian Arab Army during Nicolas Sarkozy's mandate, and at least as many were killed. Their families, if they had families, were informed that they had been "killed in action", without specifying the country where they died, nor any other information.

At the Security Council, Russia and China vetoed the project of Western military intervention. A huge crowd, close to a million citizens, took to the streets of Damascus to thank Moscow and Beijing, and to show their support for President Bashar al-Assad. The Arab League, presided by Qatar, sent an intelligence-gathering mission which revealed the stupidity of reports in the Western Press, and agreed with the Syrian Arab Republic. There was therefore no regional support nor legal status for an intervention comparable to that deployed against Libya.

Given the situation, the Western powers decided to risk everything. Washington grouped about sixty states into an alliance called the "Friends of Syria". Russia and China, who had been invited, discovered that the agenda would not allow them to express their own opinions. The participants were supposed to adopt a document which they would not see until they arrived. Moscow and Beijing therefore boycotted the meeting. The meeting was held in Tunis, and was opened late by President Moncef Marzouki because of the hostile demonstrations of his People. Marzouki enjoyed the image of a secular left-wing personality, but had in fact served as cover for the Muslim Brotherhood for a long time. He therefore gave a speech inviting President al-Assad to flee, and to seek refuge in Russia, so that the Muslim Brotherhood could take power in Syria. Alain Juppé called for the imposition of sanctions against the "Alawite dictatorship," while Hillary Clinton announced that the Western powers intended to close their embassies in Damascus.

This display clearly reveals a series of misunderstandings (honest or otherwise).

► First of all, the Western powers have still not understood why Russia supports Syria. In their eyes, it's a question of loyalty to an old ally from the Soviet era. As a result of this misinterpretation, they persist in hoping to "convince" Moscow to follow them over to the "right side of History".

▶ Then, victims of their own propaganda, they insist on affirming that Syria is a dictatorship in the grip of the Alawite cult. But although President al-Assad has authority over the army, many senior civil servants do what they have to do without waiting on his orders. Besides which, the Republic is secular and not confessional. It was founded by the Ba'ath party, which has controlled all its mechanisms for a long time. This political formation fought for the unity of the Arab People in the name of the principles of the French Revolution. All that can be said is that it is a state that has been at war since 1948, faced with an expansionist neighbour, Israel, and that it has a militarised régime largely controlled by the secular Ba'ath party.

▶ Finally, following the movement initiated by Hillary Clinton, the "Friends of Syria" deprived themselves of the legal means of checking their information by closing their embassies. Only the United States and the United Kingdom retained their vast system of satellite spying (the "Five Eyes system").

The role of the French authorities remained limited. They were first asked to supervise the Omar al-Farouq Brigade in Homs, and again during the attack on Ma'loula, the most ancient Christian city in history, with its monasteries and preservation of spoken Aramaic.

A journalist from France2, Gilles Jacquier – who was also working for the DGSE and the Mossad, in violation of the Munich Charter – died from a mortar attack in Homs, on 11 January. He was supposed to make contact with the Omar al-Farouq Brigade. He had at first asked to be embedded with the Syrian Arab Army, in order to be able to get close to Generals Maher al-Assad and Wajih Mahmud, about whom the Western secret services were trying to gather information. When he arrived in Damascus, he rushed to a hotel which was known by the security services as a meeting place for the Muslim Brotherhood and their Western sponsors. When he was invited to meet the families of the martyrs and the leaders of the internal opposition, he accused them of "disseminating régime propaganda". Refusing a governmental escort, he left on his own for Homs, persuaded that he had nothing to fear from the "revolutionaries." However, he found himself in an Alawite neighbourhood which was being bombed by the jihadists, as they did every day at the same hour, and was killed, just like many Syrians.

The DGSE tried to blame Jacquier's death on a "régime conspiracy". Alain Juppé went to the Security Council in New York, "to bow before the memory of Gilles Jaquier, the French journalist who was killed in the exercise of his functions" (an unfortunate lapse, since the expression "killed in the exercise of his functions" is usually employed for officials on an assignment, and not for journalists, even when they are working for the public service).

France also participated with the Turkish army in the supervision of jihadists, who twice attacked the tiny town of Ma'loula, the symbol of primitive Christianity. They destroyed the statue of the Virgin Mary, which overlooked the town, and plundered the relics of the "thirteenth apostle", Saint Thecla, and the monasteries of Saint Serge and Saint Bacchus, the only couple canonised by the Catholic church. Several French soldiers died in the neighbouring village of Sanayeh.

The Omar al-Farouq Brigade imposed its law on the governorate of Homs. As Nicolas Sarkozy had previously warned the Maronite patriarch, the Islamist preachers announced by loud-speaker that the Christians had to pay the tax on infidels, and then gave them a few days to leave or die. This has been a constant policy, ever since the Beaudecourt plan of 1848, implemented by France and Ottoman Turkey – displace the Catholic and Maronite Christians, who are faithful to Rome, and exterminate the Orthodox Christians.

The French Special Forces next supervised the Takfiri[9], a branch of the Muslim Brotherhood, who had barricaded themselves in a small area of Homs, Baba Amr, where they proclaimed an Islamic emirate. According to them, Muslims who did not follow the doctrine of the Brotherhood should be excommunicated, condemned to death, and executed in public. During the Iraq war, Takfiri preachers had travelled through the Syrian countryside and had managed to raise a number of adepts. Since in certain rural regions the population is not settled in villages, but on isolated farms, no one had measured their importance. They were in total about 2,000 men. Their number had been increased by about a thousand criminals who had followed them in their adventures in exchange for cash. The idea was to make

---

[9] Literally, one who calls other Muslims a *kafir*, an infidel or apostate.

this emirate the starting-point for the conquest of Syria. It was in this context that, for the second time, Russia and China used their Security Council veto against the proposed a military intervention by NATO.

The Islamic Emirate of Baba Amr remained stable, because the Syrian Arab Army could only encircle the neighbourhood which served as its territory. A unit of 70 SAA soldiers was trapped there, blockaded in a supermarket. It was therefore impossible to bomb the jihadists without risking the death of regular soldiers. It was also impossible to enter Baba Amr, because the access roads were all protected by Milan anti-tank missile batteries installed by the French Special Forces (costing €100,000 per position, more than €12,000 per shot), and Russian-built 9K115-2 Metis-M batteries. The best that could be done was to try and advance house by house, without using the streets. The little Islamic emirate was supplied with food and ammunition via a vast network of tunnels which had been carved out from the sewers during the preparations for the war.

France 24 and Al-Jazeera both had salaried correspondents in Baba Amr, including the young Abu Saleh, renowned for reporting to the whole world about the daily bombings – he showed the victims and was wounded himself. He called in vain for help from the West. The reality, though, was very different. The noise of explosions in his reports came from the destruction of the houses of Christians and partisans of the régime. The plumes of black smoke came from tyres burned on the rooftops. The wounded were movie extras. The show was so well directed, and so closely corresponded to Western desires, that everyone believed it – until a British journalist filmed Abu Saleh himself in the process of directing the scene.

The Syrian Arab Republic feared that the siege of Baba Amr would end in a bloodbath, like the coup d'état by the Muslim Brotherhood in 1982. General Assef Shawkat made contact with the French Minister for the Interior, Claude Guéant, who was as opposed to this war as he had been to the war against Libya. The two men agreed on a "Peace of the Brave". The French officers present on the ground would be allowed to evacuate freely, but the Syrian Takfiri would have to surrender. Guéant sent a brilliant officer of the DCRI (General Directorate for Internal Security) who had been attached to the French embassy, and was at that time stationed in Jordan. He was received by Michel Kassouha, the man who been unjustly declared *persona non grata* in France in 1982.

The two sides agreed that I should be their "trusted third party". This was not the first time that the Elysée had asked me for a favour, while at the same ordering the DGSE to have me "neutralised". It had already solicited me as an intermediary in secret negotiations with President Hugo Chávez, in order to avoid using the channels of the French Foreign Ministry, thus remaining secret from the United States. Of course, I acted in the interest of both Syria and France.

The negotiations were interrupted after several days so that Moscow could have time to intercede with Paris. In the end, the agreement was implemented. The French were evacuated with the "journalists". The 19 other officers who had been taken prisoner during the war were also freed. France's ambassador in Beirut, Denis Piéton, and the army Chief of Staff, Admiral Edouard Guillaud, came to collect both groups at the Lebanese border. Officially, these French soldiers were "deserters" from the Foreign Legion – and yet some of them were carrying secured NATO communications attaché-cases when they were arrested, and were welcomed by the Chief of Staff in person.

France withdrew from the war. In so doing, it pulled the rug out from under Angus McKee, the MI6 agent who was directing the operations from the British embassies in Damascus and Beirut, and Lord David Richards, British Chief of Staff, who had planned to attack Syria with 100,000 men. Washington began to panic. The NSA was ordered to hack the computers of the Elysée Palace in order to understand the French about-face. This was done.

The affair of the French prisoners was reported by the non-Western Press, particularly by Russia Today. But the Elysée intervened, and spoke to the major French media, all of whom then neglected to mention the affair.

In Paris, the time had come for some scores to be settled. The French embassy in Damascus had been closed, and the personnel repatriated. Ambassador Eric Chevallier received the journalists, and revealed "off the record" that the Minister had falsified his reports so that they would correspond with his colonial fantasies. The two men had been contradicting one another from the very start of the war, with Alain Juppé demanding that Chevallier validate the accusations by France

24 about the children whose finger-nails had allegedly been ripped out, and the existence of demonstrations for democracy. The ambassador apparently maintained that he was unable to verify the first information, and that the demonstrations had not been as numerous as was pretended, and bore no slogans in favour of democracy.

On 1 April, Alain Juppé participated in the second conference of the "Friends of Syria" in Istanbul, where 83 states and international organisations were present. That was better than the conference in Tunis. But France did not play a role. The conference took note that it would not be possible to apply the initial plan for Syria, and treat the conflict like the one in Libya, without entering into direct conflict with Russia and China. It was however considered possible to attack Syria without the authorisation of the Security Council, as had been done against Yugoslavia (currently Serbia) in Kosovo. With this aim in mind, US ambassador Stephen Rapp was tasked with creating the Syria Justice and Accountability Centre, a "NGO" based in The Hague. It was to collect all the testimony possible in order to compile a dossier of accusations which would enable the conviction of President al-Assad before an international tribunal. As for Nicolas Sarkozy, he was taking care of nothing other than his own re-election.

François Hollande and the return of the Colonial Party

Surprise – Sarkozy lost the Presidential election. Leaving the Elysée, he was employed by Qatar for an annual salary of 3 million Euros, with a directorship of Columbia Investments, a Qatari sovereign wealth fund.

Although he had been elected under the banner of the Socialist Party, François Hollande governed in the interests of the "Colonial Party". After eighteen months of his term, he announced to his astonished electors that he was not a Socialist, but rather a Social-Democrat. In reality, he had been clear about this from the day he took power. Like his predecessors, he placed the ceremony of inauguration under the auspices of a historical figure – he chose Jules Ferry (1832-1893). While it is true that Ferry organised free schooling, in his day he was extremely unpopular, and was known by the nickname of "the Tonkinese". He was indeed the man who defended the interests of the main industrial groups in Tunisia, in Tonkin and in the Congo, which launched France into a number of racist and colonial adventures. And contrary to what is commonly admitted, his interest for primary school teaching was not directed towards the education of children, but towards their preparation as the soldiers of colonisation. This is why his teachers were known as the "black hussars".

It may seem strange to use the term "French colonialism" when speaking about François Hollande, since the expression is so old-fashioned. It is often poorly understood, because it is wrongly associated with colonisation by settlement, when in fact it is above all an economic concept. In the 19th century, peasants and workers were resisting, sometimes to the death, the bosses who exploited them shamelessly. This led some of the elite to the idea that it would be easier to take advantage of less well organised populations. In order to succeed at this, they modified both the national myth and the secular organisation of the state in order to wrench the people from the influence of the Churches.

Arriving at the Elysée, François Hollande chose Jean-Marc Ayrault as his Prime Minister. Ayrault had a reputation as a reasonable man, but strongly supported the colonisation of Palestine. He became Honorary President of the Cercle Léon Blum, an association created by Dominique Strauss-Kahn in order to assemble the Zionists in the Socialist Party.

Hollande named Laurent Fabius as Minister for Foreign Affairs. The two men had once been rivals, but Fabius had negotiated with the Emir of Qatar, and especially with Israel, for their support during Hollande's electoral campaign. Fabius is a man without convictions, who has frequently changed his mind on major questions, depending on the opportunities they presented. In 1984, while he was Prime Minister, he allowed the contamination and death of 2,000 haemophiliacs in order to protect the interests of the Institut Pasteur, whose AIDS detection test was not yet ready. Thanks to François Mitterrand, who modified the rules of procedure, he was discharged by the Law Court of the Republic according to the principle "responsible but not guilty". His Minister for Health, Edmond Hervé, was convicted in his place.

Hollande chose his friend Jean-Yves Le Drian as his Minister for Defence. The two men had worked together for years as Socialist Party loyalists and protégés of President of the European

Commission, Jacques Delors. During the electoral campaign, Le Drian went to Washington, where he pledged allegiance, in Hollande's name, to the United States Empire.

Besides this, in an unprecedented decision, President Hollande maintained his predecessor's private Chief of Staff at his post – General Benoît Puga. The officer was older than the President, and shared the extreme-right convictions of the President's father. He enjoyed the right to enter the President's office at any time, and maintained a quasi-paternal relationship with him.

Before anything else, François Hollande made an assessment of the destruction of Libya. The Jamahiriya had been in possession of funds evaluated at a minimum of $150 billion. Officially, NATO had blocked, or had ordered the blockage of, at least a third of it. What happened to the rest? The Gaddafists thought they could use this money to finance the Resistance in the long term. But in April, Prefect[10] Edouard Lacroix, who had received access to a part of these investments, died in the space of one day from "lightning cancer", while the Libyan ex-Minister for Oil, Shukri Ghanem, was found drowned in Vienna. With the aid of French Minister of Finance Pierre Moscovici, economic advisor to the Elysée Emmanuel Macron,[11] and several investment bankers, the US Treasury made off with the loot – the bank heist of the century, $100 billion.

At the beginning of June 2012, France and the United Kingdom participated in a meeting of the "Friends of Syria" work group, the "International Conference for Economic Recovery and Development", which was held in Abu Dhabi in the United Arab Emirates and presided over by Germany. The point of this meeting was to get the member states to join in the war by promising them a bounty. Several years earlier, the Norwegian companies InSeis Terra and Sagex Petroleum had officially undertaken the search for hydrocarbons in Syria. Although they declared that they had detected

---

[10] A prefect is an executive of a prefecture, which is the capital city of a department, or province. The office is appointed by the central government as its representative at the local level, particularly for security matters. The department also has its own president chosen by a popularly elected council.

[11] The complete unknown Macron was handpicked to be the new prime minister in May 2017, apparently as a reward. Moscovici, an ex-Trotskyite Jew, went on to become European Commissioner for Economic and Financial Affairs, Taxation and Customs in 2014.

13 oil and gas fields in only two dimensions, they had actually explored them all in three dimensions, and thus knew the value of every one of them. Since Sagex had been bought by a Franco-US company listed on the London Stock Exchange, CGG Veritas, and then absorbed by the Schlumberger group, three states soon found themselves in possession of this precious information – but still not Syria, who did not find out until 2013. According to this research, Syria owns underground reserves at least as rich as those of Qatar!

The United Kingdom placed Osama al-Kadi, a British Gas executive, in the Syrian National Council. With his help, Paris and London allocated concessions to the attendees in the future exploitation of a country that they had not yet conquered.

Saudi Arabia was preparing to launch its army on Damascus, while the United Kingdom was to handle the Syrian media. The coordination of forces had been tested in Jordan during the exercise Eager Lion 2012, under US command. The Lebanese leaders agreed to remain neutral by signing the Baabda Declaration. Syria was expected to fall quickly. But then Russia fired two intercontinental missiles, a Topol from the shores of the Caspian Sea, and a Bulava from a submarine in the Mediterranean. The message was clear – if the Westerners had not understood the two Russian and Chinese vetoes in the Security Council, and chose to attack Syria anyway, they would have to prepare for a new World War. A dispute blew up with Sergei Lavrov to determine who was on the "right side of History".

On 30 June, in Geneva, ex-Secretary General of the UN, Kofi Annan, mandated both by his successor Ban Ki-moon and by the Secretary General of the Arab League, presided over an international conference concerning the future of the Syrian Arab Republic. No Syrian representative was invited – either from the government or the Syrian National Council. The United States and Russia agreed that they would not go to war over the Near East. They decided on the creation of a government of national union, under the presidency of Bashar al-Assad, along with a few elements of the SNC. The war was officially over. The world had once again become bipolar, as it had been during the Cold War.

Except that Secretary of State Hillary Clinton had no intention of ratifying the end of the unipolar world, nor of respecting her signature (which, according to her, had been extorted under threat), and except that the French and British Ministers expressed reservations about the interpretation of the final communiqué.

It was at that point that the DGSE managed to organise the defection of a childhood friend of President al-Assad, General Manaf Tlass, and brought him to Paris. The DGSE presented him as a top-level personality. In reality, Manaf had become a General by following in the footsteps of his father, General Mustafa Tlass, ex-Minister for Defence. Manaf Tlass was an artist who had never been interested in politics. At the start of the war, he had negotiated a compromise with the "revolutionaries" in order to bring peace to his native city of Rastan, but the agreement had been rejected by the President. Tlass bore a powerful grudge about this. Since Manaf was a friend of mine, the French press, which, like the French political class, lives only for money, concluded that he financed the Réseau Voltaire, which is untrue. In Paris, he was received by his father, who settled there when he retired in 2004; by his brother Firas, who, from Qatar, directed the construction of the jihadists' tunnel system; and by his sister, who was the mistress of Roland Dumas, and then of journalist Franz-Olivier Guisbert, with whom she still works. However, Manaf arrived too late to enjoy being nominated President in exile by the "Friends of Syria" conference.

The seeds of greed planted in Abu Dhabi proved to be fruitful indeed. Everyone rushed to the third conference of the "Friends of Syria" on 6 July 2012 in Paris. 130 states and inter-governmental organisations were present, no doubt lured by the scent of oil and gas. Despite the fact that Hillary Clinton and Sergei Lavrov had solemnly signed a peace treaty one week before, a strong US delegation was present in Paris ready to relaunch the war.

François Hollande mounted the podium and asked that Abu Saleh be seated next to him – Saleh was the young "journalist" from France 24 who had fled with the French from Baba Amr. After the meeting, Hollande lengthily praised the "revolutionaries" in full view of the cameras of the Elysée. However, these images were withdrawn from both the internal and official sites when I pointed out that Abu Saleh was an anti-Human Rights criminal who had participated in the revolutionary tribunals of the emirate, which convicted 150 Christian and Alawite civilians, and had their throats slit.

President Hollande's speech was not written by his cabinet, but composed in English in Washington, New York or Tel-Aviv, then translated into French. After having saluted the efforts of Kofi Annan as progress in the right direction, he exclaimed "Bashar Al-Assad must go, a transitional government must be constituted!" *De facto*, he changed the meaning of the word "transition" which, in the Geneva Communiqué, signified the passage from a time of disorder to a time of peace. It now meant the transition between a Syria with Bashar al-Assad and the secular institutions inspired by the French Revolution, to another, entrusted to the Muslim Brotherhood. The expression "political transition" now replaced the phrase "régime change". The SNC exulted, and Hillary rejoiced.

The unanimity of the "Friends of Syria" was certainly founded on their taste for hydrocarbons, but there was an irrational side to it. I could not help thinking that this was the largest coalition in human history, and it was still pursuing the ancient confrontation between the Roman Empire and the network of Syrian trading posts. The slogan of Cato the Elder resounded in my ears: *"Carthago delenda est"* – Carthage is to be destroyed!

Over the days that followed, François Hollande, David Cameron and Hillary Clinton kept repeating like a mantra "Bashar must go!" – thus recycling the slogans of the Colour Revolutions ("Enough of Chevardnaze!" or "Ben Ali out!"). Addressing their counterparts as if they were a street mob, they no longer referred to President al-Assad other than by his first name, "Bashar". These manners did nothing for them apart from displaying their impotence and ignorance.

On 12 July, 2012, operation "Damascus Volcano and Syrian Earthquake" began.[12] More than 40,000 mercenaries from all the Arab countries, trained by the CIA in Jordan, supervised by France and the United Kingdom, and paid for by Saudi Arabia, crossed the frontier, mostly from Jordan, and charged towards Damascus.

The French retreat during the liberation of Baba Amr, and the peace treaty signed just two weeks earlier in Geneva, were now nothing more than distant memories. A new war against Syria had begun, this time with armies of mercenaries. It was to be considerably more deadly than the first.

---

[12] http://www.voltairenet.org/article175077.html

The second war against Syria

On 18 July, 2012, an explosion destroyed the headquarters of the National Security Council in Damascus, killing General Daoud Rajiha (Minister of Defence), General Assef Shawkat (head of Military Intelligence, and brother-in-law of President al-Assad), and General Hassan Turkmani (President of the Council). General Hisham Ikhtiyar (head of counter-espionage) died soon afterwards as a result of his injuries. It seemed that a traitor had placed a bomb in a ceiling light, but it is not impossible that a missile was fired from a drone. The armies and the security services were deprived of their leaders. There was fighting everywhere. People were killed in the streets. Most of the inhabitants of the capital had fled.

Commenting on the attack that cost the lives of the members of the SNC, the Western leaders refused to condemn terrorism. Instead they announced that the dead had got no more than they deserved.

The assailants' targets had been pre-defined. A unit attacked my house in Mezzeh, where the city gives way to an expanse of Barbary figs. The army installed a mortar on the roof to keep them at bay. When the battle ended three days later, the bodies we found were those of Pakistani and Somali soldiers. But in other areas of the capital, they were Tunisians, Afghans, and men of several other nationalities. These men had received a short course in the use of weapons in Jordan, sometimes no more than a week. They had been organised per unit according to their origins, but did not constitute an army in the proper sense of the term, because they had no hierarchical structure. Many of them knew nothing about Syria, and some of them even believed that they were saving Palestinians in Israel.

A studio was set up in the basement of the Hotel Dama Rose, where General Robert Mood and the UN observers were living in luxury. Their presence guaranteed the security of the building. The governor of the Central Bank, Adib Mayaleh, appeared on TV to refute the claims of Al-Jazeera and Al-Arabiya, who had announced the collapse of the Syrian pound. ArabSat and NileSat disconnected the Syrian television stations which still functioned, while the CIA hacked the Twitter account of Al-Dounia TV to announce the retreat of the Syrian Arab Army and the fall of the régime. Syrian television signals reappeared on ArabSat and NileSat – they were not broadcast from Syria, however, but from a US National Security Agency base in Australia. In Qatar, France 24 participated in the media pool which had been requisitioned for NATO propaganda. The plan was for a coordinated broadcast of a series of reports, either filmed in an open-air studio or composed of synthetic images, attesting to the flight of President al-Assad and the fall of the "Alawite dictatorship". However, the country resisted, and the mercenaries left Damascus.

At the United Nations Security Council, Russia and China vetoed a draft resolution authorising Western military intervention, for the third time. The United States backed off. The fake Syrian TV programmes reporting the flight of President al-Assad were not broadcast.

On 24 July, King Abdallah of Arabia rewarded Prince Bandar Bin Sultan for the attack on Damascus, and named him as head of the Saudi secret services. However, four days later, his office blew up. He was seriously injured, and prematurely, I announced his death. In reality, it was his assistant Mishaal Al-Qani who died. Prince Bandar was hospitalised for a whole year, and was never able to fully recover his faculties.

The Press revealed that President Obama had signed a directive authorising a secret military intervention coordinated by NATO. Aware that all his efforts would be approved to his face and sabotaged behind his back, Kofi Annan resigned from his function as mediator on 2 August.

On 5 August, "Prime Minister" Riyad Hijab fled, with the help of the DGSE. This time, the prize had more symbolic value, but no value at all on the executive level. Syria is the oldest state in the world. Constituted 6,000 years ago on a land of passage, it had learned to survive by organising in secret. Today, only the Chief Executive, President Bashar al-Assad, remains visible. He is responsible before his people, and presides over three concentric circles of power. First of all the government, which directs the administration. His Ministers are therefore the equivalent of our directors of the central administrations. Then his Palace advisors, who have authority over the Ministers. Finally, his private advisors, with whom he makes his decisions. Syria is a republican régime, because the Executive acts in the general interest, and may be sanctioned by the People – but it is not democratic, because the most important decisions are not discussed in public. As concerns Riyad Hijab, he had never been "Prime Minister" – this function does not exist in the Constitution – but Secretary for the Council of Ministers, which is not at all the same thing in this system. His function consisted of receiving the order of the day and the directives established by the Palace, in order to transmit them to the Ministers and receive the accounts of their activities. Unlike the death of members of the National Security Council, his departure was without importance.

I remember my astonishment, during a meeting several months earlier, when General Hassan Turkmani asked me what I thought about an important subject. In my answer, I noted, among other things, that Mr. Hijab ought to be alerted. The General replied with a smile – "There's no point troubling him with such an important decision".

For Paris, no holds were barred. One of President al-Assad's advisors was recruited by the DGSE, but this source had no access to state secrets. Then, on 17 August 2012, the Minister for Foreign Affairs, Laurent Fabius, declared – "I am fully aware of the force of what I am saying – Mister Bashar al-Assad does not deserve to be on this Earth" – a somewhat surprising position for a Minister in charge of Diplomacy for a country which is opposed to the death penalty. In September, Hollande and Fabius met with Recep Tayyip Erdoğan in New York to develop a "Homo" operation (targeted assassination) against their opposite numbers, the Syrian Minister for Foreign Affairs, Walid Moallem, and President al-Assad.

It was not the first time that the France of the Fifth Republic had attempted to assassinate a foreign President. In 2008, Nicolas Sarkozy had sent a team to Caracas, commanded by "Frederic Laurent Bouquet", to assassinate President Hugo Chávez. This time, like the last time, the DGSE were unable to fulfil their mission. The plan relied on the cleaning staff of the Ministry and the Palace, Kurds whom the DGSE thought it could manipulate. But the plot was discovered.

On 12 December 2012, while he was participating in the 4th international conference of the "Friends of Syria" in Marrakech, Laurent Fabius took exception to the decision by the White House to put the al-Nusra Front (al-Qaeda) on the list of terrorist organisations. During the final Press conference, he declared that "all Arabs stand against" the US position, "because, on the ground, they (al-Qaeda) are doing a good job". "It is very clear, and the President of the Coalition also adopts this position".

In less than 10 years, France, which had been acclaimed at the Security Council during the speech by Dominique de Villepin against the Iraq war, had shrivelled to the rank of a "gangster state", using political assassination – or attempted assassination in my case – and supporting Islamist terrorists against a secular state. Worse still, it was no longer hiding the resurgence of its unspeakable ambitions – on 25 September at the UN, François Hollande asked to be allowed to "protect the liberated zones", in other words, to progressively re-establish the colonial mandate awarded to France by the League of Nations between 1923 and 1944.

During the year that followed, France maintained the fiction that the combatants were Syrians who had defected from the army. This is the myth of the Free Syrian Army (FSA), who were allegedly fighting for democracy. However, not once during the five long years of warfare did anyone provide a single image of demonstrations in favour of democracy. At best, there were slogans in favour of "liberty". But this was not the Liberté of the French Revolutionaries (by whom Ba'ath claims to be inspired). On the contrary, these demonstrators were demanding the right to apply "freely" their interpretation of Sharia law. However, several scandals dogged this tale. On 13 May 2013, one of the commanders of the Al-Farouk Brigade (Free Syrian Army) broadcast a video where he can be seen eating the entrails of a soldier of the Syrian Arab Army, declaring – "We swear before God that we will eat your hearts and your livers, soldiers of Bashar. Oh heroes of Baba Amr, massacre the Alawites. Cut out their hearts and eat them". Or again, when the Free Syrian Army massacred the Christians of al-Duvair.

On 11 January 2013, a new contradiction appeared in France's foreign policies – not between rhetoric and practise, but in terms of its alliances. "The more you eat, the hungrier you get", goes the proverb. François Hollande decided on military intervention in Mali. This was not an episode of the Arab Spring, but a direct consequence of the destruction of the Libyan Arab Jamahiriya, as had been predicted long before by Mohammed Siala, Muammar Gaddafi's Minister for Cooperation and administrator of the Libyan Investment Authority.

The Tuaregs are a nomadic people who live in the central Sahara and on the borders of the Sahel – a huge belt of semi-arid scrub land, shared between Libya, Algeria, Mali and Niger. While they have obtained the protection of the first two states, they have, on the contrary, been abandoned by the other two. Consequently, since the 1960's, they have constantly been questioning the sovereignty of Mali and Niger on their territory. With perfect logic, they decided to bring their demands to fruition in Mali. The National Movement for the Liberation of Azawad (NMLA) took power in almost all of Northern Mali, where they live. However, a small group of Islamist Tuaregs, Ansar Dine, trained by Saudi Arabia and attached to AQMI (al-Qaeda in Islamic Maghreb), profited from the occasion to impose the Sharia in a few localities.

On 21 March 2012, an astonishing coup d'état was perpetrated in Mali. A mysterious "National Committee for the Recovery of Democracy and the Restoration of the State" (CNRDRE) overthrew President Amadou Toumani Touré and declared that it wanted to restore Malian authority in the North of the country. The result was general confusion, since the putschists were incapable of explaining how their actions would improve the situation. The overthrow of the President was all the more bizarre in that a Presidential election was planned for five weeks later, and the outgoing incumbent was not running again. The CNRDRE was composed of officers who had been trained in the United States. It barred the election and handed power to one of its candidates, as it happened the Francophile Dioncounda Traoré. This piece of prestidigitation was legalised by the Economic Community of West African States, (CEDEAO), whose President was none other than Alassane Ouattara of the Ivory Coast, placed in power a year earlier by the French army.

The coup d'état accentuated the ethnic division in the country. Since the elite forces of the Malian army (trained in the USA) had a Tuareg command structure, they joined the rebellion with their arms and equipment.

Ansar Dine – supported by other Islamist groups – attacked the town of Konna. They had therefore left Tuareg territory with the intention of spreading Islamic law in the South of Mali. Transitional President Dioncounda Traoré declared a state of emergency and called for help from France. Paris intervened in the hours that followed in order to prevent the fall of the capital city, Bamako. Clairvoyant, the Elysée had pre-positioned military forces in Mali: men from its 1st Marine Infantry Parachute Regiment ("la Coloniale") and the 13th Parachute Dragoon Regiment, helicopters from Special Operations Command, three Mirage 2000D's, two Mirage F-1's, three C135's, a C130 Hercules, and a C160 Transall.

The operation was well-led, but specified al-Qaeda as the enemy, even though, in reality, the fight was against the Tuareg insurgents. Yet this was the same al-Qaeda which was "doing a good job" in Syria, and had organised the Free Syrian Army, supported by France. Panic-stricken, the Elysée ordered the French army to halt its advance in Mali, in order to allow the jihadists' Qatari military advisors to withdraw. Qatar broke off its special relations with France, while on the ground, the FSA organised demonstrations, singing – "The French are bastards. Our (Islamic) nation will be victorious".

François Hollande attempted to repair his stupid mistake and patch things up with his benefactor, Emir al-Thani. He rushed off to Doha in a panic, where he received a chilly reception. However, as Nature abhors a vacuum, Saudi Arabia and Turkey rushed in to fill the void.

The "red line"

In May 2013, NATO issued a report to its members indicating that 70% of the Syrian population supported President al-Assad. 20% supported the rebels and 10% expressed no opinion. Paris and Ankara concluded that there would be no victory unless they returned to the initial plan and bombed Syria. It would be necessary to take the initiative in order to bring pressure to bear on Washington.

On 21 August, a chemical attack affected Syrian civilians in Ghouta, a suburb of Damascus, in a zone controlled by the jihadists. In the hours that followed, a vast communications machine roared into action, accusing the Syrian Arab Republic of being responsible. This attack supposedly marked the crossing of the "red line" drawn by President Obama. The Westerners were said to be preparing to "punish the régime" by bombing its capital.

The Syrian government denied any involvement, and pointed out that on 23 May, in Adana, Turkish police had arrested 11 jihadists in possession of a large supply of sarin gas. Though the head of this group, Haytham Qassap, was of Syrian nationality, the others were Turkish. Besides this, the Free Syrian Army had itself broadcast videos of a small laboratory for the manufacture of chemical weapons, and threatened the Alawites with gassing.

The facts about Ghouta have to be examined with caution. The US secret services claimed that they had watched the Syrian Arab Army preparing the gas for four days, but without intervening. Videos were broadcast by the opposition, but one of them was dated and time-stamped by YouTube (Pacific Standard Time) at a time before sunrise in Damascus, although it was clearly filmed in daylight. The victims were either children – all the same age – or men. There were only 2 females out of the 1,429 victims counted by the United States. The dead children were revealed to have been Alawites who had been kidnapped by the jihadists a few weeks earlier. Even though they were officially absent from the country, France and the United Kingdom assured that they had taken samples on site and had tested them immediately. The tests betrayed the use of sarin gas. The problem with this result is that the only known test takes ten days to perform.

According to the French and UK intelligence services, intercepted telephone calls between officers attested to the use of chemical weapons by the Syrian army. But it soon transpired that the "telephone interceptions" had been carried out by the Israelis. It soon appears that French military intelligence was acting cautiously. It was not responsible for the intel summary distributed by the French Ministry of Defence. The summary was drawn up by Sacha Mandel, an Israelo-French bi-national, one of the Minister's advisors.

In substance, we do not understand why the use of chemical weapons would be a "red line". How are they any worse than other "weapons of mass destruction"? Why would the United States, a signatory of the Biological Weapons Convention, complain about their use by Syria, which is not a signatory, when the US itself had betrayed its own signature in 2003 in the palm groves of Baghdad?

When chemical weapons first appeared, during the First World War, they came as a surprise, and because of this, they were particularly murderous. However, the various states quickly discovered ways of dealing with them, so that none of the belligerents made significant use of them on the battlefield during the Second World War. In the Near East, Israel refused to sign the Convention, and drew with it Egypt and Syria. From 1985 to 1994, Israel had financed research in South Africa aimed at creating weapons which were racially selective. The search was for toxic agents which would kill black people or Arabs, but not Jewish people. The work was conducted under the direction of President Peter Botha's cardiologist, Colonel

Wouter Basson. We do not know if this work was crowned with success, though it seems improbable from the scientific standpoint. Several thousand human "lab rats" died during the experiments.

The British services quickly confirmed the observations mentioned above, and warned Prime Minister David Cameron about a false-flag operation. Syrian television broadcast a video of one of the jihadist's drivers. He told of having travelled to Turkey, where he had collected toxic shells from a Turkish barracks, and then secretly transported them to Damascus.

Interviewed by the Russian Press, Syrian President Bashar al-Assad replied – "The declarations made by United States and Western politicians, and also those of other countries, are an insult to common sense and an expression of contempt for the opinion of their people. It's nonsense – first they publish accusations, then they go looking for the proof (…) This sort of denunciation is exclusively political – it is a response to the series of victories won by government forces over the terrorists".

As for François Hollande, he proclaimed long and loud that his conscience was ordering him to "hit" Damascus. By these declarations, he was pursuing the work of the Colonial Party which, during the provisional governments of Charles de Gaulle and Georges Bidault, in May 1945 and November 1946, bombed, on their own initiative, the towns of Sétif, Guelma and Kherrata (Algeria), then Damascus (Syria), and finally Hải Phòng (IndoChina/Vietnam). At the moment he withdrew his troops, just after Syria's declaration of independence, General Fernand Olive ordered his army to attack Damascus, for no other reason than to express his resentment. He destroyed a part of the thousand-year old souk (just as was done recently in Aleppo) and the National Assembly, symbol of the new Republic he rejected.

Germany was the first to observe that even if Syria had used chemical weapons, the retaliatory bombing remained illegal according to international law, except in the case of a decision by the Security Council. The British and the United States finally came to the conclusion that the affair had been fabricated by Turkey with the support of France and Israel.

In London, the House of Commons forbade the Prime Minister to attack Damascus until the responsibility of Bashar al-Assad's government was proved conclusively. The deputies, many of whom were aware of the depth of involvement of their country against Syria, remembered the damage done to their reputation after joining the war against Iraq in 2003, on the basis of the fraudulent accusations by George Bush and Tony Blair. In Washington, Barack Obama left it up to Congress, which he knew was opposed to any new military adventure, whatever it might be. This was a delaying tactic, because the Syrian Accountability Act of 2003 gave him all the power needed to destroy Syria.

François Hollande, who had spoken too loud and too fast, was the only player left in the game. He hid in the Elysée while France's word was discredited on the international stage. No one questioned Turkey, especially not Anne Lauvergnon, Alexandre Adler, Joachim Bitterlich, Hélène Conway-Mouret, Jean-François Copé, Henri de Castries, Augustin de Romanet, Laurence Dumont, Claude Fischer, Stéphane Foulks, Bernard Guetta, Élisabeth Guigou, Hubert Haenel, Jean-Pierre Jouyet, Alain Juppé, Pierre Lellouche, Thierry Mariani, Gérard Mestrallet, Thierry de Montbrial, Pierre Moscovici, Philippe Petitcolin, Alain Richard, Michel Rocard, Daniel Rondeau, Bernard Soulage, Catherine Tasca, Denis Verret and Wilfried Verstraete, all of whom had received "gifts" from Turkish business leaders in the name of Recep Tayyip Erdoğan.

Russia helped the United States to extricate itself from the crisis with its head held high, by inviting Syria to sign the Chemical Weapons Convention, which it did without hesitation. President Bashar al-Assad negotiated with the Organisation for the Prohibition of Chemical Weapons to find a way of destroying the existing stocks – to be paid for by the United States.

Later, US journalist Seymour M. Hersh threw light on the hesitations of his country in this affair.[13] Professors Richard Lloyd and Theodore Postol of the Massachusetts Institute of Technology demonstrated that the chemical shells had been fired from the "rebel" zone. However, France alone persisted in accusing the Syrian Arab Republic. "Give a dog a bad name and hang him", as the popular saying goes. (In French, *"Qui veut noyer son chien l'accuse de la rage* – Who wishes to drown his dog, accuses it of rabies.")

---

[13] "Whose Sarin?" by Seymour Hersh, 19 December 2013 and "The Red Line and the Rat Line," 4 April, 2014, *London Review of Books*

In any case, the Western powers regularly accused Syria of the use of chemical weapons, even though all stocks had been destroyed jointly by Russia and the United States. This little game came to a halt, or should have, when Damascus found similar weapons in the jihadist bunkers. They had been delivered by the CIA, and had been fabricated by Chemring Defence (United Kingdom), and by Federal Laboratories and Nonlethal Technologies (USA).

Indecision

Having closed its embassy and repatriated all its personnel in 2012, having withdrawn the majority of its Special Forces after the engagement in Mali at the start of 2013, and having been disowned by Washington, Paris no longer had any presence on the ground, and no plan of action.

With no idea what to do, François Hollande turned to his perennial ally, Tel-Aviv, which had supplied him with fraudulent proof of Syrian responsibility in the false flag attack on Ghouta. Here we have to take a quick look back at Hollande's activity in favour of the colonisation of Palestine during his mandate as First Secretary of the Socialist Party:

▶ In 2000, while South Lebanon was still occupied, Hollande and the future Mayor of Paris, Bertrand Delanoë, prepared Prime Minister Lionel Jospin's visit to Palestine. The speech written for Jospin (another ex-Trotskyite) included a condemnation of the Lebanese Resistance to the Occupation, which was equated with terrorism.

▶ In 2001, Hollande demanded the resignation of Socialist Party geo-politician Pascal Boniface, who was found guilty of having criticised, in an internal memo, the blind support of Israel by the Socialists.

▶ In 2004, Hollande wrote to the Superior Audiovisual Council to question the broadcasting authorisation awarded to Al-Manar, the television channel of Hezbollah. He did not cease to apply pressure until the channel was censored.

▶ In 2005, Hollande was received behind closed doors by the Representative Council of French Jewish Institutions (CRIF). According to the minutes of the meeting, he expressed support for Ariel Sharon and sharply criticised the Gaullist Arab policy. He apparently declared – "There is an old tendency which is known as France's Arab policy, and it is inadmissible for an administration to function according to an ideology. There is a recruitment problem at the Quai d'Orsay and the Ecole Nationale d'Administration,[14] and this recruitment must be reorganised". By saying this, he turned reality on its head, because "France's Arab policy" is not a policy in favour of Arabs against the Israelis, but a policy within the Arab world.

▶ In 2006, Hollande took position against Iran's President Ahmadinejad, who had invited to Teheran a number of rabbis and historians, including certain holocaust revisionists. Hollande pretended that he did not know the purpose of the congress, which was to demonstrate that the Europeans had substituted the religion of the Holocaust for their Christian culture. And completely back to front, he absurdly claimed that the Iranian President was trying to deny the right of Israelis to exist, and that he was ready to continue the Holocaust.

▶ Hollande mobilised for the liberation of Israeli soldier Gilad Shalit, a prisoner of Hamas, on the grounds that Shalit enjoyed double nationality with France. He took no note of the fact that the young man had been arrested while he was serving in an army of occupation in a war against the Palestinian Authority, which was also an ally of France.

▶ In 2010, with Bertrand Delanoë and Bernard-Henri Levy, he published an op-ed in *Le Monde* opposing the boycott of Israeli products. He claimed that the boycott would be a collective punishment which would also affect the Israelis who were working for peace with the Palestinians. However, he did not use this logic during a similar campaign against apartheid in South Africa.

As soon as he arrived at Tel-Aviv airport, he declared "Tamid echa-er raver chel Israel", which in Hebrew means "I am, and will always be your friend".

Israeli Prime Minister Benjamin Netanyahu observed that the United States and the United Kingdom had withdrawn from the theatre of operations – which, however, did not prevent the CIA and MI6 from

---

[14] The Quai d'Orsay is the location of the Foreign Ministry, and the ENA is an exclusive university that is a training ground for top officials in the French government

pursuing their secret war. He therefore proposed to set up coordination between those states that wanted to continue the open war until the Syrian Arab Republic was overthrown – Saudi Arabia, France, Israel, Qatar and Turkey. Lebanon and Jordan would continue their logistical aid, but would not take part in the direction of operations. Since Washington did not want to advertise its involvement, the operation was to be directed by Jeffrey Feltman from the UN in New York. Speed was of the essence, because storm clouds were brewing in Washington. The partisans of an attack on Syria were pushed aside. On 8 November, General David Petraeus was forced to resign from his functions as director of the CIA, while Hillary Clinton, victim of an "accident", disappeared for a month.

Jeffrey D. Feltman was the one-man band of the Arab Spring, and also a good friend of Netanyahu.[15] Feltman had become Director of Political Affairs for the UN more than a year earlier. He ordered that a plan be drawn up by Volker Perthes for the total and unconditional surrender of Syria. Perthes is the director of Stiftung Wissenschaft und Politik (SWP), the most powerful think-tank in Europe. He had also taken charge of North Africa and the Middle East for the European External Action Service. The High Representative of the European Union, Catherine Ashton, had become his parrot. For the second time, Feltman entrusted Saudi Arabia with the training of an army of 50,000 men in Jordan. At the same time, he began re-organising the jihadist groups. Finally, on instructions from the White House, he organised the "Geneva 2" negotiations.

Benjamin Netanyahu imagined an *alliance à trois* – France would defend Israeli and Saudi interests on the international stage, in exchange for gigantic contracts, investments and bribes. It was a tactic for sabotaging the US-UN-European-Iranian negotiations, so as to maintain the monopoly of the regional directorate of Tel-Aviv and Riyadh.

The King of Arabia, one of whose most important agents, the terrorist Majed al-Majed, had just been arrested by the Lebanese army, proposed to offer $3 billion worth of French weapons if the Lebanese would agree not to record al-Majed's confession. The

---

[15] According to Wikipedia, "Feltman was born to Jewish parents in Greenville, Ohio in 1959... Jeff Feltman has no Jewish background, his family is/was Presbyterian."

terrorist chief conveniently died while the King was distributing his "gifts" to the Lebanese and the French (for example, $100 million for the unconstitutional "President", Michel Suleiman). In reality, although the beneficiaries would keep these royal "gifts", the orders for weapons would never materialise. The only French leader who did not personally receive a royal "gift", Minister for Defence Jean-Yves Le Drian, negotiated on behalf of his constituency for the financial rescue of the poultry group Doux, which was in debt to the tune of 400 million Euros. This would be partially bought and bailed out by the Saudi Al-Munajem Group.

After the resignation of Kofi Annan, the Secretary General of the UN tasked the Algerian Lakhdar Brahimi with the supervision of the Syrian dossier. Unlike Annan, he did not enjoy the title of "mediator", because Ban Ki-moon now also considered that "Bashar must go!" His mission was to steer Syria towards a "political transition, in accordance with the legitimate aspirations of the Syrian people". It is to Brahimi that we owe the creation of the "Decision Support Tool", the Secretary General's personal secret service. The UN was no longer a forum for international peace, but was equipped with a secret service to implement the policies of Washington. French diplomacy was well aware of this, given its successive roles during the end of the Lebanese civil war, the military coup d'état in Algeria and the Anglo-Saxon invasion of Afghanistan.

22 January 2014: Geneva 2 is a trap. It differs from Geneva 1, which brought together the United States and Russia in the presence of their closest partners, but without any Syrians. This time, not only were Syria and the "representatives of the opposition" invited, but so were all the states involved -- except Iran, whose invitation was cancelled after it was delivered, allegedly at the demand of the Saudis. But who could believe that Saudi Arabia enjoyed such influence in the UN? In reality, Jeffrey Feltman also organised the 5+1 negotiations with Iran, and did not intend to allow anything like the lifting sanctions on Iran. As for the representatives of the opposition, they would consist only of those who had been anointed by Arabia, in other words the new National Coalition for Syrian Revolutionary and Opposition Forces, headed by Ahmed Jarba. This man was a low-level drug trafficker who was finally enjoying his little hour of glory – because he was a member of the Saudi-Syrian tribe of the Shammars, the same as the King.

Two days before the opening of the conference, via the London law firm Carter-Ruck, Qatar announced that they were in possession of a report by three ex-international prosecutors concerning the testimony of a certain "Caesar" and the incriminating evidence that he had given them. "Caesar" claimed to be a recently defected officer of the Syrian military police, in charge of photographing crime scenes. He recounted that during the conflict, he had photographed victims of the "régime" in the morgues of military hospitals. He delivered over 55,000 photographs of 11,000 corpses, which he supposedly had taken himself. In order to appear even more distressing, every page of the communiqué announcing the report was headed with two "Confidential" stamps. The three ex-prosecutors concluded that the "prisoners" had been systematically subjected to starvation and torture by the "régime". In reality, the photographs taken in Syria show the bodies of mercenaries of various nationalities collected from the battlefield by the Syrian Arab Army, and those of civilian and military personnel who had died under the torture of jihadists because they supported the Syrian Arab Republic.

The new Secretary of State, John Kerry, who knew Bashar al-Assad well, obviously understood that this was pure propaganda, but the communiqué from Carter-Ruck provided him with a supplementary argument for his speech at Geneva 2 on 22 January 2014.

Since no one really understood what was going on after the eviction of Hillary Clinton and her supporters, TV channels from all over the world were present. Syrian Minister for Foreign Affairs, Walid Muallem – a man whom the French had attempted to assassinate – failed to adapt himself to the situation, and addressed only Syrian public opinion. He therefore missed the only occasion that he would be offered to reveal the Western conspiracy, live, before the eyes of the world. Muallem was a diplomat of rare loyalty – during a meeting of the Arab League, he had refused a 100 million-dollar bribe from his Qatari counterpart if he would turn against his own country. His speech questioned the support for terrorism provided by the "delegation of the opposition" and by their sponsors, who were present in the room.

Finally, nothing came of Geneva 2, because between the time the conference was announced and the conference itself, Washington had adopted a new strategy. The United States had no obligation to give up their dream of a unipolar world and make peace with Russia. They still had one card left to play – specifically terrorism.

While the diplomats were busy speechifying at Geneva 2, President Obama received the King of Jordan in order to agree on terms for Jordan's role. At the same time, National Security Advisor Susan Rice welcomed the heads of the Coalition secret services.

The same as every other year, Congress held a closed session during which it would approve the Pentagon's "black budgets". The existence of this session was attested by a dispatch from the British agency Reuters, but was never mentioned by the US Press, and never appeared in the official registers. The legislators authorised the continuation of the financing and arming of combatant groups in Syria, in violation of resolutions 1267 and 1373 of the Security Council. Whether they realised it or not, they had opened the gates of Hell.

The Syrian People declares itself

In spite of Bassma Kodmani, spokeswoman for the "Syrian opposition" and partner of the ex-director of the French secret services, Jean-Claude Cousseran, who declared that "the regime is incapable of organising a Presidential election, ample proof that it is a dictatorship", a new electoral Code was in fact adopted, in conformity with Western norms, and the election was held.

Until now, the President had been nominated by the Ba'ath Party, then validated by referendum. Now, for the first time, he was to be elected by direct universal suffrage. It was unlikely that the National Coalition of Opposition Forces would present a candidate, not because of the clause requiring that candidates had to have lived in Syria during the preceding ten years, but because the armed groups were violently opposed to democracy. They claimed, as formulated by the Muslim Brotherhood, "The Qu'ran is our constitution", and any ballot is illegal. There was therefore no doubt that the candidate for the régime would be elected. However, his eventual legitimacy would not depend on the percentage of votes registered in his favour, but on the number of these votes and their representativeness in terms of the whole of the population.

France was aware that out of 22 million Syrians, less than 2 million lived in the so-called "liberated zones" (under the iron rule of the jihadists), and therefore could not participate in the ballot. Another 2 million were refugees in Jordan, Lebanon, Turkey and Europe. So in order to sabotage the election, everything had to be done to prevent those Syrians who wanted to participate in the election from being able to do so. France managed to convince its European partners to follow its lead and forbid the installation of polling stations in Syrian Consulates, in violation of the Vienna Convention of 24 April 1963. Assailed by the refugees for this abuse of power, the Council of State[16] recused itself, while the "Friends of Syria" denounced a "parody of democracy" aimed at "guaranteeing the continued existence of the dictatorship".

Three candidates ran in the election – the Communist Maher el-Hajjar, the liberal Hassan al-Nouri, and the Ba'athist Bashar al-Assad. The state provided the candidates with the means for running their campaign, and also guaranteed their security. The media reported their messages. In fact, while the electorate followed their various propositions with interest, al-Assad was in a situation similar to that of de Gaulle in 1945. The choice was between standing behind him for the survival of the Syrian Arab Republic, or abstaining, and thus taking the side of the jihadists.

Expatriate refugees were allowed to vote before the voting began in Syria, although no one believed that it would make much difference. Western propaganda had convinced the Syrians that the refugees were all in favour of the "opposition". And yet, when they were questioned, most of them assured that they had left their motherland because of the fighting, and not "because of the dictatorship". On 28 and 29 May 2014, the ballot in Lebanon, where it was allowed at the embassy, attracted huge crowds – at least 100,000 people, according to Lebanese General Security. They completely blocked the capital. The army intervened to disperse the crowds, but the voters had come from all over the country. Over-run, the embassy was obliged to extend the voting hours, and then had to add additional days. It was a wonderful surprise for the Syrians from Syria and a shock for the Western embassies.

Finally, despite the calls for a boycott, 73.42% of all Syrians of voting age participated in the ballot. 360 foreign medias present on site, and all the embassies open in Damascus, confirmed that the

---

[16] A French agency roughly analogous to the Supreme Court in the USA

election had been fairly run. Bashar al-Assad got 10,319,723 votes, or 88.7% of those registered to vote, and 65% of the population of voting age. Liberal candidate Hassan al-Nouri received 500,279 votes, and Communist candidate Maher el-Hajjar received 372,301 votes.

During this campaign, France and her allies, piloted by Jeffrey Feltman, tried to force the Security Council to recognise the competence of the International Criminal Court in the Syrian civil war. Of course the draft resolution designated all the Syrian actors, both the Republic and the jihadists, but they could count on the fact that prosecutor Fatou Bensouda would legislate as her predecessor Luis Moreno Ocampo had done in Libya – on orders from NATO.

This draft resolution followed the accusations in the reports from "Caesar" and Carter-Ruck, as well as those from the daily *Le Monde*, according to which the "Alawite dictatorship" systematically raped Sunni women from the opposition. *Le Monde* journalist Annick Cojean published the testimony of a victim who declared that "We were raped every day to shouts of 'We Alawites are going to crush you all'". Cojean, president of the Albert Londres Prize, considered the French equivalent of the Pulitzer Prize, was trained by the Franco-American Foundation. It was she who published, long after the death of the Guide, the book *Gaddafi's Harem: The Story of a Young Woman and Abuse of Power in Libya*, an outlandish piece of work which accused him, without the slightest evidence, of having raped many children, thus providing an *a posteriori* justification for the destruction of Libya.

But after the triumphant democratic election of Bashar al-Assad, who could still believe in the cruelty, the generalised tortures, and the "Alawite dictatorship"? The French draft resolution was rejected by Russia and China, who opposed their fourth veto.

Daesh and the Caliphate

A conflict broke out in the ranks of al-Qaeda. The Syrians from the Iraqi Islamic Emirate (Islamic State in Iraq), who had created the Victory Front (in Arabic, "Jabhat al-Nosra" or "Al-Nusra"), entered into competition with their parent organisation when the Iraqis from the ISIS "Emirate" moved into Syria. When the conflict degenerated into a pitched battle, France and Turkey supported the Syrians against the Iraqis. Both countries sent weapons to Al-Nusra, via the empty shell of the Free Syrian Army. However, the combats between the two organisations were not generalised. For instance, in the Qalamoun mountains, on the Lebanese frontier, the same men carried both flags at once.

In May 2014, when Turkey announced to France that it was participating with Saudi Arabia, the United States, Israel, Jordan, the Iraqi Kurdish Regional Government, the Sunni tribes and the Order of Iraqi Naqshbandis, as well as Norway, in the preparation of a vast operation with the Islamic Emirate in Iraq, the internecine war was halted.

France contributed her Special Forces and the services of her multinational Lafarge Cement company. For background, in June 2008, NATO organised the annual meeting of the Bilderberg Group in Chantilly, Virginia, where Hillary Clinton and Barack Obama presented themselves to those present. Among the 120 participants were Basma Kodmani (future spokeswoman for the Syrian National Coalition) and Volker Perthes (future assistant of Jeffrey Feltman for Syria at the UN). During a debate on the permanence of US foreign policy, they underlined the importance of the Muslim Brotherhood and the role it could play in the "democratisation" [sic] of the Arab world. Jean-Pierre Jouyet (future Secretaire General for the Elysée), Manuel Valls (future Prime Minister) and Bertrand Collomb (CEO of Lafarge) were present, alongside Henry R. Kravis (future financial coordinator for Daesh).

Lafarge is the leading cement company in the world. NATO – for whom it had already worked secretly in 1991 – offered Lafarge the job of building jihadist bunkers in Syria, and the reconstruction of the Sunni part of Iraq. In exchange, Lafarge would allow the Alliance to manage its cement plants in both countries, in particular the factory in Jalabiya (on the Turkish frontier, north of Aleppo). For two years, the multinational furnished the materials for the construction of the gigantic underground fortifications which would enable the jihadists to defy the Syrian Arab Army.

The CEO of Lafarge from 2015 to 2017[17] was its long-term American manager Eric Olsen. Under him, Lafarge merged with a

---

[17] Olsen resigned in April, 2017 due to improprieties of Lafarge collaboration with ISIS. The Syrian cement plant had been finished in October 2010, only half a year before the outbreak of the Arab Spring.

Swiss cement company and absorbed the operations of the Egyptian Sawiris brothers and Firas Tlass (the brother of General Manaf Tlass, whom France had once thought of making the next Syrian President). The connections between Lafarge and the French Special Forces were facilitated by the friendship between Bertrand Collomb (who became honorary President of the multinational) and General Benoît Puga (who was still President Hollande's Chief of Staff).

When the on-line magazine *Zaman Al-Wasl* revealed that Lafarge was paying money to Daesh, the daily *Le Monde* stepped in to help. It published its own version of events, assuring that the multinational was paying for the petrol it needed to run its factory. This was untrue, because the installation in question ran on coke, which was still being delivered from Turkey. However, *Le Monde* did reveal, probably without realising it, that Lafarge was building fortifications for Daesh, insofar as it admitted that the 2.6 million tons of cement produced annually were in fact destined for the "rebel zones". Reuters and the *New York Times* admitted that Lafarge paid up to $5 million in protection money to ISIS, who eventually captured and shuttered the huge Syrian plant anyway in 2014.

The quantity of cement produced by Lafarge for Daesh – at least 6 million tons – is comparable to the amount used by the German Reich in 1916-1917 to build the Siegfried Line. As from July 2012, this was no longer a 4th generation war disguised as a revolution, but a classic war of position. Production stopped with the intervention of the Russian aviation, the only air force capable of destroying the bunkers. At the same moment, the factory in Jalibiyeh was transformed into a headquarters for NATO special forces (United States, France, Norway, United Kingdom).

On 7 January 2015, in Paris, two gunmen dressed like military commandos and claiming to be members of al-Qaeda, assassinated members of the editorial staff of satirical magazine *Charlie-Hébdo*, while a third, claiming allegiance to Daesh, killed a policewoman and took the clients of a kosher convenience store as hostages. As usual since 11 September 2001, the terrorists scattered behind them numerous clues which made them easy to identify, in this case their identity papers. The government overplayed its reaction, and the whole country went into shock, and then terror. President Hollande and his Chiefs of Staff took to the streets with more than a million and a half French citizens to shouts of "We are all Charlie!" Among them were the principal allies of France against Syria – Benjamin Netanyahu (Israel) and Ahmet Davutoğlu (Turkey), who publicly supported the jihadists. Since I contested this staged operation, and since many people refused to "be Charlie", the director of Information for France2, Nathalie Saint-Criq, appeared on the TV news to castigate the conspiracy theorists, who must be "identified, handled, integrated or reintegrated into the national community".

Shortly afterwards, we learned that the terrorists had bought their weapons from an ex-mercenary working for the police – the investigation was interrupted by the "Secret Defence" (the classification of information by the Defense Ministry, analogous to "national security secrets" in the US) – and that two of them had been trained by an agent of the DGSE, and also that the heads of state had posed separately for photographs, but had never taken part in the march through Paris. But no matter. The government decreed a state of emergency in France and its overseas possessions, which was approved by Parliament. It was renewed four times and is still in force, on the model of the USA Patriot Act.

In line with the terms of the secret Juppé-Davutoğlu Treaty of 2011, François Hollande envisaged the creation of a "Kurdistan" outside of the historic Kurdish territories, and organised a secret interview at the Elysée, on 31 October 2014, with his Turkish counterpart, Recep Tayyip Erdoğan, and the co-President of the Syrian Kurds, Salih Muslim, to whom he promised the presidency of the future puppet state for the Kurds, betraying the Turkish Kurds and their leader Abdullah Öcalan. However, at the beginning of 2015, the other co-President of the Syrian Kurds Asya Abdullah, won a victory in the battle at Kobane, and was eulogized by the United States. She was an Öcalan loyalist. Hollande reneged on his deal with Turkey, switched sides and received her publicly, on 8 February 2015, accompanied by another female officer in uniform.

The Kurds had defeated ISIS at Kobane thanks to US air support. This turning point was also was the grand play of the Kurdish card, America's backup plan to divide and conquer Syria. Kurdish independence being anathema to Turkey, this turn of events provoked the fury of Erdoğan, who most likely ordered the attacks in

Paris on 13 November.[18] On the second floor of the Bataclan Theatre, hostages were tortured and mutilated, and others decapitated. Shamefaced, François Hollande forbade the publication of this information, which was nonetheless confirmed by police agents before a parliamentary commission. Patrick Calvar, the central director of counter-espionage, attested before a parliamentary commission that his services had identified the state which gave the orders for the attack. Ducking his responsibilities, the President organised a few weepy ceremonies of commemoration, and persuaded his compatriots that terrorism is an inevitable epidemic. He inaugurated a medal for the "national recognition of the victims of terrorism", and paid compensations for the "prejudice of the anxiety of imminent death" and even the "prejudice of waiting". But he took no action against Turkey. Erdoğan sponsored another crime, five months later, against Belgium, at the Bruxelles-Zaventem airport, and in front of the headquarters of the European Commission, at the exact spot where the PKK had just demonstrated.

Far from hiding his responsibility, Recep Tayyip Erdoğan gave a resounding speech during the ceremonies celebrating the 101st anniversary of the battle of Çanakkale ("the battle of the Dardanelles"), just four days before the attacks against Belgium. He accused the Europeans of supporting the PKK, and announced what was about to happen in Brussels. The day after the attack, the media groups of Erdoğan's AKP party (Star, Akit, Internethaber) proclaimed that the Europeans got no more than they deserved.

To give the impression that it was taking the initiative against Daesh, France deployed the aircraft carrier Charles de Gaulle in February-March and in November-December 2015. It was escorted by an impressive armada, and armed with 32 aircraft (drones, helicopters and planes). During its second mission, President Hollande boarded the carrier and stressed that the ship would command a mighty international task force. In reality, the French were merely part Task Force 50 of the USNavCent, U.S. Naval Forces Central Command. To be sure, France's sixty-odd ships were commanded by rear-admiral Rene-Jean Crignola, but he was placed under the authority of the commander of the 5th fleet, vice-admiral Kevin Donegan, who was in turn under the orders of General Lloyd J. Austin III,

---

[18] Meyssan, "The motive for the attacks in Paris and Brussels," 28 March 2016, http://www.voltairenet.org/article190968.html

commander of CentCom. It is an absolute rule of the Empire that the command of Allied operations always goes to US officers – the Europeans are no more than auxiliaries.

At the end of 2015, France sent her Prime Minister, Manuel Valls, to collect some easy money from Saudi Arabia. There was once again talk of the $3 billion in orders for the Lebanese army and $10 billion worth of other contracts. But the Saudis were furious about the agreement on the Iranian nuclear programme – which France had promised to sabotage – and did not at all appreciate Paris' hesitations over Syria. The French revealed themselves as being no more than costly and inefficient vassals. The harvest was therefore much poorer than hoped for, as were the "gifts".

At the beginning of 2016, the French did not raise so much as a whisper when François Hollande nominated Laurent Fabius as President of the Constitutional Council. The Iranians received him much more noisily after the signing of the 5+1 nuclear agreement. He was hoping to establish business contacts with Iran, despite the fact that he had for years attempted to sabotage the agreement, and had confessed, during a dinner, that he had been spying for Israel, to whom he had transmitted accounts of the on-going negotiations. He was therefore received by the authorities with the formal honours due to his rank, while revolutionary associations demonstrated all along his route, from his arrival at the airport right up to his departure. They brandished posters recalling his responsibility in the death of more than 2,000 haemophiliacs in 1985-86, as well as his support for al-Qaeda which was "doing a good job", killing several tens of thousands of Syrians.

Jean-Marc Ayrault replaced him as Minister for Foreign Affairs. Preoccupied by the widening gap between France and Germany, he decided to concentrate his energy on preventing their separation. By doing so, he sacrificed the Syrian dossier, and after a few weeks of hesitation, he decided to follow in the footsteps of his predecessors, Juppé and Fabius.

Ayrault did not work with the new Prime Minister, Manuel Valls, but dealt directly with François Hollande, the President, who decided to take charge of the Syrian question himself.

While Ayrault is a moderate supporter of Israel – although he was the honorary President of the Cercle Léon Blum, the Zionist club within the Socialist Party – Valls is much more hard. He came into conflict with President Hollande about the archaeological excavations in Jerusalem, ordered by Tel-Aviv, which were damaging Muslim monuments. Previously a supporter of the Palestinian cause, Valls attributed his change of views to his marriage to the Franco-Israeli violinist Anne Gravoin.

During the national celebrations on 14 July 2016, an individual who claimed to be a member of Daesh, Mohamed Lahouaiej-Bouhlel, drove a truck at random over the passers-by on the Promenade des Anglais in Nice, killing 86 people and injuring 484. Although never, anywhere, had anyone managed to kill and injure so many people with one vehicle, the investigators confirmed that the man had received no particular training, and had acted alone. And yet his family in Tunisia had just received 100,000 Euros, without any enquiry as to who had paid for the crime. Although the country was in a state of emergency, it transpired that the terrorist had been able to act more easily because 60 gendarmes had been transferred from Nice to Avignon to ensure the safety of President Hollande, who was dining with a group of actors.

In Paris, there were comments about the jihadist breakthrough in Syria, claiming that the régime now controlled no more than 20% of the territory, and would soon fall. In reality, two thirds of Syria are desert that no one controls, neither the Republic, nor the jihadists. President al-Assad made the choice of defending his population rather than his territory. At least 8 million Syrians chose to flee the jihadists to seek refuge in the towns of the Republic. No one has heard of refugees fleeing into the jihadist zones.

François Hollande was therefore furious when he learned, in February 2015, of the visit to Damascus by two senators, Jean-Pierre Vial of the Republican party and François Zocchetto of the Center Party, and two deputies, Jacques Myard (Republican) and Gérard Bapt (Socialist). On a second visit, in September 2015, Gérard Bapt was this time accompanied by the representative Jerôme Lambert (Socialist) and Christian Hutin (Chévénementist). On a third visit, in March 2016, a group of Republican representatives around Thierry Mariani, with Valérie Boyer, Nicolas Dhuicq, Denis Jacquard and Michel Vision. And finally, a fourth group, in January 2017, with the same players plus Jean Lassalle (Centrist). They were all received by President al-Assad, with the exception of Gérard Bapt.

In fact, the Socialist Bapt – he too – had come for business reasons. He represented the Grande Loge de l'Alliance Maçonnique Française (GLAMF) – which is headed by Prince Edward, duke of Kent. It is a breakaway group from the Grande Loge Nationale Française (GLNF), created on behalf of the British by Alain Juillet (ex-head of Economic Intelligence for the General Secretariat of National Defence). He met with businessmen and promised that, in return for cash bribes, he would have them removed from the European sanctions list. Of course, he had no such power in the matter. He was accompanied by another crook, Jerôme Toussaint, who is today in prison in France.

The third visit revealed the presence in Syria of the association SOS Chrétiens d'Orient, which recruited mainly within the National Front. Although these volunteers worked devotedly, and at their own expense, their activity in favour of Christians loyal to Rome established a form of discrimination against Orthodox Christians. The millions of Euros they claimed to have collected in France were hijacked and never arrived in Syria. Local religious authorities were annoyed when these Western Christians, adopting the spirit of the Crusades, celebrated a mass in the ruins of the Krak des Chevaliers, the imposing 12th century Crusader fortress. These young people were not aware that the Christians of the Levant had defended their country against the invading Crusaders, whom they saw as imperialist conquerors.

Finally, while France was sinking into decline, her leaders were unable to form an anti-imperialist front, which is nonetheless an indispensable prerequisite for economic recovery. Only a few formations took position against this colonial war – Le Front National of Marine Le Pen and Florian Philippot, the Christian-Democrat Party of Jean-Frédéric Poisson, Nicolas Dupont-Aignan's Debout la France, François Asselineau's Union Populaire Républicaine, the group of Republicans around François Fillon, and Jean-Luc Mélenchon's group, Les Insoumis.

Deprived of information on the ground since the closing of its embassy, incapable of analysing the origins of events, but always seeking to pretend that it had initiated them, France had obviously not foreseen what was about to happen.

The Russian intervention

Hollande's government was stupefied when it learned of the Russian military deployment in September 2015. They had never imagined this, although Russia and Syria had been preparing it for three years. France was to be even more surprised, in August 2016, when Russia installed another base, this time in Iran – which had been in preparation for a year.

The Russian army presented a plethora of new weapons, and used the battlefield to promote its defence industry. In the space of a few months, one by one, it destroyed all the fortifications and bunkers that Lafarge had built. However, Paris did not immediately understand what was happening, particularly since Washington was in no hurry to bring it up to speed. Russia had installed a system in Latakia which inhibited NATO controls and commands, rendering the Alliance deaf and blind within a range of 300 kilometres. In addition, when NATO aircraft crossed the zone, they were unable to activate their weapons. In order to demonstrate the efficiency of this new type of electronic warfare, Russia carried out tests, trespassing on Lebanese and Cypriot territory (including the huge British military base), and then over Iraq.

The same system was deployed in Crimea and in Kaliningrad. *De facto*, Russia had become the world's major conventional military power, overtaking the United States, as the Supreme Commander of NATO recognised. Whatever – Paris withdrew behind the Juppé-Davutoğlu project while participating in the [US] International Coalition against Daesh. The Coalition published triumphant communiqués about its bombing of the jihadists. But on the ground, numerous witnesses attested to the fact that it was not fighting Daesh, but dropping them weapons and ammunition, while the Syrian Arab Republic, in view of future reparations, addressed to the UN the lists of oil and gas installations that the Coalition have destroyed.

Since the Russian economy had suffered greatly from the European sanctions imposed during the Ukrainian conflict, Moscow was unable to pursue its bombing campaign indefinitely. Although it should have ended on 6 January (date of the Orthodox Christmas), it nonetheless continued until mid-March.

The struggle for civilisation by Syria and Russia was celebrated on 5 and 6 May (anniversaries of the Syrian Army and the Allied victory over Nazism) by the concerts in liberated Palmyra. Presidents Vladimir Putin and Bashar al-Assad both spoke, relayed by a giant screen, while symphony orchestras played in the midst of the antique ruins. The "desert city" is the incarnation of the ancient people's resistance to Roman imperialism. It is also one of the most strategic points of the war – it had been occupied by Daesh.

Before withdrawing her bombers, Moscow signed an agreement with the US State Department. The United States swore that they were acting in good faith, and claimed that they had no idea what Jeffrey Feltman at the UN was up to with Daesh. John Kerry and Sergei Lavrov therefore decided to take the Geneva negotiations in hand. They agreed to impose a cease-fire on both parties – the regime and the opposition, but excluding the "terrorists" – to send humanitarian aid to the besieged populations, and to form the next Syrian government themselves. Good resolutions which did not last for long.

Macron the Undecided

In May 2017, the French people, scalded by the catastrophic mandates of Nicolas Sarkozy and François Hollande, chose a political stranger, Emmanuel Macron, as their President. A senior civil servant from the Treasury who had made a noticeable detour via the Rothschild bank, Macron was a "mandarin," a bureaucrat, with no political party, but who represented the 300 members of the Inspection Générale des Finances. As such, he knew nothing about international politics. He therefore relied on a few advisors, some of whom shamelessly displayed in their offices at the Elysée the certificates of congratulations offered them by a foreign authority, the US State Department.

President Macron hoped to maintain good relations with all of them. He therefore began his mandate with a few words favourable to the restoration of diplomatic relations with Damascus, and sent emissaries to Syria. To his great surprise, they were not received by President al-Assad, who told them to inform President Macron that Syria would not accept a French embassy until Paris ceased its military support for the jihadists. It was at that moment that

Emmanuel Macron discovered the amplitude of France's secret engagement in this war.

Finally, he left the Syrian dossier to his Minister for Foreign Affairs, Jean-Yves Le Drian, who, when he was François Hollande's Minister for Defence, had pushed harder than anyone else for the destruction of the Syrian State.

Provisional balance sheet

It is a mistake to speak of French policies in the context of the Arab Spring. On one hand, because Paris did not understand who was triggering these events, nor why they were doing so, and on the other, because successive French governments have made no attempt to defend the interests of their country. At best, we may note the erratic behaviour of France as it hunts for potentially lucrative opportunities for her leaders.

From now on, on this subject and many others, the distinction Right-Left no longer has any meaning. Nicolas Sarkozy, Alain Juppé, François Hollande and Laurent Fabius have all conducted the same privatisation of national politics, even though Sarkozy showed himself to be more flexible, and had ceased to attack Syria once he understood that victory was impossible. However, there exists within almost every political faction a colonialist vs. anti-imperialist split, and a few men who have attempted to save the honour of the country.

This absence of cohesion in French politics was expressed by ex-President Valery Giscard d'Estaing, in *Le Parisien*, 27 September 2015. Offering his support to his left-wing successor, this right-wing politician declared – "I wonder about the possibility of creating a UN mandate for Syria for a period of five years" – an elegant formula for reintroducing the mandate exercised by France, from 1920 to 1946, with the approval of the League of Nations. The mandate was a politically correct expression for the colonisation of Syria, as it had been planned during the First World War by Sir Mark Sykes, François Georges-Picot and Sergei Sazonov, representing respectively the United Kingdom, France and the Tsarist Empire (the "Sykes-Picot agreement"). As it happens – and this is no coincidence – Valery Giscard d'Estaing is a third cousin of François Georges-Picot.

If they were made to face a Nuremberg-type trial, the members of the Sarkozy administration would have to answer for the privatisation of national politics and the 160,000 deaths caused by the operation in Libya (numbers from the International Red Cross). Of course, they would share this responsibility with others, mainly from the United States, Britain, Qatar and Turkey. However, they would benefit from a dismissal for their crimes in Syria, in view of their change of position in February 2012, and the peace treaty signed with the Syrian Arab Republic. As for the Hollande administration and its accomplices, they would have to answer for 260,000 Syrian deaths (numbers from the UN General Secretary) and the 200,000 to 300,000 jihadists who were also killed (evaluation by the Syrian Arab Army).

Unless they opt for a Revolution, to dissolve their liabilities, the French and their allies would have to pay reparations for the destruction of two thirds of Syria (at least $300 billion, according to the World Bank), including almost all the oil and gas infrastructures, and also a major part of the antique monuments.

Part Two:
The "Arab Spring" as experienced by the Muslim Brotherhood

In 1951, building on the foundations of the old organisation of the same name, the Anglo-Saxon secret services put together a secret political society called the Muslim Brotherhood. At first they used it to assassinate personalities who resisted them, and then, starting in 1979, as mercenaries against the Soviets. At the beginning of the 1990's, they incorporated the Brotherhood into NATO, and in 2010, attempted to force it into power in the Arab countries. The Muslim Brotherhood and the Sufi Order of the Naqshbandi were financed with at least $80 billion annually by the ruling Saudi family, which made them one of the most powerful armies in the world. All jihadist leaders, including the leaders of Daesh, belong to this military structure.

The Egyptian Muslim Brotherhood

Four empires disappeared during the First World War – the German Reich, the Austro-Hungarian Empire, the Tsarist Holy Russian Empire, and the Ottoman Sublime Porte. The victors utterly lacked any sense of reason in the conditions they imposed on the defeated. Thus, in Europe, the Treaty of Versailles determined conditions which were unacceptable and unbearable for Germany, falsely blamed as the sole responsible for the conflict. In the Orient, the carving up of the Ottoman Caliphate was not going well. At the San Remo Conference (1920), in accordance with the secret Sykes-Picot agreements (1916), the United Kingdom was authorised to set up a Jewish homeland in Palestine, while France was allowed to colonise Syria (which included, at the time, what is now Lebanon). However, in what was left of the Ottoman Empire, Mustafa Kemal led a revolt both against the Sultan, who had lost the war, and against the Western powers, who were taking control of his country. At the Sèvres Conference (1920), the Caliphate was chopped into little pieces in order to create a variety of new states, including a Kurdistan. The Turko-Mongol population of the provinces of Thrace and Anatolia rose up and carried Kemal to power. Finally, the Lausanne Conference (1923) traced the frontiers we know today, gave up on the idea of Kurdistan, and organised gigantic population transfers which caused more than half a million deaths.

But just as in Germany, Adolf Hitler was to contest his country's lot, so, in the Near East, a man stood up against the new division of the region. An Egyptian schoolteacher founded a movement to re-establish the Caliphate which the Westerners had defeated. This man was Hassan al-Banna, and his organisation was the Muslim Brotherhood (1928).

In principle, the Caliph was the successor of the Prophet, to whom all owe obedience – it was therefore a very coveted title. There had been several great lines of Caliphs in succession – the Omeyyads, the Abbassids, the Fatimids and the Ottomans. The next Caliph would have to be the man who seized the title – and as it happened, this was the "General Guide" of the Brotherhood, who was quite comfortable with the idea of becoming the master of the Muslim world.

The secret society spread rapidly. Its intention was to work from within the system in order to re-establish Islamic institutions. Applicants had to swear fealty to the founder not only upon the Qu'ran, but also on a sabre or a revolver. The aim of the Brotherhood was exclusively political, even though it expressed itself in religious terms. Hassan al-Banna and his successors never spoke about Islam as a religion, nor did they evoke Muslim spirituality. For them, Islam is no more than a dogma, a submission to God and the exercise of Power. Obviously, the Egyptians who supported the Brotherhood did not see it this way. They followed it because it claimed to follow God.

For Hassan al-Banna, the legitimacy of a government was not to be measured by its representativeness, the way we evaluate that of Western governments, but by its capacity to defend the "Islamic way of life", in other words, the way of life of 19th century Ottoman Egypt. The Brotherhood never considered that Islam has a History, and that Muslim ways of life vary considerably according to region and era. Neither did it imagine that the Prophet had revolutionised the Bedouin society in which he lived, or that the way of life described in the Qu'ran is no more than a stage meant for those particular men. For them, the disciplinary rules of the Qu'ran – Sharia – do not correspond to a given situation, but fix inalterable laws upon which Power can rely.

For the Brotherhood, the fact that the Muslim way of life had often been imposed by the sword justified the use of force. The Brotherhood would never admit that Islam may have been spread by example. This did not prevent al-Banna and his Brothers from standing for election – and losing. If they condemned political parties, it was not because of opposition to the multi-party system, but because by separating religion from politics, they would succumb to corruption.

The doctrine of the Muslim Brotherhood was the ideology of "political Islam" – "Islamism" – a word which was destined to become all the rage.

In 1936, Hassan al-Banna wrote to Egyptian Prime Minister Mostafa El-Nahas Pasha. He demanded:

► legislative reform, and the conformity of all tribunals with Sharia law;

► recruitment within the armies to create a volunteer force under the banner of jihad;

► connection between all Muslim countries, and the preparation for the restoration of the Caliphate, in realization of the unity demanded by Islam.

During the Second World War, the Brotherhood declared itself to be neutral. In reality, it mutated into an Intelligence service for the Reich. But from the point at which the United States entered the war, when the fortune of arms seemed to be changing sides, it played a double game, and sold information about Germany to the British. In this way, the Brotherhood revealed its total absence of principles and pure political opportunism.

On 24 February 1945, the Brothers tried their luck and assassinated the Egyptian Prime Minister in the middle of a parliamentary session. This was followed by an escalation of violence – a movement of repression against the Brotherhood, and a series of political assassinations, going as far as the murder of the new Prime Minister on 28 December 1948, and in retaliation, the killing of Hassan al-Banna himself, on 12 February 1949. A short time afterwards, a tribunal instituted by martial law condemned most of the Brotherhood to prison sentences, and dissolved their association.

This secret organisation was in reality no more than a band of assassins who hoped to grab power by masking their ambition behind the Qu'ran. Its story should have ended there. Unfortunately, it did not.

The Brotherhood reinstated by the Anglo-Saxons, and the separate peace with Israel

The capacity of the Brotherhood to mobilise people and turn them into assassins obviously intrigued the major Powers.

Two and a half years after its dissolution, a new organisation was formed by the Anglo-Saxons, who re-used the name "Muslim Brotherhood". Because all its historical leaders were incarcerated, ex-judge Hassan al-Hudaybi was selected as General Guide. Contrary to what is often believed, he represented no historical continuity between the old and the new Brotherhood. It transpired that a unit of the old secret society, the "Secret Section", had been tasked by Hassan al-Banna with perpetrating attacks for which he denied all responsibility. This organisation within the organisation was so secret that it had not been affected by the dissolution of the Brotherhood, and was now available to his successor. The Guide decided to disown the "Secret Section", and declared that he wanted to attain his objectives only by peaceful means. It is difficult to establish exactly what happened at that moment between the Anglo-Saxons, who wanted to recreate the old society, and the Guide, who believed he was simply reviving its audience from within the masses. In any case, the "Secret Section" survived, and the authority of the Guide waned in favor of other Brotherhood leaders, triggering a great internecine struggle. The CIA gave Sayyid Qutb a leadership position within the Brotherhood. Qutb, a Freemason, was the theoretician of jihad, whom the Guide Hudaybi had condemned, before being forced to come to terms with MI6.

It is impossible to specify the relations and degrees of hierarchy between these men, on one hand because each foreign branch enjoyed its own autonomy, and on the other, because the secret units within the organisation no longer necessarily answered either to the General Guide, or the local Guide, but sometimes directly to the CIA and MI6.

During the period following the Second World War, the British attempted to re-organise the world in order to keep it out of Soviet hands. In September 1946, in Zurich, Winston Churchill launched the idea of the United States of Europe. On the same principle, he also launched the Arab League. In both cases, the aim was to unify these regions without Russia. From the beginning of the Cold War, the United States, for their part, created associations tasked with accompanying this movement for their own profit – the American Committee on United Europe and the American Friends of the Middle East. In the Arab world, the CIA organised two coups d'état, first of all in favour of General Hosni Zaim in Damascus (March 1949), then with the Free Officers in Cairo (July 1952). The goal was to support the nationalists who were believed to be hostile to the Communists. It was in this state of mind that Washington sent SS General Otto Skorzeny to Egypt, and Nazi General Fazlollah Zahedi to Iran, accompanied by hundreds of ex-Gestapo officers, with whom they hoped to direct the anti-Communist conflict.

Unfortunately, Skorzeny schooled the Egyptian police in a tradition of violence. In 1963, he chose the CIA and the Mossad over Nasser. As for Zahedi, he created the SAVAK, the cruelest political police force of the time.

While Hassan al-Banna had defined the objective – seizing power by manipulating religion – Sayyid Qutb defined the means – jihad. Once the adepts had admitted the supremacy of the Qu'ran, it could be used as a foundation for organising them into an army and sending them into combat. Qutb developed a Manichean theory which distinguished "Islamist" from "evil". This brainwashing enabled the CIA and MI6 to use adepts to control the nationalist Arab governments, then to destabilise the Muslim regions of the Soviet Union. The Brotherhood became an inexhaustible reservoir of terrorists under the slogan – "Allah is our goal. The Prophet is our leader. The Qu'ran is our law. The jihad is our way. Martyrdom is our vow".

Qutb's ideas were rational, but not reasonable. He applied an ironclad rhetoric of Allah – Prophet – Qu'ran – Jihad – Martyrdom, which left no room for any discussion at any point. He placed the superiority of his logic over human reason.

The CIA organised a conference at Princeton University on "The Situation of Muslims in the Soviet Union". It was the occasion for the United States to receive a delegation of the Muslim Brotherhood led by Sa'id Ramadan, one of the heads of its armed branch. In his report, the CIA officer in charge of the summary noted that Ramadan was not a religious extremist, but rather resembled a fascist – a way of underlining the exclusively political character of the Muslim Brotherhood. The conference ended with a reception at the White House, hosted by President Eisenhower, on 23 September 1953. The alliance between Washington and jihadism was formed.

The CIA, which had resuscitated the Brotherhood to use against the Communists, first of all used it to help nationalists. At that time, the Agency was represented in the Middle East by middle-class anti-Zionists. They were rapidly ousted and replaced by senior civil servants of Anglo-Saxon and Puritan origin, graduates from major universities, all favourable to Israel. Now Washington entered into conflict with the nationalists, and the CIA turned the Brotherhood against them.

Sa'id Ramadan   had commanded a few combatants from the Brotherhood during the brief war against Israel in 1948, then helped Sayyid Abul Ala Maududi to create the paramilitary organisation Jamaat-i-Islami in Pakistan. The point was to fabricate an Islamic identity for the Muslim Indians so that they could constitute a new state, Pakistan. Jamaat-i-Islami in fact drew up the Pakistani constitution. Ramadan married the daughter of Hassan al-Banna, and became the head of the armed branch of the new "Muslim Brotherhood".

Meanwhile, in Egypt, the Brotherhood had taken part in the coup d'état by General Mohammed Naguib's Free Officers – Sayyid Qutb was their liaison officer. They were tasked with eliminating one of their leaders, Gamal Abdel Nasser, who had opposed Naguib. Not only did they fail, on 26 October 1954, but Nasser took power, subdued the Brotherhood, and put Naguib under house arrest. Sayyid Qutb would be hanged a few years later.

Forbidden in Egypt, the Brotherhood fell back to the Wahhabi states (Saudi Arabia, Qatar and the Emirate of Sharjah), and to Europe (Germany, France and the United Kingdom, plus neutral Switzerland). Each time, they were received as Western agents fighting the growing alliance between the Arab nationalists and the Soviet Union. Sa'id Ramadan was issued a Jordanian diplomatic passport, and settled in Geneva in 1958. From there that he directed the destabilisation of the Caucasus and Central Asia (both Pakistan-Afghanistan and the Soviet Fergana Valley). He took control of the Committee for the construction of a mosque in Munich, which enabled him to supervise almost all the Muslims in Western Europe. With the assistance of the American Committee for the Liberation of the Peoples of Russia (AmComLib), which is to say the CIA, he had at his command Radio Liberty /Radio Free Europe, a radio station financed directly by the US Congress to spread the philosophy of the Brotherhood.

After the Suez Canal crisis and the spectacular about-face of Nasser to join the Soviets, Washington decided to provide unlimited help to the Muslim Brotherhood in the fight against the Arab nationalists. A senior officer of the CIA, Miles Copeland, was charged – in vain – with selecting a personality within the Brotherhood who could play, in the Arab world, a role equivalent to that of Pastor Billy Graham in the United States. It was not until the 1980's that a preacher of that calibre was found – the Egyptian Yusuf al-Qaradawi.

In 1961, the Brotherhood established a connection with another secret society, the Order of the Naqshbandis. This was a sort of Muslim Freemasonry which mixed Sufi initiation with politics. One of their Indian theorists, Abu al-Hasan Ali al-Nadwi, published an article in the Brotherhood's magazine. The Order is ancient, and represented in many countries. In Iraq, the grand master was none other than the future vice-President, Izzat Ibrahim al-Douri. He would support the attempted coup d'état by the Brotherhood in Syria, in 1982, and then the "Return to Faith Campaign" organised by President Saddam Hussein in order to restore an identity to his country after the imposition of the Western no-fly zone.

In Turkey, the Order would play a more complex role. It would include as its directors both Fethullah Gülen (founder of the Hizmet movement) and President Turgut Özal (1989-1993), as well as Prime Minister Necmettin Erbakan (1996-1997), founder of the Justice Party (1961) and the Millî Görüş movement (1969). In Afghanistan, ex-President Sibghatullah Mojaddedi (1992) was the Order's grand master. In 19th century Russia, with the help of the Ottoman Empire, the Order had raised up Crimea, Uzbekistan, Chechnya and Daghestan against the Tsar. Until the fall of the USSR, we would hear nothing more of this branch – just as in the Chinese Xinjiang region. The proximity between the Brotherhood and the Naqshbandis is very rarely studied, given the *a priori* Islamist opposition to mysticism and Sufi orders in general.

In 1962, the CIA encouraged Saudi Arabia to create the Muslim World League and finance both the Brotherhood and the Naqshbandi Order to work against the nationalists and the Communists. The organisation was first of all financed by Aramco (Arabian-American Oil Company). Amongst the twenty or so founding members, we note the presence of three Islamist theorists whom we have already mentioned – the Egyptian Sa'id Ramadan, the Pakistani Sayyid Abul Ala Maududi, and the Indian Abu al-Hasan Ali al-Nadwi.

De facto, Arabia, which suddenly disposed of enormous liquidities thanks to the commerce in oil, became the godfather of the Muslim Brotherhood all over the world. At home, the monarchy entrusted them with the educational system for schools and universities, in a country where almost no one knew how to read or write. The Brotherhood had to adapt to its hosts. Indeed, their allegiance to the King prevented them from swearing loyalty to the General Guide. In any case, they organised around Mohamed Qutb, Sayyid's brother, in two tendencies – the Saudi Brotherhood on one side, and the "Sururists" (adepts of Sheikh Surur) on the other. The Sururists, who are Saudis, attempted to create a synthesis between the Brotherhood's political ideology and Wahhabi theology. This cult, of which the royal family are members, lived by an interpretation of Islam which was born of the Bedouin tradition, iconoclast and anti-historic. Until Riyadh came into all its petro-dollars, it made traditional Muslim schools anathema, which, in return, considered it heretical.

In reality, the politics of the Brotherhood and the Wahhabist religion have nothing in common, although they are compatible – except that the pact linking the Saud family with the Wahhabist preachers cannot exist within the Brotherhood – the idea of a "divine right" monarchy clashes with the Brotherhood's greed for power. It was therefore agreed that the Sauds would support the Brotherhood everywhere in the world, on the condition that they abstain from entering politics in Arabia.

The Saudi Wahhabi support for the Brotherhood provoked extra rivalry between Arabia and the two other Wahhabi states – Qatar and the Emirate of Sharjah.

From 1962 to 1970, the Muslim Brotherhood took part in the civil war in North Yemen, and attempted to re-enlist the monarchy on the side of Saudi Arabia and the United Kingdom against the Arab nationalists, Egypt and the USSR – a conflict which foreshadowed what was to happen over the next half-century.

In 1970, Gamal Abdel Nasser managed to negotiate an agreement between the Palestinian factions and King Hussein of Jordan, which put an end to the "Black September" terrorist group. But on the evening of the Arab League summit which met to ratify the agreement, he died, officially from a heart attack, but was far more probably assassinated. Nasser had three vice-Presidents – one from the left wing who was extremely popular; a centrist, a very public figure; and a conservative at the bidding of the United States and Saudi Arabia – Anwar el-Sadat. Under pressure, the left-wing vice-President declared himself unfit for the function. The centrist vice-President preferred to abandon politics. Sadat was therefore designated as the Nasserian candidate. This drama is played out in many countries – the President chooses a vice-President from among his rivals in order to extend his electoral base, but when he dies, the vice-President replaces him and ruins his heritage.

Sadat, who had served the Reich during the Second World War, and professed great admiration for the Führer, was an ultra-conservative soldier who served as Sayyid Qutb's alter-ego, a liaison officer between the Brotherhood and the Free Officers Movement, the group of nationalist authors who instigated the 1952 revolution in Egypt. As soon as Sadat gained power, he freed the Muslim Brothers who had been imprisoned by Nasser. The "faithful President" was the Brotherhood's ally for anything concerning the Islamisation of society (the "Corrective Revolution"), but its rival when politically profitable for him. This ambiguous relationship was illustrated by the creation of three armed groups, which were not factions within the Brotherhood, but exterior units under its orders – the Islamic Party of Liberation, the Islamic Jihad (under Sheikh Omar Abdul Rahman), and Excommunication and Immigration (the "Takfiri"). All of them claimed to be following the instructions of Sayyid Qutb. Armed by the secret services, the Islamic Jihad launched attacks against the Coptic Christians. Far from mitigating the situation, the "faithful President" accused the Copts of sedition, and imprisoned their Pope and eight of their bishops. Finally, Sadat intervened in the government of the Brotherhood and took a stance in favor of the Islamic Jihad against the General Guide, whom he arrested.

On instructions from US Secretary of State Henry Kissinger, Sadat convinced Syria to join with Egypt to attack Israel and restore Palestinian rights. On 6 October 1973, while the Israelis were celebrating Yom Kippur, the two armies took the Hebrew country in a pincer movement. The Egyptian army crossed the Suez Canal, while the Syrian army attacked from the Golan Heights. However, Sadat only partially deployed his anti-aircraft cover, and halted his army 15 kilometres to the East of the Canal – meanwhile, the Israelis attacked the Syrians, who discovered that they were trapped and screamed conspiracy.[19]

It was only when the Israeli reserve forces had been mobilised, and the Syrian army was surrounded by Israeli troops, that Sadat ordered his army to continue its progression, before halting it once again to negotiate a cease-fire. Observing the Egyptian treason, the Soviets, who had already lost an ally with the death of Nasser, threatened the United States and demanded an immediate cessation of combat.

Four years later – still pursuing the CIA plan – President Sadat went to Jerusalem and signed a separate peace treaty with Israel, to the detriment of the Palestinians and of Syria. From then on, the alliance between the Muslim Brotherhood and Israel was sealed. All the Arab peoples decried this treason, and Egypt was excluded from the Arab League, whose headquarters were moved to Algiers.

In 1981, Washington decided to turn the page. The Islamic Jihad was ordered to eliminate Sadat, who had outlived his usefulness. He was assassinated during a military parade, while the Parliament was preparing to proclaim him the "Sixth Caliph". In the presidential box, seven people were killed and 28 wounded, yet sitting next to the President, his vice-President General Mubarak survived. He was the only person in the box wearing body armour. He succeeded the "faithful President", and the Arab League could now be repatriated to Cairo.

---

[19] https://www.counterpunch.org/2012/02/22/what-really-happened-in-the-yom-kippur-war/

The Brotherhood in the service of the Carter-Brzeziński strategy

In 1972-1973, an official from the Foreign Office – and probably MI6 as well – Sir James Craig, together with the British ambassador to Egypt, Sir Richard Beaumont, began an intense lobbying campaign aimed at harnessing the Muslim Brotherhood for use by the United Kingdom and the United States in the struggle against the Marxists and the nationalists, not only in Egypt, but also all over the Muslim world. Sir James was soon to be nominated as Her Majesty's ambassador in Syria, then in Arabia, and would find an attentive ear at the CIA. Much later, he was to become the designer of the "Arab Springs".

In 1977, Jimmy Carter was elected President of the United States. He appointed Zbigniew Brzeziński as his National Security Advisor. Brzeziński decided to use Islamism against the Soviets. He gave the Saudis the go-ahead to increase their payments to the Islamic World League, organised regime changes in Pakistan, Iran and Syria, destabilised Afghanistan, and made US access to oil from the "Greater Middle East" a national security objective. Finally, he entrusted the Brotherhood with military equipment.

This strategy was clearly explained by Bernard Lewis during the meeting of the Bilderberg Group, organised by NATO in Austria, April 1979. Lewis, an Anglo-Israeli-US Islamologist, assured that the Muslim Brotherhood could not only play a major role against the Soviets and provoke internal trouble in Central Asia, but also balkanise the Near East in favour of Israel.

Contrary to a widely-held belief, the Brotherhood was not happy about following the Brzeziński plan – it was looking further afield. It had obtained the assistance of Riyadh and Washington for the creation of other branches of the Brotherhood in other countries – branches that were to come to fruition later on. The King of Arabia granted an average of $5billion annually to the Muslim World League, which extended its activities in 120 countries and financed various wars. As a point of reference, $5 billion was the equivalent of the military budget of North Korea. The League obtained advisory status for the Economic and Social Council of the United Nations, and the post of observer for UNICEF.

In Pakistan, General Muhammad Zia-ul-Haq, the Army Chief of Staff, trained at Fort Bragg in the United States, overthrew President Zulfikar Alî Bhutto and had him hanged. A member of the Jamaat-e-Islami, in other words the local version of the Muslim Brotherhood, he went on to Islamise Pakistani society. The Sharia was progressively established – including the death penalty for blasphemy – and a vast network of Islamic schools was set up. It was the first time that the Brotherhood had been in power outside of Egypt.

In Iran, Brzeziński convinced the Shah to abdicate, and organised the return of Imam Ruhollah Khomeini, who defined himself as a "Shiite Islamist". In his youth, in 1945, Khomeini had met Hasan al-Banna in Cairo, and convinced him not to exacerbate the Sunni/Shiite conflict. Later, he translated two books by Sayyid Qutb. The Brotherhood and the Iranian Revolutionaries agreed on social subjects, but not at all on political questions. Brzeziński realised his mistake the very day that the Ayatollah arrived in Teheran. Khomeini immediately went to pray at the tombs of the martyrs of the Shah's régime, and called on the army to revolt against imperialism. Brzeziński committed a second error by sending Delta Force to save the US spies who were being held hostage in their embassy in Teheran. Even if he was able to hide from Western eyes the fact that these "diplomats" were actually spies, he made a laughing-stock of his soldiers with the failed mission "Eagle Claw", and convinced the Pentagon that it was necessary to find a way of defeating Iran.

Brzeziński set up "Operation Cyclone" in Afghanistan. Between 17,000 and 35,000 Muslim Brothers from about 40 countries came to fight the USSR, which had come to the defence of the Democratic Republic of Afghanistan, at its request. There had never been a "Soviet invasion", as US propaganda pretended.

The men of the Brotherhood came to reinforce a local coalition of conservative combatants and the local Muslim Brotherhood, including the Pashtun Gulbuddin Hekmatyar and the Tajik Ahmad Shah Massoud. They received the major part of their armament from Israel – officially their sworn enemy, but now their partner. All these forces were commanded from Pakistan by General Muhammad Zia-ul-Haq, and financed by the United States and Saudi Arabia. This was the first time that the Brotherhood had been used by the Anglo-

Saxons to wage war. Among the combatants present were the future commanders of the wars in the Caucasus, of the Indonesian Jemaah Islamiyah, the Abu Sayyaf group in the Philippines, and of course al-Qaeda and Daesh. In the United States, the anti-Soviet operation was supported by the Republican Party and a small group from the extreme left, the Trotskyists of Social Democrats USA.

The Carter-Brzeziński strategy represented a change of scale. Saudi Arabia, which up until then had been financing the Islamist groups, found itself tasked with managing the war funds for the fight against the Soviets. The general director of Saudi Intelligence, Prince Turki (son of King Faisal), became an indispensable personality for all the Western summits on Intelligence.

In the early phases, so many problems arose between the Afghans and Arabs that it was impossible to get them to fight together against the Communists. Prince Turki first sent the Palestinian Abdallah Azzam, the "Imam of Jihad", to bring order to the Brotherhood, and run the Kabul office of the Muslim World League, but the office did not do well and was closed. Azzam was then succeeded by billionaire Osama Ben Laden. Both of them had been trained in Saudi Arabia by Sayyid Qutb's brother.

During Carter's term, the Muslim Brotherhood also undertook a long campaign of terror in Syria, including the assassination, by the Muslim Brotherhood's "Fighting Vanguard", of non-Sunni cadets at the Military Academy of Aleppo. The "Vanguard" were able to use training camps in Jordan, where the British handled their military instruction. During these "Years of Lead", the CIA managed to broker an alliance between the Muslim Brotherhood and the small group of ex-Communists under Riyadh al-Turk. He and his Syrian dissident friends, Georges Sabra and Michel Kilo, had split with Moscow during the Lebanese civil war to support the Western camp. They affiliated themselves with the US Trotskyist group, Social Democrats USA. Together, the three men drew up a manifesto in which they affirmed that the Muslim Brotherhood formed the new proletariat, and that Syria could only be saved by US military intervention. Finally, the Brotherhood attempted a coup d'état in Syria in 1982, with the support of the Iraqi Ba'ath Party (which was collaborating with Washington against Iran) and Saudi Arabia. The combats which followed at Hama caused 2,000 deaths according to the Pentagon, 40,000 according to the Brotherhood and the CIA.

After that, hundreds of prisoners were slaughtered in Palmyra by the brother of President Hafez al-Assad, Rifaat, who was dismissed and forced into exile in Paris when he attempted, in his turn, a coup d'état against his own brother. The Trotskyists were imprisoned, and most members of the Brotherhood fled either to Germany (home of ex-Syrian Guide Issam al-Attar), or to France (like Abu Musab the Syrian). Chancellor Helmut Kohl and President François Mitterrand granted them asylum. Two years later, a scandal broke out within the opposition – which was in exile at the moment of division – $3 million had disappeared out of an envelope of $10 million donated by the Muslim World League.

Towards the constitution of an Internationale for jihad

During the 1980's, the Muslim World League received instructions from Washington to transform Algerian society. Over a period of ten years, Riyadh paid for the construction of mosques in the villages of Algeria. Each time, a dispensary and a school were built alongside the mosques. The Algerian authorities were delighted with this assistance, especially since they were no longer able to guarantee the people's access to health care and education. Progressively, the Algerian working classes distanced themselves from the state which was no longer much use to them, and grew ever closer to these generous mosques.

When Prince Fahd became the King of Saudi Arabia in 1982, he nominated Prince Bandar (son of the Minister for Defence) as ambassador to Washington, a post he retained for the duration of Fahd's reign. His function was double – on one side, he looked after Saudi-US relations, on the other, he served as an interface between the Director of Turkish Intelligence and the CIA. He became friends with the vice-President and ex-Director of the CIA, George H. W. Bush, who considered him as his "adopted son" (whence his nickname "Bandar Bush), then with Secretary for Defense Dick Cheney and the future Director of the CIA, George Tenet. He made his way into the social life of the elite and also had an entrée into the Christian cult of the Pentagon Chiefs of Staff, called The Family, as well as the ultra-conservative Bohemian Club of San Francisco.[20]

---

[20] See Sharlett, *The Family: The Secret Fundamentalism at the Heart of American Power*, Harper and Collins, 2009. The Bohemian Club has a townhouse in downtown San Francisco, plus the Bohemian Grove retreat in the

Bandar directed the jihadists from the Muslim World League. He negotiated with London for the purchase of weapons from British Aerospace for his kingdom, in exchange for oil. These record-breaking "pigeon" contracts, in Arabic "Al Yamamah", would cost Riyadh between 40 and 83 billion pounds sterling, of which an important part would be transferred to the Prince by the British. A corruption and fraud scandal arose, but was suppressed by the Saudi and British governments.

In 1983, President Ronald Reagan entrusted Carl Gershman, ex-leader of the aforementioned Trotskyites, Social Democrats USA, with the directorship of the new National Endowment for Democracy [sic]. This was an agency which depended on the "Five Eyes" agreement, camouflaged as a NGO. It was the legal window for the secret services of Australia, Britain, Canada, the United States and New Zealand. Gershman had already worked with his Trotskyist comrades and his Muslim Brotherhood friends in Lebanon, Syria and Afghanistan. He set up a vast network of associations and foundations that the CIA and MI6 used to help the Brotherhood wherever possible. He pledged allegiance to the "Kirkpatrick Doctrine", which basically states that all alliances are justified so long as they serve the interests of the United States (against its rivals, who are *ipso facto* "totalitarians".

In 1985, the United Kingdom, faithful to its tradition of academic expertise, equipped itself with an institute tasked with studying Muslim societies and the ways in which the Brotherhood could influence them – the Oxford Centre for Islamic Studies.

In 1989, the Brotherhood succeeded in perpetrating a second coup d'état, this time in Sudan, on behalf of Colonel Omar el-Bechir, who wasted no time in nominating the local Guide, Hassan al-Turabi, as President of the National Assembly. In a conference held in London, al-Turabi announced that his country was going to become the rear base for all the Islamist groups in the world.

Also in 1989, the Islamic Salvation Front (FIS) arose in Algeria, based around Abassi Madani, while the party in power collapsed under the weight of numerous scandals. The FIS was supported by the mosques "gifted" by the Saudis, and as a result, by the Algerian

---

California countryside, made famous by Alex Jones as the site of annual rites of the Illuminati.

people who had been frequenting them for a decade. FIS won the local elections, due more to rejection of the country's leaders than by belief in the ideology of FIS. Considering the failure of the politicians and the categorical impossibility of negotiating with the Islamists, the army carried out a coup d'état and cancelled the elections. The country sank into a long and murderous civil war about which we knew very little, but which claimed more than 150,000 victims. The Islamists did not hesitate to practise both individual and collective punishments, for example when they massacred the inhabitants of Ben Talha – guilty of having voted despite the fatwa forbidding them to do so – and destroyed the village. Evidently, Algeria served as a laboratory for new operations. The rumour spread that it was the army, not the Islamists, who had massacred the villagers. In reality, several senior officers from the secret services, who had been trained in the United States, joined the Islamists and spread confusion.

In 1991, Osama Bin Laden, who returned to Saudi Arabia as a hero of the anti-Communist struggle at the end of the war in Afghanistan, officially fell out with the King, while the "Sururists", or followers of Sheikh Surur, rose up against the monarchy. This insurrection, the "Islamic Awakening", lasted for four years, and ended with the imprisonment of the principal leaders. It showed the monarchy – who imagined that they enjoyed total authority – that by mixing religion and politics, the Brotherhood had created the conditions for a revolt via the mosques.

In this context, Osama Bin Laden claimed that he had proposed the aid of a few thousand veterans of the Afghan war to fight Saddam Hussein's Iraq, but astonishingly, the King seemed to prefer the million soldiers from the US and their allies. Allegedly as a result of this disagreement, Bin Laden left for exile in Sudan – but in reality, his mission was to regain control of the Islamists who had escaped the authority of the Brotherhood and had risen up against the Saudi monarchy. With the Sudan's Islamist leader Hassan al-Turabi, he organised a series of popular pan-Arab and pan-Islamic conferences, to which he invited the representatives of Islamist and Nationalist movements from about fifty countries. The aim was to create, at the party level, the equivalent of what Saudi Arabia had already succeeded in doing with the Organisation of Islamic Cooperation, which brought States together. The participants did not know that these meetings were paid for by the Saudis, and that the hotels where they met were under CIA surveillance. Everyone participated, from Yasser Arafat to the Lebanese Hezbollah.

The FBI managed to convict the BCCI, a gigantic Muslim bank which had become, over time, the bank used by the CIA for its secret operations, particularly the financing of the war in Afghanistan – but also the narco-traffic in Latin America. When the BCCI was declared bankrupt, its smaller clients were not reimbursed, but Osama Bin Laden managed to recover $1.4 billion to continue the Muslim Brotherhood's work for Washington. The CIA then transferred its activities to the Faysal Islamic Bank and its subsidiary, Al-Baraka.

The Islamists controlled by the Pentagon

At the beginning of the 1990's, the Pentagon decided to work with the Islamists, who had hitherto depended only on the CIA. This was operation Gladio B, by reference to the secret services of NATO in Europe (Gladio A).[21] For a decade, all the Islamist chiefs – including Osama Bin Laden and Ayman al-Zawahiri – travelled on aircraft of the US Air Force. The United Kingdom, Turkey, and Azerbaidjan participated in the operation. As a direct result, the Islamists – who had so far been secret combatants – were publicly integrated into the NATO forces.

Saudi Arabia – which is both a state and the private property of the Saud family – officially became the company charged with the management of world Islamism. In 1992, the King proclaimed a Fundamental Law, which stated "The state protects Islamic Law and applies the Sharia. It imposes Good and fights Evil. It obeys the duties of Islam (…) The defence of Islamism, of society and of the Muslim homeland is the duty of every subject of the King".

In 1993, Charles, the Prince of Wales, placed the Oxford Centre for Islamic Studies under his patronage, while the head of the Saudi secret services, Prince Turki, took over its direction.

London openly became the nerve centre of Gladio B, to the point where people spoke of "Londonistan". Under the umbrella of the Muslim World League, the Arab Muslim Brotherhood and the

---

[21]For more on Gladio see Cottrell, *Gladio: NATO's Dagger at the Heart of Europe*, 2015, Progressive Press.

Pakistani Jamaat-i-Islami created a large number of cultural and cult-based associations around the mosque in Finsbury Park. This system enabled the recruitment of many kamikazes, from those who attacked the Russian school in Beslan to Richard Reid, the "shoe bomber". Above all, Londonistan was the home for a number of medias, publishing houses, newspapers (al-Hayat and Asharq al-Awsat – both directed by the children of the present King Salman of Arabia) – and television channels (the group MBC of Prince Walid ben Talal broadcasts about twenty channels). They are not destined for the Muslim diaspora in the United Kingdom, but are broadcast in the Arab world. And since the agreement between the Islamists and Saudi Arabia had been extended to the United Kingdom, they enjoyed total freedom of action, although they were banned from interfering in domestic UK politics. The system employed several thousand people and handled gigantic quantities of money. It was to remain publicly in place until the attacks of 11 September 2001, when it became impossible for the British to continue to justify such open collaboration.

Abu Musab "The Syrian" – a survivor of the aborted coup d'état in Hama, who had become a liaison officer between Bin Laden and the Groupe Islamique Armé (GIA) of Algeria – posited the theory of "decentralised jihad". In his Call for a Global Islamic Resistance, he advanced, in Islamic terms, the well-known doctrine of the "strategy of tension". This concerned provoking the authorities in order to spark fierce repression which would lead the people to rise against them. This tactic had already been used by the CIA/NATO Gladio networks in manipulating the European extreme left wing in the 1970's and 1980's (the Baader-Meinhof Complex, the Red Brigades, Action Directe). Of course, there was no question that the strategy would allow the people to prevail, and the CIA/NATO knew that it had no chance of doing so – they were never victorious anywhere – but it was intended to use the repressive reaction of the state to topple the existing élite and place its men in power.

"The Syrian" pointed to Europe – but above all, away from the United States – as the next Islamic battlefield. He fled France after the attacks of 1995. Two years later, he created the Islamic Conflict Studies Bureau in Madrid and Londonistan, on the model of Aginter Press, the Gladio cell which the CIA had created in Lisbon during the 1960's and 1970's. Both these structures excelled in the organisation of false-flag terrorist attacks (from those attributed to the extreme left at the Piazza Fontana, in 1969, to those blamed on Muslims in London in 2005[22]).

Simultaneously, the Brotherhood elaborated a vast programme of training for pro-US Arab leaders. The Libyan Mahmud Jibril El-Warfally, professor at the university of Pittsburg, taught them how to speak the language known as "politically correct". Thus he trained Emirs and Generals from Saudi Arabia, Bahrain, Egypt, the Emirates, Jordan, Kuwait, Morocco and Tunisia (but also Singapore). Mixing the principles of public relations with studies of reports by the World Bank, the most brutal dictators were now able to expound straight-faced on their Democratic Ideal as well as their profound respect for Human Rights.

The war against Algeria spilled over into France. Jacques Chirac and his Minister for the Interior, Charles Pasqua, interrupted French support for the Muslim Brotherhood and even banned books by Yusuf al-Qaradawi (the Egyptian Brotherhood preacher). For them, it was essential to maintain French presence in the Maghreb, which the British wanted to wipe off the map. The Armed Islamic Group of Algeria (GIA) took the passengers of an Air France Algiers-Paris flight hostage (1994), exploded bombs in the Métro and various points of the French capital (1995) and planned a gigantic attack – which was foiled – during the World Football Cup in France (1998), including the crash of an aircraft onto a nuclear power plant. Each time, the suspects who managed to flee were able to find refuge in Londonistan.

The war in Bosnia-Herzegovina began in 1992. On instructions from Washington, the Pakistani secret services (ISI), still supported financially by Saudi Arabia, sent 90,000 men to participate in the fight against the Serbs, who were supported by Moscow. Osama Bin Laden received a Bosnian diplomatic passport and became the military advisor to President Alija Izetbegović (for whom US citizen Richard Perle was diplomatic advisor, and the Frenchman Bernard-Henri Levy was Press advisor). Bin Laden formed an Arab Legion with ex-combatants from Afghanistan and supplied financing from the Muslim World League. Either by a sense of confessional solidarity or in competition with Saudi Arabia, the Islamic Republic

---

[22] See Kollerstrom, *Terror on the Tube*, 2009-2016, Progressive Press.

of Iran also came to the help of the Bosnian Muslims. With the Pentagon's blessing, it sent several hundred Guardians of the Revolution and a unit of the Lebanese Hezbollah. Above all, it delivered the main weapons used by the Bosnian army. The Russian secret services, who penetrated Bin Laden's camp, found out that the Arab Legion's entire bureaucracy was written in English, and that the Legion was taking its orders directly from NATO. After the war, a special International Tribunal was created. It launched criminal proceedings against a number of combatants for war crimes, but not one was a member of the Arab Legion.

After three years of quiet, the war between Muslims and Orthodox Christians started up again in ex-Yugoslavia, this time in Kosovo. The Kosovo Liberation Army (UÇK) was composed of mafia-style groups trained in combat by the German Special Forces (KSK) at the Turkish base of Incirlik. The Albanians and the Muslim Yugoslavs shared a Naqshbandi culture. Hakan Fidan, the future head of the Turkish secret services, was a liaison officer between NATO and Turkey. The veterans of the Arab Legion joined the UÇK, of which one brigade was commanded by a brother of Ayman al-Zawahiri. He systematically destroyed Orthodox churches and monasteries and forced the Christians to flee.

In 1995, reviving the tradition of political assassination, Osama Bin Laden attempted to eliminate Egyptian President Hosni Mubarak. He did the same a year later with the Libyan Guide, Muammar Gaddafi. This second attack was paid for with £100,000 by the British secret services, who sought to punish Libya for supporting the Irish resistance. However, the operation failed. Several Libyan officers fled to the United Kingdom. Among them was, Ramadan Abidi, whose son, many years later, was to be tasked, still by the British secret services, with carrying out a terrorist attack in Manchester. Libya transmitted its evidence to Interpol and issued the first international arrest warrant for the person of Osama Bin Laden, who still maintained a public relations bureau in Londonistan.

In 1998, the Arab Commission for Human Rights was founded in Paris. It was financed by the NED. Its President was the Tunisian Moncef Marzouki, and its spokesman was the Syrian Haytham Manna. Its objective was to defend members of the Muslim Brotherhood who had been arrested in different Arab countries for their terrorist activities. Marzouki was a left-wing doctor who had been working with the Brotherhood for a long time. Manna was a writer who managed the financial investments of Hassan el-Turabi and the Sudanese Brothers in Europe. When Manna retired, his partner stayed on as the Director of the association. Manna was replaced by the Algerian Rachid Mesli, a lawyer. He was incidentally the lawyer for Abassi Madani and the Algerian Brotherhood.

In 1999 (after the war in Kosovo and the power grab by the Islamists in Grozny), Zbigniew Brzeziński, with a cohort of neo-conservatives, founded the American Committee for Peace in Chechnya. While the first war in Chechnya had been an internal Russian affair in which a few Islamists had taken part, the second war was aimed at the creation of the Islamic Emirate of Ichkeria. Brzeziński, who had been preparing this operation for several years, attempted to reproduce the Afghan experience. The Chechen jihadists, like Shamil Basayev, had not been trained in Sudan by Bin Laden, but in Afghanistan by the Taliban. Throughout the whole war, they benefited from the "humanitarian" support offered by Necmettin Erbakan and Recep Tayyip Erdoğan's Turkish Millî Görüş, and the "IHH – Human Rights and Freedoms". This Turkish association had been created in Germany under the name of Internationale Humanitäre Hilfe (IHH). Thereafter, they organised several major operations – notably against the Moscow Theatre (in 2002 – 170 dead, 700 wounded); against a school in Beslan (in 2004 – 385 dead, 783 wounded); and against the town of Nalchik (in 2005 – 128 dead, 115 wounded). After the massacre in Beslan and the death of jihadist leader Shamil Basayev, Millî Görüş and the IHH organised an extravagant funeral service at the Fatih mosque in Istanbul – the body was not present, but tens of thousands of militants attended the ceremony.

During this period, three important terrorist attacks were attributed to al-Qaeda. But however important these operations may have been, they represented an abasement for the Islamists, who were an integral part of NATO, but at the same time found themselves relegated to the level of anti-American terrorists.

▶ In 1996, a truck bomb exploded in front of an eight-story tower in Khobar, Saudi Arabia, killing 19 US soldiers. First attributed to al-Qaeda, responsibility for the attack was next pinned on Iran, and then finally, on no one at all.

▶ In 1998, two bombs exploded in front of the US embassies in Nairobi, Kenya, and Dar-es-Salam, Tanzania, killing 298 Africans –

but no US citizens – and wounding more than 4,500. These attacks were claimed by a mysterious "Islamic Army for the Liberation of Holy Places". According to US authorities, the attacks had been committed by members of the Egyptian Islamic Jihad in response to the extradition of four of their members. And yet the same authorities accused Osama Bin Laden of being the instigator of the attacks, and the FBI issued – finally – an international arrest warrant for him.

► In 2000, a suicide boat exploded against the hull of the destroyer USS Cole, harboured in Aden, Yemen. The attack was claimed by al-Qaeda in the Arab Gulf Peninsula, but a US tribunal blamed Sudan.

These attacks occurred while the collaboration between Washington and the Islamists was on-going. Osama Bin Laden therefore held onto his bureau in Londonistan until 1999. Situated in the neighbourhood of Wembley, the Advice and Reformation Committee (ARC), served to disseminate Bin Laden's declarations and also to cover the logistical activities of al-Qaeda, including matters of recruitment, payments, and the acquisition of equipment. Among his collaborators in London, we find the Saudi Khalid al-Fawwaz and the Egyptians Adel Abdel Bary (father of the suspected Jihadi John) and Ibrahim Eidarous, three men who were the objects of international arrest warrants, but had nonetheless received political asylum in the United Kingdom. It was in perfect legality in London that Bin Laden's bureau published, in February 1998, his famous appeal for a jihad against Jews and Crusaders. Seriously ill with kidney disease, Bin Laden was hospitalised, in August 2001, at the American Hospital in Dubai. A head of one of the Gulf states assured me that he had visited him in his room, where security was provided by the CIA.

The fusion of the two "Gladio" networks and preparation of Daesh

Following the same logic, the Bush administration blamed the Islamists for the gigantic attacks which occurred on 11 September 2001 in the United States. The official version prevailed, although it contains innumerable incoherences. The Justice Secretary assured that the planes were hijacked by the Islamists, despite the fact that, according to the airline companies themselves, none of the suspects were on board. The Department of Defense published a video in which Bin Laden claimed responsibility for the attacks, despite the fact that he had publicly denied it, and that experts in facial and vocal recognition affirmed that the man in the video was not Bin Laden.[23] In any case, these events served as the pretext for Washington and London to launch the "Endless War" on terrorism and attack their ex-allies, the Taliban in Afghanistan, and Saddam Hussein's Iraq.

Although Osama Bin Laden suffered from chronic kidney disease, he died on 15 December 2001 from the consequences of Marfan Syndrome. A representative of MI6 was present at his funeral in Afghanistan. For a while, several more or less life-like body doubles kept his image alive, one of whom was himself assassinated in 2005 by Omar Sheikh, according to Pakistani Prime Minister Benazir Bhutto.

In August 2002, MI6 organised a conference in London for the Muslim Brotherhood on the theme "Syria for All". The speakers developed the idea that Syria was oppressed by the Alawite cult, and that only the Muslim Brotherhood could offer true equality.

After Sayyed Qutb and Abu Musab "the Syrian", the Islamists found a new strategist, Abu Bakr Naji. In 2004, this character, who seems never to have existed, published a work on the Internet, "The Management of Savagery", a chaos theory. Although certain authors believed they could recognise the style of an Egyptian writer, it seemed that the book had been written in English, sprinkled with superfluous Qu'ranic quotes, and then translated into Arabic. The "Savagery" in the book's title did not refer to a recourse to terrorism, but a return to the state of nature before civilisation created the state. It was about dragging Humanity back to the time when "Man is a wolf for Man". The strategy of chaos is explained in three phases:

▶ First, demoralise and exhaust the state by attacking its least-protected flanks. Choose secondary targets, often without strategic value, but easy to destroy and disperse. The point is to give the impression of a general uprising, a revolution.

▶ Second, when the state has withdrawn from the suburbs and the countryside, conquer certain zones and administer them. It will be necessary to rely on the Sharia to signal the passage to a new form of state. During this period, build alliances with all those who are

---

[23] See Tarpley, *9/11 Synthetic Terror,* Guyénot, *JFK-9/11*, Curtis, *Power of Nightmares*, among many other works, for innumerable proofs that 9/11 was a false flag operation.

opposed to Power – they must be given weapons. Then the war will become a war of position.

▶ Third, proclaim the Islamic state.

This treatise draws on contemporary military science. It places much importance on psychological operations, notably the use of spectacular violence. In practise, this strategy has nothing to do with revolution, but with the conquest of a country by exterior powers, because it supposes a massive investment. As always in subversive literature, the most interesting aspects are those which are not clearly stated, or quoted only incidentally.

▶ The preparation of populations to gladly welcome the jihadists supposes the previous construction of a network of mosques and social works, as was done in Algeria before the "civil" war.

▶ The primary military operations require arms, which must be imported beforehand. Above all, after the campaign, the jihadists will have no possibility of acquiring weapons, and even less ammunition. They will therefore need to be supplied from outside.

▶ The administration of the occupied zones supposes the participation of senior executives who have been trained in advance, like those of regular armies tasked with "rebuilding states".

▶ Finally, the war of position supposes the construction of enormous infrastructures which will require a great deal of equipment, materials, engineers and architects.

By invoking this treatise the Islamists revealed their intent to continue playing a military role on behalf of external forces, but this time on a massive scale.

In 2006, the British asked Emir Hamad of Qatar to place his pan-Arab TV channel, al-Jazeera, at the service of the Muslim Brotherhood. The Libyan Mahmud Jibril, who had trained the royal family to speak in democratic language, was tasked with carefully introducing the Brotherhood into the channel, and creating channels in foreign languages (English, and then later, Bosnian and Turkish), as well as a channel destined for children. The preacher Yusuf al-Qaradawi became the "religious advisor" for al-Jazeera. Of course, the channel broadcast and validated the audio and video recordings of the various "Osama Bin Ladens".

During the same period, US troops in Iraq were faced with a growing uprising. After having been utterly demoralised by the suddenness and brutality of the invasion (the "Shock and Awe technique"), the Iraqis were beginning to organise their resistance. John Negroponte, US ambassador in Baghdad, and then Director of National Intelligence, proposed to overcome the resistance fighters by turning their anger against themselves, and transforming the resistance to the occupation into a civil war. An expert in secret operations, he had notably participated in Operation Phoenix in Vietnam, then organised a civil war in Salvador and the Iran-Contras operation in Nicaragua, and guided the collapse of the Free and Sovereign State of Chiapas in Mexico. Negroponte called on one of the men he had worked with in Salvador, Colonel James Steele. He entrusted him with creating Iraqi Shiite militias against the Sunnis, and Sunni militias against the Shiites. For the Sunni militia, Steele used the Islamists. From al-Qaeda in Iraq, he armed a tribal coalition, the Islamic Emirate in Iraq (future Daesh), under cover of the Special Police ("the Wolf Brigade"). In order to terrify the victims and their families, he trained the Emirate in torture, according to the methods of the School of the Americas and the Political Warfare Cadres Academy in Taiwan, where he taught.

Within a few months, a new terror came crashing down on the Iraqis and divided them according to their religion. Thereafter, when General David Petraeus took command of the US troops in-country, he designated Colonel James H. Coffman to work with Steele and provide him with reports on the operation, while Brett H. McGurk advised the President directly. The principal heads of the Islamic Emirate were recruited at the detention center at Camp Bucca, but were conditioned at Abu Ghraib prison, according to the "brainwashing" techniques of professors Albert D. Biderman and Martin Seligman. The whole programme was supervised from Washington by the Secretary for Defense Donald Rumsfeld, who was Steele's direct superior.

In 2007, Washington informed the Brotherhood that it intended to overthrow the secular régimes in the Greater Middle East, including those of the allied states, and that it should prepare to exercise power. The CIA organised the alliances between the Brotherhood and the secular parties or personalities from all the states in the region. At the same time, it connected the two "Gladio" branches by reinforcing the ties between the Western Nazi groups and the Oriental Islamist groups.

These alliances were sometimes unstable – for example during the "National Conference of the Libyan Opposition", in London, the Brotherhood was only able to bring together the Islamic group fighting in Libya (al-Qaeda in Libya) and the Wahhabi Senussi Brotherhood. The platform of the programme involved re-establishing the monarchy and making Islam the state religion. More convincing was the constitution of the National Salvation Front, in Berlin, which officialised the cooperation of the Brotherhood and ex-Syrian vice President Abdel Halim Khaddam.

On 8 May 2007, in Ternopol (West Ukraine), a number of small Nazi and Islamist groups created an anti-Imperialist Front in order to fight Russia. Organisations from Lithuania, Poland, Ukraine and Russia participated, including the Islamist separatists from Crimea, Adygea, Dagestan, Ingushetia, Kabardino-Balkaria, Karachay-Cherkessia, Ossetia, and Chechnya. Since he could not travel there because of international sanctions against him, Doku Umarov – who had abolished the Republic of Chechnya and proclaimed the Islamic Emirate of Ichkeria – had his contribution read on his behalf. The Front was presided over by Dmytro Yarosh, who, during the coup d'état in Kiev, in February 2014, was to become Assistant Secretary of the National Security Council of Ukraine.

In Lebanon, May-June 2007, the national army began the siege of the Palestinian camp of Nahr al-Bared, after members of Fatah el-Islam had taken refuge there. The combats lasted for 32 days and cost the lives of 76 soldiers, about thirty of whom were decapitated.

In 2010, the Brotherhood organised the Gaza Freedom Flotilla, via the IHH. Officially, it was intended to brave the Israeli embargo and bring humanitarian aid to the citizens of Gaza. In reality, the main ship in this flotilla changed its flag of convenience during the crossing, and continued under Turkish colours. Numerous spies mingled with the non-violent militants taking part in the expedition, including the Irish CIA agent, Mahdi al-Harati. Falling into the trap laid for him by the United States, Israeli Prime Minister Benjamin Netanyahu ordered the assault of the ships in international waters. The whole world condemned this act of piracy, under the mocking eyes of the White House. Israel, which had supplied weapons to the jihadists in Afghanistan, and supported the creation of Hamas against

Yasser Arafat's PLO, turned against the Islamists in 2008 and bombed them, along with the population of Gaza. In this way, Netanyahu paid for Operation "Cast Lead," which it had led with Saudi Arabia against the advice of the White House. Finally, the passengers from the Flotilla were freed by Israel. The Turkish Press then showed Prime Minister Recep Tayyip Erdoğan visiting Mahdi al-Harati in hospital.

The beginnings of the "Arab Spring" in Tunisia

On 17 December 2010, a street vendor, Mohamed Bouazizi, set himself on fire after the police had seized his wheelbarrow. The Brotherhood seized on the affair and circulated false information that the young man was an unemployed university student, and that he had been slapped by a female police agent. Immediately, men from the National Endowment for Democracy (or NED, the fake NGO run by the secret services of the five Anglo-Saxon states) paid the dead man's family so that they would not reveal the truth, and began to foment a revolt throughout the country. A series of demonstrations against unemployment and police violence followed, and Washington asked President Zine El-Abidine Ben Ali to leave the country, while MI6 organised the triumphal return from London of the Guide of the Tunisian Brotherhood, Rached Ghannouchi.

This was the "Jasmine Revolution". The plan for this régime change borrowed both from the abdication of the Shah of Iran, followed by the return of Imam Khomeini, and from the technique of colour revolutions.

Rached Ghannouchi had created a local branch of the Muslim Brotherhood and attempted a coup d'etat in 1987. Arrested and imprisoned several times, he took exile in Sudan, where he was offered the support of Hassan al-Turabi, then in Turkey, where he became close to Recep Tayyip Erdoğan (then the director of Millî Görüş). In 1993, he obtained political asylum in Londonistan, where he lived with his two wives and their children.

The Anglo-Saxons helped him to improve the image of his party, the Movement of Islamic Tendency, renaming it the Renaissance Movement ("Ennahdha"). In order to soothe the population's fear of the Brotherhood, the NED called on its extreme left-wing puppets. Moncef Marzouki, President of the Arab Committee for Human Rights, offered moral sanction. He claimed that the Brotherhood had truly changed, and had become democrats. He was elected President of Tunisia. Ghannouchi won the general election and managed to form a government between December 2011 and August 2013. He nominated other puppets from the NED, like Ahmed Nejib Chebbi, ex-Maoist, then Trotskyist, converted by Washington. Following the example of Hassan al-Banna, Ghannouchi formed a militia within the party, the "Leagues for the Protection of the Tunisian Revolution", which proceeded with political assassinations, including that of the leader of the opposition, Chokri Belaid.

However, despite conclusive support from part of the Tunisian population when he returned, his party soon sank into the minority. Before leaving power, Rached Ghannouchi forced a vote on the tax code which was aimed, in the long term, at ruining the secular bourgeoisie. He hoped in this way to transform his country's social structure and return once again to the front of the stage.

In May 2016, the 10th congress of Ennahdha was organised by Innovative Communications & Strategies, a company created by MI6. The speakers gave assurances that the party had become "civil," with a separation of political and religious activities. But this had no connection with secularism, it simply required a division of labor between members, who must refrain from being both an elected official and an Imam at the same time.

The "Arab Spring" in Egypt

On 25 January 2011, just one week after President Ben Ali had fled, the Egyptian national holiday was transformed into a demonstration against the authorities. The protests were supervised by the US team traditionally used for colour revolutions – the Serbs trained by Gene Sharp (a NATO theorist specialised in non-violent régime change, in other words, without recourse to war) and the men from NED. Their books and brochures, translated into Arabic, including the rules for demonstrations, were widely distributed from the first day. Most of the spies were arrested later, and judged, condemned, then expelled. The demonstrators were mainly mobilised by the Muslim Brotherhood, who enjoyed the support of 15% to 20% of the population throughout the country, and also by Kifaya ("That's enough!"), a group created by Gene Sharp. This was the "Lotus Revolution". The protests took place mainly in Cairo, on Tahrir

Square, but also in the seven other major cities. Yet it was very different from the revolutionary wave which had swamped Tunisia.

The Brotherhood used weapons right from the start. On Tahrir Square, they moved their wounded into a mosque which was fully equipped to provide them with first aid. The TV channels of the petro-dictatorships – al-Jazeera for Qatar, and al-Arabiya for Saudi Arabia – called for the overthrow of the régime, and carried live broadcasts which gave out strategic information. The United States called on the ex-Director of the Atomic Energy Agency, Nobel Peace Prize-winner and President of the National Association for Change, Mohamed El-Baradei. He had been honoured for calming the anger of Hans Blix, who, in the name of the UN, had denounced the lies that the Bush administration used to justify the war against Iraq. For more than a year, El-Baradei presided over a coalition created on the model of the Damascus Declaration – a reasonable text, signatories from all sides, plus the Muslim Brotherhood, whose own programme was in reality totally opposed to that of the platform.

Finally, the Brotherhood was the first Egyptian organisation to call for the overthrow of the régime. The television channels of all the member states of NATO and the Gulf Cooperation Council predicted the flight of President Hosni Mubarak. President Obama's special envoy, ambassador Frank Wisner (Nicolas Sarkozy's father-in-law by marriage), first of all pretended to support Mubarak, then pretended to withdraw and hide behind the crowd. He pressed Mubarak to resign. Finally, after two weeks of rioting and demonstrations gathering up to a million people, Mubarak gave in. However, the United States wanted to change the Constitution before putting the Brotherhood in power. Power was therefore retained, temporarily, in the hands of the army. Marshal Mohammed Hussein Tantawi presided over the military committee which administered current affairs. He nominated a Commission of 7 members, two of whom were Muslim Brothers. Indeed, it was one of these, judge Tariq Al-Bishri, who presided over the work of the Commission.

However, the Brotherhood held demonstrations every Friday after prayers at the mosques, and continued lynching Coptic Christians, without the police interfering.

No to Revolution in Bahrain and Yemen

Although the Yemenite culture has nothing in common with North Africa, other than the Arabic language, an important dispute had been troubling Bahrain and Yemen for months. Revolutionary fervor had unexpectedly spilled over from Tunisia and Egypt, an unwelcome development for the Empire. Bahrain harboured the 5th US Fleet and controlled maritime traffic in the Persian Gulf, while Yemen and Djibouti controlled the entrance and exit of the Red Sea and the Suez Canal.

The reigning Sunni dynasty in Bahrain feared that the popular revolt could overthrow the monarchy, and automatically blamed Iran for organising it. Indeed, in 1981, an Iraqi Shiite ayatollah had attempted to export Imam Khomeini's revolution and topple the puppet régime which had been set up by the British upon independence in 1971. Perhaps 70 to 80% of the Bahraini population is Shiite, and they have many grievances, including the destruction of their mosques and lack of representation in the Sunni-dominated government, in addition to the economic and political grievances shared with ordinary Sunnis, who also joined the protests.

Secretary of Defense Robert Gates visited the area and authorised Saudi Arabia to nip these authentic revolutions in the bud. The repression was directed by Prince Nayef. He belonged to the Sudairi clan, as did Prince Bandar, although Nayef was his elder, and Bandar was only the son of a slave. The sharing of roles between the two men was clear – the uncle would maintain order by repressing popular movements, while the nephew would destabilise States by organising terrorism. They only needed to know which states were to receive which treatment.

Seldom had the hypocrisy and contradictions of imperialist policy been more evident. The grip of a Sunni minority dictatorship would be imposed against a real popular uprising in Bahrain, while a fake uprising was to be armed against a popular government, nominally headed by a member of the Alawite minority in Syria. Bahrain would be occupied by 5,000 Saudi military police indefinitely, along with 7,000 US troops stationed at the US Naval Base in Bahrain, the peninsula of the two seas.

The "Arab Spring" in Libya

While Washington had planned to overthrow the governments of Ben Ali and Mubarak without waging war, the situation was very different in Libya and Syria, ruled by the revolutionaries Gaddafi and Assad.

At the beginning of February 2011, in Cairo, while Hosni Mubarak was still President of Egypt, the CIA launched the next phase of the operations. A meeting was held with representatives of several power centers, such as the NED (Republican senator John McCain and Democrat Joe Lieberman), France (Bernard-Henri Levy), and the Muslim Brotherhood. The Libyan delegation was led by Brother Mahmud Jibril (the man who had trained the Gulf leaders and reorganised al-Jazeera). He entered the meeting as the number two of the Jamahiriya government, Libya's head of planning and economic development and a protégé of Saif al-Islam Gaddafi. On his way out, his new job was ... head of the opposition to the "dictatorship". He did not return to his luxurious offices in Tripoli, but landed in Benghazi, in Cyrenaica. The Syrian delegation included Anas al-Abdeh (founder of the Syrian Observatory for Human Rights) and his brother Malik al-Abdeh (director of Barada TV, an anti-Syrian channel financed by the CIA). Washington gave instructions to begin the civil wars in Libya and in Syria both at the same time.

On 15 February, Fathi Terbil, attorney for the victims of the 1996 massacre at Abu Salim prison, ran through the city of Benghazi claiming that the local prison was on fire, and calling for help to free the prisoners. He was briefly arrested and freed the same day. The next day, 16 February, still in Benghazi, rioters attacked three police stations, the buildings of Internal Security and the offices of the Prosecutor. The police killed 6 people while defending the armoury of Internal Security. Meanwhile, in Al-Bayda, between Benghazi and the Egyptian border, other rioters also attacked police stations and Internal Security. They took the Hussein Al-Jawf barracks and the air force base of Al-Abraq. They captured a large quantity of weapons, beat the guards and hanged a soldier. Other less spectacular incidents took place, in coordinated fashion, in seven other towns.

These attackers claimed to be members of the Libyan Islamic Fighting Group, (LIFG-al-Qaeda). They were all members or ex-members of the Muslim Brotherhood. Two of their commanders had been brainwashed in Guantánamo according to the techniques of professors Albert D. Biderman and Martin Seligman.[24]

At the end of the 1990's, on the demand of MI6, the LIFG had made four attempts to assassinate Muammar Gaddafi and establish a guerrilla warfare operation in the Fezzan mountains. They were bitterly opposed by General Abdel Fattah Younès, who forced them to flee the country. Since the attacks of 2001, LIFG has figured on the list of terrorist organisations established by Committee 1267 of the UN, but still maintained an office in London, under the protection of MI6.

The new head of LIFG, Abdelhakim Belhaj, who fought in Afghanistan alongside Osama Bin Laden, and also in Iraq, had been arrested in Malaysia in 2004, then transferred to a secret CIA prison in Thailand, where he was subjected to truth serum and torture. After an agreement between the United States and Libya, he was sent back to Libya, where he was again tortured, this time by British agents, in Abu Salim prison. In 2007, the LIFG and al-Qaeda joined forces.

However, in the context of negotiations with the United States during the period 2008-2010, Saif el-Islam Gaddafi (as naïve as he was idealistic) had negotiated a truce between the Jamahiriya and the LIFG (al-Qaeda). Belhaj had published a long document, entitled "Corrective Studies", in which he admitted that he had committed an error by calling for a jihad against co-religionists in a Muslim country. In three successive waves, all the members of al-Qaeda were amnestied and freed on the sole condition that they renounce violence in writing. Of 1,800 jihadists, only a hundred or so refused the agreement and preferred to stay in prison. As soon as he was freed, Abdelhakim Belhaj left Libya and settled in Qatar. They all managed to return to Libya without attracting attention.

On 17 February, 2011, the Brotherhood organised a protest in Benghazi, in memory of the 13 people who had died at the Italian Consulate there during the demonstration against the Danish Mohamed cartoons in 2006. A vicious rumour had been spread by Hizb ut-Tahrir, a media group of the Muslim Brotherhood that agitates for the Caliphate, that Muammar Gaddafi himself was behind the blasphemous cartooning, in league with an ally of the US

---

[24] Biderman was the author of *The Manipulation of Human Behavior,* while Seligman is known for his discovery of "learned helplessness".

and Israel, the Italian Northern League. This fake news was widely believed in Benghazi. At the anniversary the demonstration went from bad to worse than before, with 14 people killed and shot, both police and demonstrators. One may conjecture that the shooters were most likely special forces provocateurs, as this is the very template of an insurgency sparked by death squad snipers shooting from the roofs at both sides during a public demonstration. Such was precisely the starting gun for the Syria insurgency a month later, and on the Maidan in Kiev, three years afterwards.[25]

This massacre was the beginning of the "revolution". In reality, the demonstrators were not seeking to overthrow the Jamahiriya, but to proclaim the independence of Cyrenaica. So, in Benghazi, tens of thousands of flags of King Idris (1889-1983) were distributed. Modern Libya is composed of three provinces of the Ottoman Empire (Tripolitania in the west, Fezzan in the southwest, and Cyrenaica in the east); it has only been a single country since 1951. Cyrenaica was governed between 1946 and 1969 by the Senussi monarchy – a Wahhabi family supported by the Saudis – who extended their power across all of Libya.[26]

Muammar Gaddafi promised to "spring rivers of blood" to save his population from the Islamists. In Geneva, an association created by the NED, the Libyan League for Human Rights, took these declarations out of context and inverted them in the Western Press as threats against the Libyan People. It asserted that Gaddafi was

---

[25] See "Daraa, the Spark of the Storm" in *ISIS IS US* for the use of snipers in false flag operations in Syria and Ukraine, as well as in numerous CIA coups, according to Gearóid Ó Colmáin; most recently in Nicaragua, June 2018.

[26] "Libya has the largest oil reserves in Africa." "Approximately 80 percent of Libya's oil is in the eastern region of Cyrenaica." "Libya's oil export revenues accounted for 95 percent of its hard currency earnings and 75 percent of government receipts."
The math and motives for breaking up Libya are clear. The Empire has always preferred to limit oil revenues to fiefdoms like the Gulf Emirates, where the wealth can be controlled and recycled via petrodollars, and not wasted by idealistic dreamers like Gaddafi on raising living standards for millions of useless eaters in foreign lands. Thus Bush's war for Kuwait; the attempt to break off "Biafra" from Nigeria, 50 years ago; the current attempt to carve out "Kurdistan" from oil-rich zones of Syria and Iraq.
Quotes from https://en.wikipedia.org/wiki/Oil_reserves_in_Libya;
https://www.globalsecurity.org/military/world/libya/petrol-background.htm; and
https://www.loc.gov/rr/frd/cs/profiles/Libya-new.pdf

bombing Tripoli. The League itself was an empty shell which housed the men who were chosen to become future Ministers of the country after the NATO invasion.

On 21 February, on al-Jazeera, sheikh Yusuf al-Qaradawi issued a fatwa ordering the Libyan military to save their people by assassinating Muammar Gaddafi.

The Security Council, basing its work on that of the United Nations Human Rights Council in Geneva – which had auditioned the League and the Libyan ambassador – and at the request of the Gulf Cooperation Council, authorised the use of force to protect the population from the dictator.

The commander of AfriCom, General Carter Ham, hit the roof when the Pentagon ordered him to coordinate with the LIFG (al-Qaeda). How could he work in Libya with the same people he was fighting in Iraq, combatants who had killed GI's? He was immediately relieved of his concerns, and replaced by the commander of EuCom and NATO, Admiral James Stavridis.

Intermission: on 1 May 2011, Barack Obama announced that in Abbottabad, Pakistan, US Navy Seal Team 6 had eliminated Osama Bin Laden, of whom we had seen no credible life signs for almost 10 years. This announcement closed the al-Qaeda file, and made it possible to recast the jihadists as allies of the United States, just like in the good old days of the wars in Afghanistan, Bosnia-Herzegovina, Chechnya and Kosovo. "Bin Laden's body" was buried at sea, far offshore from prying eyes.

For six months, the Libyan front line remained unchanged. The LIFG controlled Benghazi and proclaimed an Islamic emirate in the town of Derna, the hotbed of extremism where most of its members originated. In order to terrorise the Libyans, LIFG death squads would kidnap people at random. Their bodies would be found later, dismembered, their limbs scattered in the streets. The jihadists had originally been normal people, but they were put on a regime of natural and synthetic drugs which made them lose all sensitivity. They were then able to commit atrocities without being aware of what they were doing.

The CIA, which suddenly needed large quantities of Captagon – an amphetamine derivative – contacted the Mafia capo, Boyko Borissov. As the Bulgarian Prime Minister he holds the presidency of the European Council for the first half of 2018. Borissov is an ex-bodyguard who joined the Security Insurance Company, one of the major Mafia organisations in the Balkans. This company has a number of clandestine laboratories which produce the drug for German sports professionals. Borissov manufactures these miracle pills by the ton, to be ingested while smoking hashish.

General Abdel Fattah Younès defected and joined the "revolutionaries". At least, this is the story that was circulated in the West. In reality, he remained in the service of the Jamahiriya at the same time as becoming the head of the armed forces of independent Cyrenaica. The Islamists, who remembered his actions against them a decade earlier, lost no time in discovering that he was still in contact with Saif el-Islam Gaddafi. They laid a trap for him, killed him, burned him and devoured part of his corpse.

Emir Hamad of Qatar hoped to get rid of the Jamahiriya and install the new power structure, as he had done with the unconstitutional President of Lebanon. While NATO settled for airborne intervention, Qatar built an airstrip in the desert and landed men and equipment there. But the population of Fezzan and Tripolitania remained loyal to the Jamahiriya and its Guide.

When NATO rained a deluge of fire on Tripoli, in August, Qatar massed Special Forces and unloaded its tanks in Tunisia. These thousands of men were of course not Qataris, but mercenaries – mainly Colombian – trained by Academi (ex-Blackwater Xe) in the United Arab Emirates. They joined al-Qaeda (now once again the good guys, even though they were still considered as terrorists by the UN) in Tripoli, dressed and hooded in black, so that their eyes could not be seen.

Only two groups of Libyans participated in the taking of Tripoli – the fighters from Misrata, under the command of Turkey, and the Tripoli Brigade[27] (al-Qaeda – LIFG), commanded by the Irishman Mahdi al-Harati, and supervised by regular officers from the French army.

Even before Muammar Gaddafi had been lynched, a provisional government was formed by Washington. We note the presence of all the "heroes" of this story – under the presidency of Moustafa Abdul Jalil (who had covered up the torture of the Bulgarian nurses and the

---

[27] Wikipedia has useful details on the Tripoli Brigade

Palestinian doctor), Mahmud Jibril (who taught the Emirs of the Gulf, reorganised Al-Jazeera and underwent metamorphosis in the February meeting in Cairo), and Fathi Terbil (who launched the "revolution" in Benghazi). The head of the LIFG and world ex-number 3 of al-Qaeda, Abdelhakim Belhaj (implicated in the attacks on Atocha train station in Madrid), was named as "military governor of Tripoli".

The "Arab Spring" in Syria

As of 4 February 2011, date of the opening of the meeting in Cairo, the coordination of the Arab Spring in Syria was handled by the Facebook account "Syrian Revolution 2011". The title alone is enough to indicate that the operation was intended to quickly overthrow the Syrian Arab Republic, as had been the case for the other "colour revolutions", since the objective was not to change the mentalities, but only the leading elites and a few of the country's laws. On the same day as its creation, "Syrian Revolution 2011" launched an appeal for a demonstration in Damascus which was relayed by al-Jazeera, while Facebook reported tens of thousands of "Followers". Computer magic. This account was to play a central role over the next five years. Every Friday, the Muslim day for prayer, it dedicated itself to one of the Brotherhood's objectives.

On 22 February, John McCain was in Lebanon. He met various leaders of the pro-Saudi Coalition of 14 March, including deputy Okab Sakr, to whom he entrusted the delivery of arms to the Islamists responsible for terrorist attacks in Syria. He then left Beirut and went off to explore the Syrian border. He chose the village of Ersal as the future base of operations.

In spite of the appeals from the mysterious Syrian Revolution 2011 account, it was not until mid-March that events began to heat up in Syria. The Brotherhood gathered in Daraa, a town in the South of Syria, near the border with Jordan. It was reputed for being heavily Ba'athist, and also home to ex-jihadists from Afghanistan and Iraq. The Brotherhood hijacked a demonstration by civil servants who were demanding a pay rise, and began destroying the Palace of Justice. The same day, supervised by Mossad officers, they attacked a centre of Syrian military intelligence outside the town, used exclusively for surveillance if Israeli activity in the occupied Golan Heights.

Reporting on the event, al-Jazeera claimed that the inhabitants of Daraa were protesting after the police had tortured children who had tagged slogans hostile to President Assad. Confusion reigned while the vandals continued the destruction of the town centre. Over the following weeks, three groups of Islamists rambled through the country, attacking poorly-defended secondary targets. The impression of instability was generalised, even though the attacks concerned only three distinct locations at a time. In the space of a few weeks, there were more than 100 deaths, mainly policemen and soldiers.

President Assad's reaction was the opposite of what was expected – instead of imposing a local Patriot Act, he abrogated the state of emergency which was still in force – Syria is still at war with Israel, which occupies the Golan Heights – and dissolved the State Security Court. He passed a law guaranteeing and organising the right to demonstrate, denounced an operation instigated from overseas, and called on the People to support the Institutions. He convened the Chiefs of Staff and forbade soldiers to use their weapons if there was any risk of causing collateral civilian deaths.

Taking the President at his word, the Brotherhood attacked a military convoy in Banias (hometown of the traitorous ex-vice President Abdel Halim Khaddam) for several hours, in full view of the population. Fearing that the spectators might be killed or wounded, the soldiers obeyed their President and did not use their weapons. A dozen of them were killed. The sergeant who was commanding the detachment lost both his legs when he covered a grenade with his body to protect his men. The operation was organised from Paris by Khaddam's Salvation Front and the Muslim Brotherhood. On 6 June, 120 policemen were killed in a similar situation in Jisr al-Shughur.

Demonstrations hostile to the Syrian Arab Republic were held in several towns. Contrary to the image that was propagated by the Western medias, the demonstrators never called for democracy. The slogans they chanted most were – "The People want the régime to fall", "Christians to Beirut, Alawites to the grave", "We want a God-fearing President", "Down with Iran and the Hezbollah". Several other slogans mentioned "liberty", but not in the Western sense of the word. The demonstrators were calling for the freedom to practise Sharia law.

At that time, people believed that only al-Jazeera and al-Arabiya were trustworthy sources of information – media that had supported the régime changes in Tunisia and Egypt. They were therefore persuaded that in Syria too, the President would abdicate and that the Muslim Brotherhood would take power. The vast majority of Syrians were witnessing what they thought was a "revolution", and were preparing for a new Islamist government. It is very difficult to count the number of Syrians who demonstrated against the Republic, or who supported the Muslim Brotherhood. We can only report that hundreds of small-scale demonstrations took place throughout the country, and that the largest of them gathered close to 100,000 people in Hama.[28] Its organisers were received by President Assad in Damascus. When he asked them what they were demonstrating for, they answered that they wanted to "forbid Alawites to enter Hama". The astonished President – himself an Alawite – ended the interview.

On 4 July in Paris, there was a public conference, organized by the Brotherhood and the Israeli government behind the scenes, to get the French leaders on board. Responding to the appeal of "philosopher" Bernard-Henry Levy and the ex- and future Ministers for Foreign Affairs Bernard Kouchner and Laurent Fabius,[29] representatives from the right, centre, and left, and some ecologists, lent their support to what was presented to them as a struggle for democracy. No one noticed the presence in the room of the real organisers of the event – Alex Goldfarb (advisor to the Israeli Minister for Defense) and Melhem Droubi (world head of external relations for the Brotherhood), who had come specially from Saudi Arabia.

In August, a Syrian National Council was founded in Istanbul, on the model of the Libyan National Transitional Council. It consisted of long-time expatriates from Syria, others who had recently left, and the Muslim Brotherhood. The bizarre idea that this group was seeking to establish a "democracy" was ostensibly made plausible by personalities from the extreme left wing, such as professor Burhan

---

[28] Anti-Assad protesters in Homs, alleged "cauldron of the revolution," were paid youngsters who had been bussed in, according to local witnesses. *ISIS IS U.S.*, p. 127.

[29] Coincidentally, of course, all three of these politicians are Jewish, or of Jewish extraction, as were both the major French presidential candidates, Nicholas Sarkozy and Dominique Strauss-Kahn, until the latter was eliminated by scandal.

Ghalioun, who was named its President. Yet this man had been working for years with the NED and the Muslim Brotherhood. Although he was a layman, he had been writing speeches for Abassi Madani (President of the Islamic Salvation Front of Algeria) since he was exiled in Qatar. This was also the case of George Sabra and Michel Kilo, who had been working with the Brotherhood for more than thirty years, and who had followed the Trotskyists to the NED in 1982. Under the direction of the Libyan Mahmud Jibril, Sabra notably worked on the foreign versions of the children's TV programme "Sesame Street", produced by the French Lagardère Media and by al-Jazeera of Qatar, with RAND Corp. researcher Cheryl Benard, wife of Zalmay Khalilzad, US ambassador to the UN and then Iraq. Similarly, human rights careerist Haytham Manna was manager of investments for the Sudanese Brotherhood.

Qatar bought the rotating presidency of the Arab League from the PLO for $400 million. In violation of the statutes, it suspended the Syrian Arab Republic, even though it was a founding member of the organisation. Then it proposed an on-site Observer Mission presided by Sudan (still governed by the Brotherhood). It designated the ex-head of the secret services and ex-ambassador to Qatar, General Mohammed Ahmed Mustafa al-Dabi, to direct the work. Every member state sent observers, in order to represent all tendencies. The Syrian Arab Republic agreed to host the League and allowed the Mission to deploy over all its territory. This was the first and only time that a pluralist organisation had gone into the field, met with all the protagonists, and visited the whole country. It was actually the only trustworthy external source of information throughout the whole conflict.

The nomination of General al-Dabi was unanimously saluted by all parties. He had negotiated the separation of Sudan and South Sudan, and was proposed by many Arab states for the Nobel Peace Prize. However, it appeared from a reading of the preliminary reports that the Sudanese had no intention of writing a report made to order, but to conduct an authentic and pluralist investigation. Suddenly, the international media changed their tune, and accused al-Dabi of responsibility for the genocide in Darfur. All those who had approved his nomination now demanded his resignation. The General resisted angrily.

Finally, a status report was published, attesting to the fact that there was no revolution in Syria. The Mission confirmed that the violence had been considerably exaggerated, that the army had withdrawn from the towns, that there was no repression, that the victims were mostly soldiers and policemen, that more than 5,000 prisoners whose names had been transmitted to the authorities had been freed, and that foreign medias who request to cover the events had been allowed to do so.

Qatar, in a fit of anger, paid $2 billion to Sudan to recall General al-Dabi, but he refused to allow the League to nominate his successor. Bereft of its commander, the Mission was dissolved at the beginning of 2012.

Furious at seeing the Syrian Arab Republic pull through, the Brotherhood decided to create an Islamic emirate. After several attempts, they chose a new neighbourhood of Homs, Baba Amr, where tunnels had previously been dug and fitted to ensure a supply route in case of a siege. 3,000 combatants gathered there, including 2,000 Syrian Takfiri. They were members of a sub-group of the Brotherhood, "Excommunication and Immigration", created under Sadat.

They set up a "Revolutionary Tribunal", judged and condemned to death more than 150 inhabitants of the neighbourhood, and then cut their throats in public. The rest of the inhabitants fled, with the exception of about forty families. The Takfiri then built barricades at all the points of access to the area, and these were heavily armed by the French Special Forces. The terrorist campaign of the first year gave way to a war of position, in conformity with the plan laid out in 2004 in "The Management of Savagery". From that point on, the Islamists received weapons from NATO which were more sophisticated than those of the Syrian Army, which had been under an embargo since 2005.

One morning, the Syrian Arab Army entered Baba Amr, whose defences had been de-activated. The French, the journalists and a few leaders fled, to reappear a few days later in Lebanon. The Takfiri surrendered. The war that had just begun seemed to be ending already, like in Lebanon in 2007, when the Lebanese army defeated Fatah al-Islam. But the Islamists were not done yet.

A new operation was being prepared from Jordan, under NATO command. The plan was to attack Damascus in the context of a gigantic psychological operation, but this was cancelled at the last moment. The Islamists who had been abandoned by France in Baba Amr were now decommissioned by the United States, who were discussing a possible sharing of the Middle East with Russia. A promise of peace was signed in Geneva, on 30 June 2012.

The end of the "Arab Spring" in Egypt

In Egypt, the Brotherhood dominated the new parliament, or "constituent assembly," which was of the opinion that the new Constitution – drawn up specifically to expedite its election – did little more than reiterate a slightly amended old text, although it had been approved by referendum at 77%. It therefore designated a Constituent Assembly of 100 members, this time including 60 Brothers.

The Brotherhood stressed that the young democrats could undermine the power of the army. Its campaign for the Presidential election was the occasion to call for the regeneration of the country by the Qu'ran. Yusuf al-Qaradawi preached that it was more important to fight homosexuals and re-instate the Faith than to fight Israel for the recognition of the rights of the Palestinian People. While the Sunni population massively boycotted the election, the Brotherhood prevented the election from being held in Christian villages and towns, so that 600,000 citizens were unable to vote. However, the election results favoured General Ahmed Shafik, Mubarak's ex-Prime Minister, who won by a slim margin of 30,000 votes. The Brotherhood then threatened the members of the Electoral Commission and their families until, 13 days later, it decided to proclaim victory for Brother Mohamed Morsi. The "international community" praised the democratic character of the election.

Mohamed Morsi was an engineer who had worked for NASA. He had United States nationality and secret defence security clearance in the Pentagon. As soon as he came to power, he began work to rehabilitate and favour his own clan, and to reinforce the bonds with Israel. On the anniversary of Sadat's execution, he received the assassins at the Presidential palace. He nominated Adel Mohammed al-Khayat, one of the leaders of Gamaa Al-Islamiya, (the group responsible for the 1997 massacre in Luxor), as governor for that district. He persecuted the democrats who had demonstrated against certain aspects of Hosni Mubarak's politics (but not his resignation). He supported a vast campaign of pogroms by the Muslim Brotherhood against the Christians, and covered up their abuses – lynchings, destruction of the archbishoprics, and the burning of churches. Simultaneously, he privatised major businesses and announced the possible sale of the Suez Canal to Qatar, which was then sponsoring the Brotherhood. From the Presidential palace, he telephoned Ayman al-Zawahiri, world leader of al-Qaeda, at least four times.

Finally, opposition to Morsi became unanimous; excepting the Brotherhood, all political parties, even the Salafists, demonstrated against him. 33 million citizens took to the streets and called on the army to give the country back to the People. Taking no notice of the street, President Morsi ordered the army to prepare to attack the Syrian Arab Republic in order to come to the assistance of the Syrian Muslim Brotherhood. That was to be the final straw.

On 3 July 2013, at the hour that Washington's offices close for the long weekend of the Independence Day national holiday, the army carried out a coup d'état. Mohamed Morsi was imprisoned, while the streets became a battlefield – the Muslim Brotherhood and their families on one side, and the law enforcement agencies on the other.

The war against Syria

It is said that "in politics, promises only bind those who believe in them". One month after the Geneva 1 conference and the peace agreement, and a few days after the "Friends of Syria" Conference in Paris, war was authorised once again. Instead of a NATO action supported by a few jihadists, this was a jihadist attack supported by NATO. Its code name was "Damascus Volcano and Syrian Earthquake".

An army of 40,000 men, trained in Jordan, crossed the border and charged towards the Syrian capital, at the same time as a terrorist bombing killed top Syrian leaders at a meeting of the National Security Council. The army and the intelligence services lost their commanders in the attack.

The jihadists were mercenaries who had been recruited from among the poor of the Muslim world. Many of them did not speak Arabic, and had received only one week of military training. Some of them believed they were fighting Israelis. After suffering considerable losses, they retreated.

In the long war which followed, the Syrian Arab Army attempted to defend its population centers, against the jihadists, who tried to make life impossible in the vast expanses of the desert. They enjoyed an infinite supply of reinforcements. Every month, new fighters arrived to replace the dead and the deserters. All the petty criminals of the Muslim world came to try their luck for a few hundred dollars a month. Recruitment centres were opened publicly in countries like Tunisia and Afghanistan, and more discreetly in countries like Morocco and Pakistan. However, the fatality rate of these legionnaires was extremely high.

In July 2013, according to Interpol, some very sophisticated escape operations were carried out in nine states in order to free the Islamist leaders and transfer them to Syria. For example:

► On 23 July, between 500 and 1,000 prisoners escaped from the prisons in Taj and Abu Ghraib (Iraq).

► On 27 July, 1,117 prisoners escaped from Kouafia prison in Benghazi district, Libya by a riot inside the prison combined with an attack from outside.

► On the night of 29 to 30 July, 243 Taliban escaped from the prison in Dera Ismail Khan in the Pakistani tribal areas.

The Syrian Arab Army cremated most of the combatants' corpses, while retaining those that could be identified. They were sent back to their families. Several states discreetly set up repatriation networks, for example Algeria, with the Emir Abdelkader Foundation. Yet the Syrian Arab Army still holds more than 30,000 corpses that were identified, but never claimed.

Those Western states which had at first sent Special Forces recruited from amongst their own soldiers with double nationality – generally Muslims with origins in the Maghreb – later organised their own networks to recruit jihadists. Thus, in France, a network was set up in prisons with Salafist mosques, like the one in the Rue Jean-Pierre Timbaud in Paris. These several thousand individuals were added to the tens of thousands from the "Greater Middle East". Although we do not know for certain how many people took part in the war, it is estimated that the total number of jihadists fighting in Syria and Iraq, both locals and foreigners, has been more than 350,000 since 2011. This is more than any regular army of the European Union, and twice that of the Syrian Arab Army.

The ideological unity of the jihadists was guaranteed by the "spiritual head of the Free Syrian Army", sheikh Adnan al-Aroor. This colourful personality was able to reach a vast public by way of his weekly TV programme. He inflamed passions by calling for the overthrow of the tyrant, and supported a paternalistic, authoritarian vision of society. As time went on, he drifted towards sectarian appeals for the massacre of Christians and Alawites. He originally he came from a family of delinquents, betrayed his brothers to the police, and escaped a prison sentence by joining the Syrian Arab Army. As a non-commissioned officer, he was arrested for raping young recruits. He then fled to Saudi Arabia, where he became a sheikh in the service of Allah.

The jihadists usually received basic weaponry, and had access to an unlimited supply of ammunition. They were organised in *katibas* or brigades, small units of a few hundred men, whose commanders received ultra-sophisticated equipment, notably portable communication kits relaying live satellite images of the movements of the Syrian Arab Army. They were therefore fighting an asymmetrical war against the Syrian Arab Army, who were certainly better trained, but whose weapons all dated from before 2005, and who had no access to satellite imagery.

In contrast to the Syrian Arab Army, whose units were all coordinated and placed under the authority of President Bashar al-Assad, the jihadist *katibas* were continually skirmishing between themselves, as on all battlefields where rival "warlords" struggle for superiority. However, all the factions received reinforcements, arms, ammunition and intelligence from a single central command, NATO LandCom, situated in Izmir (Turkey), and whom they were therefore obliged to obey. But the United States had great difficulty in making this system work, because many of the participants were attempting to conceal their operations from their allies – for example, the French in secret from the British, or the Qataris to the detriment of the Saudis.

As soon as a territory was evacuated by the Syrian Arab Army, the jihadists who occupied it dug in. They built tunnels and bunkers. The

Saudis had sent the billionaire Osama Bin Laden to Afghanistan because he was a specialist in public works. He supervised the construction of tunnels in the mountains – or more exactly, the enlarging of subterranean riverbeds. In Syria, NATO civil engineers came to supervise the construction of gigantic lines of defence, comparable to those of the Central Powers during the First World War.

Daesh and the Caliphate

The early membership of the al-Nusra Front (al-Qaeda in Syria) were Syrians who went to fight in Iraq after the fall of Baghdad in 2003. They returned to Syria to participate in the planned insurgency against the Republic, which was later postponed until July 2012. For two years – until 2005 – they benefited from the aid of Syria, which allowed them to circulate freely, believing they had come to fight the US invader. However, when General David Petraeus arrived in Iraq, it became apparent that their true function was to fight the Iraqi Shiites, to the greater glory of the occupiers. In April 2013, the Islamic Emirate in Iraq, from which they all originated, was reactivated under the name of the Islamic Emirate in Iraq and the Levant (ISIL or ISIS). The members of the al-Nusra Front, who now had their own leading roles of in Syria, refused to rejoin to their parent company.

In May 2013, an American Zionist association, the Syrian Emergency Task Force, organised a trip by Senator McCain to rebel-occupied areas in Syria. He met various criminals, including Mohammad Nour, spokesman for the *katiba* Northern Tempest (al-Qaeda), which had kidnapped and imprisoned 11 Shiite Lebanese pilgrims in Azaz, Syria. A photograph published by his Press service showed McCain in deep discussion with leaders of the Free Syrian Army, some of whom also displayed the black Al-Qaeda flag of the al-Nusra Front. Some doubt arose about the identity of one of these men. I wrote later that he was actually Daesh's future Caliph, which the Senator's spokesperson vehemently denied. As this man had also been a translator for journalists, there was room for doubt. The spokesperson insisted that my theory was absurd, since Daesh had several times made death threats against the Senator. But shortly afterwards, with no worries about contradicting himself, John McCain declared on TV that he knew the leaders of Daesh personally, and was "in permanent contact with them". Supposedly he entertained no illusions about the Islamists, but he could brag that he had learned a thing or two in Vietnam, and was supporting them against "Bashar's régime" out of strategic necessity. So even before the events in Syria began, McCain had organised their weapons supply from Lebanon, where he chose the village of Arsal as a rear base of operations. His fact-finding tour of jihadist Syria would help in planning Daesh's future operations.

In December 2013, the Turkish police and Ministry of Justice determined that for a number of years, Prime Minister Recep Tayyip Erdoğan had been secretly meeting with Yasin al-Qadi, the banker of al-Qaeda. Photographs showed that he came in a private plane, and was welcomed once the surveillance cameras of the airport had been switched off. US vice-President Dick Cheney was at that time (and probably still is) a personal friend of Al-Qadi. He was taken off NATO's wanted list only on 5 October 2012, and off the State Department list on 26 November 2014, but had been coming to see Erdoğan for a long time before that. He admitted financing Bin Laden's Arab Legion in Bosnia-Herzegovina (1991-95), as well as Bosnian President Alija Izetbegović. According to the FBI, he also played a central role in the financing of the attacks against the US embassies in Tanzania and Kenya (1998). The FBI also pointed to Al-Qadi as the owner of the software firm Ptech, (now Go Agile) suspected of having play a role in international terrorism (the 9/11crimes, in particular).

A short time afterwards, the Turkish police searched the headquarters of the IHH and interrogated Halis B., the suspected leader of al-Qaeda in Turkey, and İbrahim Ş., second-in-command of the organisation for the Near East. Erdoğan managed to fire the policemen and free the suspects.

In January 2014, the United States began a vast programme for the development of an unnamed jihadist organisation. Three training camps were set up in Turkey, in Şanlıurfa, Osmaniye and Karaman. Huge supplies of weapons arrived for ISIL, arousing the envy of al-Nusra. For several months, the two groups fought each other mercilessly. France and Turkey, who were not aware of the plan, at first of sent ammunition to al-Nusra (al-Qaeda) to help them get their hands on ISIL's treasure trove. Saudi Arabia demanded to be given the leadership of ISIL, and proclaimed that would now be commanded by Prince Abdul Rahman al-Faisal, brother of the Saudi ambassador to the United States and the Saudi Minister for Foreign Affairs.

Gradually, the situation became clearer – on 18 February, the White House convened the heads of the secret services of Saudi Arabia, Jordan, Qatar and Turkey. The US National Security Advisor, Susan Rice, told them that Prince Bandar was not recovering from his injuries, and would be replaced by Prince Mohammed bin Nayef as supervisor of the jihadists. But Nayef had no natural authority over people, and this only whet Turkish appetites. Rice also shared the new organization chart of the Free Syrian Army, and told the assembled spy chiefs that Washington would entrust them with a vast secret operation to redraw the borders. At the beginning of May, Abdelhakim Belhaj (ex-officer of al-Qaeda, military governor of Tripoli, and founder of the Free Syrian Army) went to Paris to inform the French government about the US-jihadist plans, and to end the war waged by France against ISIL. Notably, he was received at the Quai d'Orsay, the Foreign Ministry. From 27 May to 1 June, several jihadist chiefs were invited for consultations in Amman, the capital of Jordan.

According to the minutes of the meeting, the Sunni combatants were to be regrouped under the banner of ISIL (Islamic Emirate of Iraq and the Levant). They would receive vehicles and massive amounts of Ukrainian weaponry. They were to take control of a vast zone straddling Syria and Iraq, mainly desert, and would proclaim an independent state there. Their mission was to cut the Beirut-Damascus-Baghdad-Teheran route and obliterate the Franco-British frontiers of Syria and Iraq. Iraqi ex-vice-President Izzat Ibrahim al-Douri, who was master of the Order of the Naqshbandis in his country, announced that he would bring 80,000 veteran soldiers of Saddam's army with him. The CIA confirmed that 120,000 combatants from the Sunni tribes of Al-Anbar province would join ISIL as soon as it arrived, and would supply them with heavy weaponry that the Pentagon would deliver, officially for the Iraqi army. Masrour "Jomaa" Barzani, head of the secret services of the Kurdistan Regional Government, brokered an agreement allowing his government to annex the disputed territories of Kirkuk as soon as ISIL annexed Al-Anbar. Less obvious is the reason for the presence of Mullah Krekar, who was serving a prison sentence in Norway, and who nonetheless arrived in a special NATO aircraft. For many years he had been playing an important role in the ideological preparation of the Islamists for the proclamation of the Caliphate. But that question would not be examined during the meeting.

At the same moment, at West Point military academy, President Barack Obama announced the resumption of the "war on terrorism" with an annual budget of $5 billion. The White House later announced that this programme included the training of 5,400 "moderate rebels" annually (therefore not the Muslim Brotherhood).

In June, the Islamic Emirate launched attacks, first of all in Iraq, then in Syria, and proclaimed a caliphate. Until then, Daesh – this was the name it was given, based on its Arab acronym – was only supposed to be composed of a few hundred combatants, but miraculously, it was suddenly swollen by several hundred thousand mercenaries. The gates of Iraq were opened to them by ex-officers of Saddam Hussein, who were taking revenge on the government of Baghdad, and by Shiite officers who had emigrated to the United States. Daesh grabbed the weapons that the Pentagon had just delivered to the Iraqi army, and cash reserves from the Central Bank of Mosul. Simultaneously, and in coordinated fashion, the Regional Government of Kurdistan annexed Kirkuk and announced that there would be a referendum on self-determination. In order to prevent jihadists from competing groups of the Islamic Emirate from crowding into Turkey, Ankara closed its frontier with Syria.

As soon as it was settled in, Daesh installed civil administrators trained at Fort Bragg, North Carolina, some of whom had recently taken part in the US administration of Iraq. Instantaneously, Daesh had a state administration apparatus at its disposition, in conformity with the US army's theory of state-building. This was a miraculous makeover for what had been only a minor terrorist group a few weeks earlier.

Almost everything had been planned in advance. So, when Daesh took the Iraqi military airports, it immediately inherited combat-ready airplane and helicopter pilots. These could not have been ex-Iraqi air force pilots, since combat efficiency was considered to be lost after six months without flight experience. But the planners had forgotten to supply the necessary technical teams, which meant that part of the equipment could not be used.

Daesh also was given a media arm, apparently composed mostly of MI6 specialists, who were tasked with editing newspapers as well as staging the violence of Allah. This was another change for the jihadists. Until now, they had used violence to terrorise the population. From now on, they would magnify it in order to shock and hypnotise them. Remarkably polished and well-filmed, their videos would burn into people's minds and recruit the fans of snuff movies.

The astonishing success of Daesh attracted Islamists from all over the world. If al-Qaeda had been their reference during the time of Osama Bin Laden and his cohort of look-alikes, Caliph "Ibrahim" was now their new idol. One by one, the majority of jihadist groups in the world swore allegiance to Daesh. On 23 February 2015, the Prosecutor General of Egypt, Hichem Baraket, notified Interpol that Abdelhakim Belhaj, military governor of Tripoli, was the head of Daesh for the whole of Maghreb.

Daesh exploited Iraqi and Syrian oil. Crude oil was transported either via the pipe-line controlled by the Kurdistan Regional Government of Iraq, or by tank trucks owned by the Turkish companies Serii and SAM Otomotiv, via the border posts of Karkamış, Akçakale, Cilvegözü and Öncüpınar. A part of the crude oil was refined for Turkish use by Turkish Petroleum Refineries Co. (Tüpraş) in the city of Batman. It was then shipped to Ceyhan, Mersin and Dortyol on ships of the Palmali Shipping & Agency JSC, the company of Turko-Azeri billionaire Mubariz Gurbanoğlu. Most of the crude oil was transported to Israel, where it received false certificates of origin, thence to Europe (including France, at Fos-sur-Mer, where it was refined). The rest was sent directly to Ukraine.

This system was perfectly well known to industry insiders, and was mentioned at the World Petroleum Council (15 to 19 June in Moscow). The speakers assured that Aramco (USA/Saudi Arabia) organised the distribution of Daesh's oil in Europe, while Exxon-Mobil (the Rockefeller company that rules Qatar) sold the oil stolen by al-Nusra. A few months later, during a hearing of the European Parliament, the representative for the European Union in Iraq, ambassador Jana Hybaskova, would confirm that the member states of the EU were sponsoring Daesh by buying their oil.

At first, the UN Security Council was incapable of denouncing this traffic – at best, its President noted that trading with terrorist organisations was forbidden. We had to wait until February 2015 for the vote on resolution 2199. Mubariz Gurbanoğlu then retired, selling several of his ships (*Mecid Aslanov, Begim Aslanova, Poet Qabil, Armada Breeze* and *Shovket Alekperova*) to BMZ Group Denizcilik ve İnşaat A.Ş., the maritime company belonging to Bilal Erdoğan, son of President Recep Tayyip Erdoğan. Bilal continued the traffic. It was only in November 2015, during the G20 summit in Antalya, that Vladimir Putin accused Turkey of violating the UN resolution and selling Daesh's oil. When President Erdoğan denied it, the head of operations for the Russian army, General Serguei Rudskoy, presented satellite images at a public Press conference, showing 8,500 tanker trucks crossing the Turkish border.   The Russian air force immediately destroyed the trucks present in Syria, but the greater part of the traffic continued via Iraqi Kurdistan, under the responsibility of its President Massoud Barzani. Work was then begun on expanding the oil terminal "Yumurtalık" (linked to the Turko-Iraqi Kirkuk-Ceyhan pipeline), boosting its storage capacity up to 1.7 million tons.

These tank trucks all belonged to Powertans, a company which had obtained the monopoly for the transport of oil on Turkish territory, without it being put out for competitive bids. It was owned by the very mysterious Grand Fortune Ventures, based first in Singapore, then transferred to the Cayman Islands. Behind this financial set-up was Çalık Holding, the company belonging to Berat Albayrak, President Erdoğan's son-in law and his Minister for Energy.

The oil which travelled via the Kurdish pipeline was also sold in the same way. However, when the Iraqi government denounced the Barzani clan's complicity with Daesh, and the theft of Iraqi public property which they had organised together, Ankara feigned surprise. Erdoğan blocked the income of the Iraqi Kurds in a Turkish bank account, while waiting for Erbil (the capital of Iraqi Kurdistan) and Baghdad to clarify their positions. Although this money was supposedly blocked, income was generated by investing it, which was not declared to the Turkish Budget, but paid to Erdoğan's AKP (Justice and Development Party).

In September 2014, the Caliph purged the cadres of his organisation. The North African officers in general and the Tunisians in particular were accused of disobedience, condemned to death and executed. They were replaced by Georgian Chechens and Chinese Uyghurs.

The Georgian Military Intelligence officer Tarkhan Batirashvili became the Caliph's right-hand man, under the name of "Abou Omar al-Chichani". Innocently, Georgian Minister for Defence and ex-head of the "Abkhazian government in exile" (sic) Irakli Alassania, announced at the same time that his country was preparing to set up training camps for Syrian jihadists.

On 13 September, reacting to the large-scale atrocities and the execution of two US journalists, President Obama announced the creation of an anti-Daesh Coalition. During the battle of Kobane in northern Syria, the USAF kept the game going by bombing Daesh on certain days and dropping them weapons and ammunition on other days.

The Coalition declared it was leading an operation against a certain Khorasani group of al-Qaeda in Syria. Although there is no proof whatsoever that this group actually existed, the US media claimed that it was led by an explosives expert on mission for the French secret services, David Drugeon, which the French Defense Minister denied. The American media then claimed that Drugeon, on behalf of the French secret services, had trained Mohammed Mera (accused in the attacks in Toulouse and Montauban in 2012) and the Kouachi brothers (blamed for the attack on Charlie Hébdo in Paris in 2015).

In order to increase its resources, Daesh levied taxes in the territories it controlled, ransomed prisoners, and smuggled antiques. The latter activity was supervised by Abu Sayyaf al-Iraqi. The stolen artefacts were brought to Gaziantep, in Turkey, not far from Aleppo. Then they were either delivered directly to the collectors who had ordered them, via transport companies like Şenocak, Devran, Karahan and Egemen, or sold at the Coppersmith Bazaar in Gaziantep.

Additionally, when Afghan President Hamid Karzai left power, he took the transport of opium and Afghani heroin from the Kosovars and handed it over to the Islamic State Caliphate. For many long years, the family of the Afghan President – notably his brother Ahmed Wali Karzai, until his assassination – had reigned over the main opium cartel. Under the protection of US armed forces, Afghanistan produced 380 tons of heroin per year of the 430 tons available on the world market. This commerce had enriched the Karzai clan by $3 billion in 2013. Daesh was tasked with transporting the drugs to Europe via its African and Asian subsidiaries.[30]

The Liquidation of Daesh

On 21 May 2017, President Donald Trump announced in Riyadh that the United States had abandoned the idea of creating a Sunnistan (Daesh Caliphate) straddling the border between Iraq and Syria, and would cease to support international terrorism. He directed all Muslim states to do the same. This speech had been carefully prepared with the Pentagon and Prince Mohamed Ben Salman, but not with London.

While Saudi Arabia obediently began dismantling the gigantic system of support for the Muslim Brotherhood that it had developed over sixty years, the United Kingdom, Qatar, Turkey and Malaysia refused to follow this US initiative.

In August 2017, London launched the Arakan Rohingya Salvation Army against the Burmese government. For a month, international public opinion was force-fed truncated information claiming that the exodus of Rohingha Muslims from Myanmar to Bengal was due to persecution by the Buddhist Burmese army. This is an attempt to launch a second phase of the war of civilisations – after the war of Muslims against Christians, we are now served the war of Buddhists against Muslims. However, the operation was interrupted when Saudi Arabia ceased its support for the Arakan Rohingya Salvation Army, whose headquarters are in Mecca.

Finally, the United States, Iran and Iraq chased Daesh out of Iraq, while Syria and Russia threw them out of Syria. This raises the question as to whether the West will settle for abandoning the idea of a jihadist State, the Caliphate, or whether it will continue to clean house by eliminating the other terrorist groups, as President Trump wishes.

---

[30] See "Karzai family hands over heroin trafficking to Islamic State", 1 Dec. 2014, http://www.voltairenet.org/article186109.html

Part Three:
The "Arab Springs" organised
by Washington and London

When the Soviet Union collapsed, the US elite believed that a period of commerce and prosperity would follow the Cold War. However, a section of the military-industrial complex imposed rearmament in 1995, followed by a very aggressive imperialist policy as from 2001. This faction, which identifies itself with the "Continuity of Government" group, stands ready to take over power in case of the destruction of elected institutions. It prepared the wars in Afghanistan and Iraq in advance, although they were not launched until after 11 September 2001. Faced with its military failure in Iraq and the impossibility of attacking Iran, this group changed its strategy. It adopted the British project of overthrowing the secular régimes of the Greater Middle East and remodelling the region into small states administered by the Muslim Brotherhood. Progressively, it took control of NATO, the European Union and the UN. It was only several millions of deaths and trillions of dollars later that it was challenged in the United States by the election of Donald Trump.

US Supremacy

When the Second World War ended, the United States was the only victorious nation which had not experienced war on its own soil. Profiting from its advantage, Washington chose to succeed London in the control of its Empire, and to enter into conflict with Moscow. Over the next 44 years, a Cold War followed the hot war of World War II. When the Soviet Union began to fall apart, President George H. Bush Sr. decided that it was time to get back to doing business. He began to scale down his armies, and ordered a revision of foreign policy and military doctrine.

Washington then claimed, in its publication "National Security Strategy of the United States" (1991) that "the United States remains the only state with truly global strength, reach and influence in every dimension — political, economic and military... There is no substitute for American leadership".[31]

This is why they reorganised the world during operation "Desert Storm" – first they pressured their Kuwaiti ally to steal Iraqi oil, and at the same time, to demand arrears on the reimbursement of Iraq's allegedly free aid against Iran. Next they encouraged their Iraqi ally to resolve the problem by annexing Kuwait, which had been arbitrarily carved out by the British 30 years earlier. Finally, they invited every state on the planet to support them – instead of the United Nations – in the reaffirmation of international law.

But since the two empires were propped up one against the other, the disappearance of the USSR ought logically to have brought about the fall of the other super-power, the United States. In order to prevent its collapse, Congress forced President Bill Clinton to rearm in 1995. The armed forces, which had just demobilised a million men, began to rearm, although at that time they had no enemy who could equal them. The dream of Bush Sr. of a unipolar world led by United States business gave way to an insane chase to hold onto the imperial project.

US domination of the world has been imposed through four wars which were waged without the approval of the United Nations – in Yugoslavia (1995 and 1999), in Afghanistan (2002), in Iraq (2003) and in Libya (2011). This period came to an end with the six Chinese and seven Russian vetoes before the UN Security Council, which explicitly forbade open conflict with Syria.

The Gulf War had hardly ended when Republican George H. Bush Sr. asked Paul Wolfowitz to write the Defense Policy Guidance (a classified document, but extracts were published by the New York Times and the Washington Post). Wolfowitz, a militant Trotskyist and at that time the future Assistant Secretary for Defense, presented his theory concerning US supremacy.

> Our first objective is to prevent the re-emergence of a new rival, either on the territory of the former Soviet Union or elsewhere, that poses a threat on the order of that posed formerly by the Soviet Union. This is a dominant consideration underlying the new regional defense strategy and requires that

---

[31] The White House, Aug. 1, 1991, http://nssarchive.us/NSSR/1991.pdf

we endeavor to prevent any hostile power from dominating a region whose resources would, under consolidated control, be sufficient to generate global power. These regions include Western Europe, East Asia, the territory of the former Soviet Union, and Southwest Asia.

There are three additional aspects to this objective: First, the U.S. must show the leadership necessary to establish and protect a new order that holds the promise of convincing potential competitors that they need not aspire to a greater role or pursue a more aggressive posture to protect their legitimate interests. Second, in the non-defense areas, we must account sufficiently for the interests of the advanced industrial nations to discourage them from challenging our leadership or seeking to overturn the established political and economic order. Finally, we must maintain the mechanisms for deterring potential competitors from even aspiring to a larger regional or global role.[32]

The "Wolfowitz Doctrine" was supposed to prevent a new Cold War and guarantee the United States its place as the "world policeman". President Bush Sr. massively demobilised his armies, because they were no longer to be anything more than a police force.

And yet what we saw was the opposite of that – first of all with the four wars mentioned above, as well as the war against Syria, then the war against Russia in Ukraine.

▶ It was in order to demonstrate the "necessary leadership" that Washington decided, in 2001, to take control of all the hydrocarbon reserves in the "Greater Middle East" – a decision that launched the wars in Afghanistan and Iraq.

▶ It was in order to "dissuade [their allies] from challenging [their] leadership", that it modified its plan in 2004 and decided to apply the British suggestions (1) to annex the non-recognised Russian states – starting with South Ossetia – and (2) to overthrow the secular Arab governments for the benefit of the Muslim Brotherhood – the "Arab Spring".

---

[32] "Excerpts From Pentagon's Plan: 'Prevent the Re-Emergence of a New Rival'", *New York Times*, March 8, 1992, https://www.nytimes.com/1992/03/08/world/excerpts-from-pentagon-s-plan-prevent-the-re-emergence-of-a-new-rival.html

► Finally, it is in order to dissuade Russia from playing "a global role" that it is currently using the jihadists and ex-jihadists in Syria and Crimea.

To be efficiently implemented, the Wolfowitz Doctrine thus required not only financial and human means, but also a powerful political will. A group of political and military officials hoped to find their man by promoting the candidacy of the son of George Bush Sr. – George Bush Jr. This group asked the Kagan family to create a lobbying group within the American Enterprise Institute – the Project for a New American Century. They were obliged to falsify the Presidential election in Florida – with the help of Governor Jeb Bush, Jr.'s brother – in order to allow W to clamber into the White House. But well before that, the group was actively militant for the preparation of new wars of invasion, particularly in Iraq.

However, the new President was not particularly obedient, which forced his backers to organise a shock for public opinion, which they compared to a "New Pearl Harbor", on 11 September 2001.

The Collapse of 11 September

Everyone thinks that they know about 9/11, and can quote from memory about the planes that hit the Twin Towers and the destruction of part of the Pentagon. But behind these events and their interpretation by the Bush administration, something quite different happened.

When two planes smashed into the World Trade Center, and explosions were heard in the Pentagon, the Coordinator for Counterterrorism, Richard Clarke, launched the procedure for "Continuity of Government" (CoG). Developed during the Cold War, in case of a nuclear exchange and the decapitation of the Executive and Legislative branches, this procedure was intended to save the country by assigning responsibility to a provisional authority which had been secretly nominated beforehand.

But on that day, none of the elected leaders died.

Nevertheless, by 10 a.m., George W. Bush was no longer President of the United States of America. The Executive Power was transferred from the White House in Washington to site "R", the Raven Rock Mountain bunker complex in Pennsylvania. Units of the army and the Secret Services moved about the capital, to collect and "protect" the members of Congress and their teams. Almost all of them were taken, "for their safety", to another mega-bunker close to the capital.

The alternative government, whose composition had not changed for at least nine years, included – as if by a miraculous coincidence – several personalities who had been in politics for a long time, including Vice-President Dick Cheney, Secretary for Defense Donald Rumsfeld and ex-Director of the CIA, James Woolsey.[33]

During the afternoon, Israeli Prime Minister Ariel Sharon interceded in the crisis and addressed the nation, while no one knew the Continuity of Government plan was in effect, and there was no news of George W. Bush. Sharon declared the solidarity of his people, who had also been suffering from terrorism for many years. He spoke as if he was convinced that the attacks were over, but without indicating his sources, and as if he represented the American state.

Finally, at the end of the afternoon, the provisional government handed back executive power to President Bush, who made a televised speech, and the members of Congress were freed.

These are proven facts, and not the outlandish fairy-tale that the Bush administration concocted, with kamikaze warriors hatching a plot in an Afghan cave to destroy the greatest military power in the world.

In a book published thirty years earlier, destined to become the bedtime reading of the Republicans during the electoral campaign of 2000, *Coup d'état – A Practical Handbook*, historian Edward Luttwak explained that a coup d'état is all the more effective when no one realises that it has happened, and therefore do not oppose it. He should also have added that in order for the legal government to obey the conspirators, it is necessary not only to maintain the illusion that the same team is in "Power", but for the conspirators to be included in it.

The decisions imposed by the provisional government on 11 September were approved by President Bush during the days that followed. Concerning domestic policy, the Bill of Rights – the first ten amendments to the Constitution – was suspended by the USA Patriot Act for all affairs of terrorism. Concerning foreign policy,

---

[33] Editors note – Progressive Press has published a number of books on this topic. Please see ProgressivePress.com/911.html

régime changes and wars were planned, both to hinder the development of China and to take control of the energy reserves in the Greater Middle East.

President Bush held the Islamists responsible for the attacks of 9/11, and declared the "War on Terrorism" – an expression which sounds macho enough, but is nonetheless nonsensical. Indeed, terrorism is not a world power, but a method of action. Within a few years, the terrorism that Washington claimed to be fighting had increased 20-fold throughout the world. Strangely enough, Bush had called this new conflict "a task that never ends."[34]

Four days later, President Bush presided over an improbable meeting at Camp David, during which it was decided on a long series of wars to destroy all the as yet uncontrolled states in the "Greater Middle East", along with a plan for political assassinations around the world. CIA Director George Tenet dubbed it the "Worldwide Attack Matrix". This meeting was first mentioned by the Washington Post, then denied by the ex-Supreme Commander of NATO, General Wesley Clark. By "Matrix", it is important to understand that this was only the first phase of a much more far-reaching strategy.

Who governs the United States?

In order to understand the institutional crisis which was brewing, we have to take a step back.

The founding myth of the United States tells us that a few Puritans, realizing the impossibility of reforming the British Church and monarchy, decided to build a "New Jerusalem" in the Americas. In 1620, they sailed to the New World on board the Mayflower, where they gave thanks to God for letting them cross the Red Sea (i.e., the Atlantic Ocean) and to escape the dictatorship of Pharaoh (the King of England). These thanks are at the origin of the feast of Thanksgiving.

---

[34] "George Bush first called it a 'crusade,' then a 'War for Civilization,' then 'A Task That Never Ends,' then 'A Global War on Terror,' then a 'Titanic War on Terror.'" The FBI itself estimated Al Qaida's strength at less than 200 individuals, while Bush claimed we were at war with up to 60 countries. -- Aijaz Ahmad In *War and the Media: Reporting Conflict 24/7*, Sage Publications, 2003, p. 18.

The Puritans claimed to obey God by respecting both the teaching of Christ and the Jewish Law. They did not venerate the Gospels in particular, but the whole Bible; the Old Testament was as important as the New. They practised an austere form of morality – they were persuaded that they had been chosen by God, and thus blessed by Him by means of their wealth. Consequently, they believed that no man can improve himself, no matter what he does, and that Money is a gift from God for His faithful.

This ideology has many consequences. It is reflected in the obstinate opposition to Social Security by US elites, or by the belief that some people are born criminals. This is what led the Manhattan Institute for Policy Research to promote laws in many states that punished repeat offenders with very heavy prison terms, even for minor infractions, like taking the subway without a ticket.

Even though the national myth has by now mostly papered over the fanaticism of the "Pilgrim Fathers", the truth remains that they set up a sectarian community, established corporal punishment, and obliged their women to wear veils. There are clearly many similarities between their way of life and that of contemporary Islamists.

The War of Independence arose at a time when the demographics of the colonies had undergone a profound change. The settlers were no longer exclusively from the British Isles, but now included Europeans of many nationalities. The patriots who fought the King of England hoped to become masters of their own destiny, and create institutions which were both Republican and Democratic. It was for them that Thomas Jefferson wrote the Declaration of Independence in 1776, inspired by the Enlightenment in general and the philosopher John Locke in particular. However, after victory was won, it was a very different source which inspired the Constitution. It was founded on the Mayflower Pact, the Puritan ideology, and the desire for institutions like those of Great Britain, but without a hereditary nobility. This is why, in place of popular rule, it placed power in the governors of the federal states. As this system was absolutely unacceptable, it was immediately "balanced" by ten constitutional amendments, which form the Bill of Rights. The final text therefore reserves political responsibility for the elites of the federal states and gives citizens the right to defend themselves in court against the arbitrary state power.

By suspending the Bill of Rights in all affairs which may be connected to terrorism, the USA Patriot Act has dragged the Constitution two centuries in reverse. By depriving citizens of their legal rights, it has disturbed the checks and balances. This has submitted Power to the Puritan ideology and guaranteed only the rights of the elites of federal states, or the oligarchy.

The coup d'état of 11 September split these elites into two groups, depending on whether they supported it or pretended to ignore it. A few personalities openly opposed to it, like Senator Paul Wellstone, have been physically eliminated. Some citizens chose to speak out nonetheless, notably two real estate billionaires. Thus, on the evening of 11 September, on Channel 9 in New York, Donald Trump contested what was already becoming the official version. After having reminded his listeners that the engineers who built the Twin Towers had since joined his company, he observed that it was impossible for Boeings to break through the steel frames of the towers, and that it was impossible for such an accident to provoke their collapse. He concluded that there had to be other factors involved which were as yet unknown. Another contractor, Jimmy Walter, spent a great part of his fortune buying pages of publicity in the newspapers and distributing DVD's analysing the trickery behind this grand show.

Over the next fifteen years, these two groups – the conspirators and the passive accomplices – although they were pursuing the same objective of foreign and domestic domination – were to confront one another regularly, until both were apparently overthrown by a popular movement led by Donald Trump.

Washington's strategy

In 2001, Washington had worked itself up into a fit of anxiety about an imminent shortage of energy resources. The National Energy Policy Development Group (NEPD), headed by Dick Cheney, had interviewed the private and public officials concerned with fossil fuel supplies. At the time, having met the General Secretary of the NEPD, which the Washington Post called a "secret society", I was impressed by his determination and his plans to deal with the shortage. So much so, knowing little about the matter, that for a short time I supported his Malthusian viewpoint.

In any case, Washington concluded that it was necessary to take control of all the known reserves of oil and gas as quickly as possible, in order to keep its economy going. This policy would be abandoned when the US elite realized the availability of other sources of oil than Saudi Arabia, Texas or the North Sea. By taking control of Pemex, the United States would then take over the reserves in the Gulf of Mexico and proclaim their energy independence, while hiding its scarcity behind the promotion of shale oil and gas. Today, giving the lie to Dick Cheney's predictions, the supply of oil is greater than ever, and is still cheap.

In order to control the "Greater Middle East", the Pentagon demanded that it be given complete latitude and be permitted to set its strategic objectives independently of the desires of the oil companies. Basing on British and Israeli studies, it planned to remodel the region, in other words, to redraw the borders inherited from the European Empires, dissolve the major states which had the capacity to resist, and to create small, ethnically homogeneous, dependent states. Not only was this a programme of domination, but it was a one-size-fits-all plan for the region as a whole, without accounting for local peculiarities. Although ethnic religious groups in the Middle East are sometimes concentrated in their own areas, they are more often thoroughly commingled, so that dividing the map with a jigsaw is impossible without resorting to huge massacres.

But no matter... it was time to get started.

The wars against Afghanistan and Iraq

The plan was launched with the war against the Afghan Taliban, applying Cheney's One Percent Doctrine,[35] after the breakdown of negotiations for the construction of a pipeline through Afghanistan in mid-July 2001. Already then, senior Pakistani diplomat Niaz Naik, who represented Pakistan during the Berlin negotiations with the Taliban, returned to Islamabad convinced that a US attack was inevitable. His country had already begun preparing for the consequences. The British fleet was deployed in the Gulf of Oman, NATO had transported 40,000 men to Egypt, and the prominent Afghan Tajik leader Ahmad Shah Massoud had been assassinated

---

[35] Cheney spoke of taking the threat of a "low-probability, high-impact event" seriously, in response to the unlikely event that Al-Qaeda might obtain a nuclear weapon.

Sept. 9, two days before the attacks in New York and Washington. Massoud was Afghanistan's most gifted commander and an adversary of the Taliban, who many hoped would become the leader of a reunited Afghanistan.

The representatives for the United States and the United Kingdom at the UN, John Negroponte and Sir Jeremy Greenstock, assured public opinion that President George W. Bush and Prime Minister Tony Blair were applying their right to legitimate defence by attacking Afghanistan, for allegedly harbouring Osama bin Laden, whom the US was framing as the mastermind of the 9/11 attacks. But the assembled ambassadors knew that Washington and London had wanted to launch this war well before 9/11. At best, they concluded that they were using the crime as an excuse. However, I had managed to raise doubts across the world about what had happened on 11 September. In France, President Jacques Chirac had my work evaluated by the DGSE (Direction Générale de la Sécurité Extérieur). After a wide-ranging enquiry, the DGSE noted that all the elements on which I had based my work were true, but they were unable to confirm my conclusion [that it had been carried out by the deep state in the US itself, as a false flag operation.]

The daily Le Monde, which had begun a campaign to discredit me, mocked my predictions that the United States was preparing to invade Iraq. However, the inevitable happened. Washington accused Baghdad of sheltering members of al-Qaeda and preparing weapons of mass destruction for an attack on the "Land of Liberty". So it was to be war on Iraq again, just like in 1991. In reality, of course, Saddam Hussein was staunchly opposed to Al-Qaeda, and he had no WMD capability at all.

Everyone was therefore faced with a question of conscience. By ignoring the coup d'état of 11 September, one could avoid being ridiculed as a conspiracy theorist, but one also lost the only effective means of silencing the war drums, and was thus obliged to allow the next crime, which was the invasion of Iraq.

Alone on the stage, one senior international civil servant, Hans Blix, decided to defend the truth. This Swedish diplomat was the ex-Director of the International Atomic Energy Agency (IAEA). He was head of the United Nations Monitoring, Verification and Inspection Commission (UNMOVIC), tasked with keeping an eye on Iraq. Standing up to Washington, he attested that Iraq did not possess the means of which it was accused. Unparalleled pressure soon came to bear on him – not only the United States Empire, but also all its allies, demanded that he cease his childishness and allow the world superpower to get on with destroying Iraq. He did not give in, even when his successor at the IAEA, Egyptian Mohamed el-Baradei, pretended to play the peace-maker.

On 5 February 2003, Secretary of State and ex-Joint Chief of Staff Colin Powell gave a speech before the Security Council, which had been written by Cheney's team. He accused Iraq of being the root of all evil – after all, they offered protection to the authors of the attacks of 11 September, and were preparing weapons of mass destruction to attack the West. In passing, he revealed the existence of a new face in al-Qaeda, Abu Musab al-Zarqawi.

But in his turn, Jacques Chirac refused to take part in this criminal enterprise, although he did not dare denounce Washington's lies. He sent his Minister for Foreign Affairs, Dominique de Villepin, to the Security Council. De Villepin left the reports by the DGSE behind him in Paris, and concentrated his improvised speech on the difference between war as an obligation and war as a choice. It was clear that the invasion of Iraq had nothing to do with 11 September, but was in fact an imperial choice, a war of conquest. De Villepin went on to underline the results already obtained by Blix in Iraq. He then deflated US accusations and showed that the use of force was not justified at this stage, and concluded by stating that nothing proved that war could obtain anything more than the continuation of inspections. Believing that this formulation would offer a way out for Washington, and that war could be avoided, the Security Council applauded. This was the first time that diplomats had ever applauded one of their own in this room.

Not only did Washington and London impose their war, but forgetting Hans Blix, the United States undertook all sorts of operations to "make Chirac pay". The French President quickly caved in and began toeing the line for his US overlord even more eagerly than was necessary.

We have to draw lessons from this crisis. Hans Blix, like his compatriot Raoul Wallenberg during the Second World War, refused the idea that the United States, (or the Germans), were superior to others. He decided to save people who had committed no other crime than being Iraqi (or Hungarian Jews). Jacques Chirac would have liked to resemble these two brave Swedes, but his previous errors and private secrets made him vulnerable to blackmail, leaving him no choice other than to resign or submit. [Indeed, under our putative system of democracy, especially since JFK, the oligarchy will not allow the election of any candidate who cannot be blackmailed.]

Washington planned to hand over power in Baghdad to the Iraqis in exile which it had selected from a British association, the Iraqi National Congress, headed by Ahmed Chalabi. The fact that he was a convicted criminal, found guilty of embezzlement in the collapse of his own Petra Bank in Jordan, was of no consequence, if it was not a qualification for the post. The aircraft company Lockheed Martin generously founded a Committee for the Liberation of Iraq, headed by George Shultz, ex-Secretary of State and mentor of Bush Jr. This Committee and the Chalabi Council sold the war to US public opinion. They promised that the United States would restrict itself to helping the "Iraqi resistance," and that the war would not last long. (It is not yet over.)

Like the attack on Afghanistan, the invasion of Iraq had been prepared before the attacks on New York and Washington. In early 2001, Vice-President Dick Cheney had personally negotiated the installation of US military bases in Kirghizstan, Kazakhstan and Uzbekistan, in the context of the development of the Central Asia Battalion (CENTRASBAT) agreements with the Eurasian Economic Community (EAEC or EurAsEC). Since the planners had anticipated that in the war on Iraq, their troops would need 60,000 tons of equipment per day, the Military Traffic Management Command had been tasked with getting an early start and setting up the logistics in place.

The training of the troops only began after 9/11. These were the biggest military manoeuvres in History – "Millennium Challenge 2002". War games mingled real troop movements with simulations in the Staff control centre, using technological tools developed by Hollywood for the film "Gladiator". 13,500 men were mobilised between 24 July and 15 August 2002. The islands of San Nicolas and San Clemente, off the coast of California, and training grounds in the Nevada desert, had been evacuated for a theatre of operations. This extravagant spending spree gobbled up a budget of $235 million. The soldiers playing the part of the Iraqi troops, commanded by General

Paul Van Riper, used a non-conventional strategy and decimated the US contingent. The Staff decided to end the exercise early.

Taking no notice of the reports by Hans Blix, nor the objections of France, Washington launched "Operation Iraqi Liberation" on 19 March 2003. When the acronym for the invasion – OIL – was noticed, the operation was re-baptised "Operation Iraqi Freedom". An unprecedented deluge of fire fell on Baghdad, the so-called "Shock and Awe" tactic. The citizens of Baghdad were dumbfounded, while the United States and their allies seized the country.

Government was first of all assumed by an office of the Pentagon, the ORHA (Office of Reconstruction and Humanitarian Assistance), then, after a month, the Defense Secretary named a civilian administrator, L. Paul Bremer III, Henry Kissinger's private assistant. He soon assumed the title of Administrator for the Coalition Provisional Authority (CPA). However, contrary to what its title may suggest, this Authority had not been created by the Coalition, which had never met and whose composition was unknown.

For the first time, an organisation appeared which answered to the Pentagon, but which had never featured in any organisation chart in the United States. It was an arm of the group which took power on 11 September 2001. In the documents published by Washington, the Authority is defined as an organ of the Coalition if the document is intended for foreigners, and as an organ of the US government if it is intended for Congress. With the exception of one British official, all the employees of the Authority are paid by US administrations, but are not subject to US law. Thus they have a free hand giving out public works contracts. The Authority seized the $5 billion in the Iraqi Treasury, but only one billion appeared in its accounts. What happened to the other four billion? The question was asked at the Madrid Conference on Reconstruction in Iraq. It was never answered.

Paul Bremer's assistant was none other than Sir Jeremy Greenstock, the United Kingdom's representative at the Security Council, who had justified the invasions of Afghanistan and Iraq. During the occupation, the United States examined the possibilities for remodeling Iraq, in this case, its partition into three states. Bremer sent Ambassador Peter Galbraith – who had organised the partition of Yugoslavia into seven separate states – as advisor to the Kurdish Regional Government.

Bremer worked directly with Assistant Secretary for Defense, Paul Wolfowitz, who had defined US strategy during the collapse of the USSR. He is a Trotskyist Jew who had been trained in the philosophy of Leo Strauss. He brought many adepts of this German-Jewish philosopher to the Pentagon. Known as the neo-conservatives, or neo-cons, they formed a well-structured, solidly coherent, and unified group. According to them, after the weakness of the Weimar Republic vs. the Nazis, Jewish people can have no faith in democracies to protect them from a new genocide. Instead, they must join the side of authoritarian régimes, and occupy a place close to Power. In this way, the idea of a world dictatorship was legitimised as a preventative measure.

Wolfowitz set the broad outlines for the work of the Coalition Provisional Authority (CPA), in other words, the plunder of Iraq's economy, and the de-Ba'athification of the country – which meant the sacking of all officials and officers who were members of the secular Ba'ath Party. On his instructions, Bremer gave all public contracts to companies owned by friends, generally without a call for tender – excluding, on principle, the French and Germans, who were guilty of having opposed this imperial war.

Every one of the members of the Project for a New American Century (the think tank which prepared the 11 September attacks) was incorporated, either directly or indirectly, into the Coalition Provisional Authority, or worked with it.

From the very start, these people were regarded with distrust – first of all, by the representative of the UN Secretary General, the Brazilian Sergio Vieira de Mello. He was assassinated on 19 August 2003, allegedly by the jihadist Abu Musab al-Zarqawi, whom Powell had denounced at the United Nations. But those close to the diplomat pointed to the conflict which opposed him to Paul Wolfowitz, and directly accused a US faction of the killing. Then General James Mattis, commander of the 1st Division of the Marines, who worried about the disastrous consequences of de-Ba'athification. In the end, though, he stepped back into line.

Carried away by their "successes" in the United States, Afghanistan and Iraq, the men of 11 September guided their country towards new heights.

Theopolitics

Between 12 and 14 October 2003, there was a strange meeting at the King David Hotel in Jerusalem. The invitation announced: "Israel is the moral alternative to Eastern totalitarianism and Western moral relativism. Israel is the 'Ground Zero' of the central battle for the survival of our civilisation. Israel can be saved, and the rest of the West with it. It is time for us to meet in Jerusalem".

Several hundred personalities from the extreme right of the United States and Israel were received at the expense of the Russian Mafia. Avigdor Lieberman, Benjamin Netanyahu and Ehud Olmert were there to congratulate Elliot Abrams, Richard Perle and Daniel Pipes. They all shared the same belief system– theopolitics. According to them, the "End Time" is close. Soon the world will be governed by a Jewish institution based in Jerusalem.

This meeting upset Israeli progressives, particularly since some orators identified Baghdad, which had been conquered six months earlier, as the antique "Babylon". It was evident for them that the theopolitics claimed by the congress was a renaissance of Talmudism. This school of thought – of which Leo Strauss was a specialist – interprets Judaism as a millennial prayer by the Jewish people to avenge the crimes of the Egyptians against their ancestors, their deportation to Babylon by the Assyrians and even the destruction of European Jews by the Nazis. It considers that the "Wolfowitz doctrine" is a preparation for Armageddon (the final battle) which will begin with the fomenting of chaos, first of all in the Greater Middle East, then in Europe. This general destruction will mark the divine punishment of those who have caused the suffering of the Jewish people.

Ex-Prime Minister Ehud Barak realised the mistake he had made by refusing the peace that he had himself negotiated with Presidents Bill Clinton and Hafez al-Assad; a peace which would have preserved the interests of all the populations in the region, which the theopoliticians did not want. He began to re-assemble officers who tried in vain to block the re-election of Benjamin Netanyahu to the Commanders for Israel's Security. He continued this struggle until he gave a speech in June 2016, at the Herzliya Conference, in which he denounced Netanyahu's "worst case politics" (cacocracy) and his desire to institutionalise Apartheid. He called on his compatriots to save their country by blocking these fanatics.

The extension of the war

President Bush wrote to his opposite numbers in Libya and Syria ordering them to "either destroy their weapons of mass destruction, or watch them being destroyed by the United States – everything will be destroyed without discussion". On 6 May 2002, the Director of Disarmament for the State Department, John Bolton, designated Libya, Syria and Cuba as the next targets. Libya – which was already under embargo – decided to play for time, while Syria refused to disarm unilaterally and prepared for war. There was no further talk of Cuba.

Baghdad had hardly fallen when Congress began debating the next move. The ex-leader of the Lebanese Christians, General Michel Aoun, came to give testimony against Syria before Congress, accusing it of protecting numerous terrorist organisations – none of which he named. The war against Damascus was voted, then ratified by President Bush, on 12 December 2003. This was the Syrian Accountability Act, drawn up on the model of the Iraq Liberation Act of 1998. As for Muammar Gaddafi, he announced, on 19 December, that his country renounced all of its weapons of mass destruction, and accepted the principle of international inspections.

During the offensive in Afghanistan, Secretary of State Colin Powell created the US-Middle East Partnership Initiative (MEPI). This office was so important that it was directed by Liz Cheney, the daughter of Vice-President and member of the alternative government, Dick Cheney. His civil servants worked in collaboration with those of the Department of Commerce (for access to and control of the Internet) and the National Endowment for Democracy (NED), the common agency of the secret services of the "Five Eyes" group. On the occasion of the 20th anniversary of the NED, President Bush confirmed that the Middle East and North Africa were the strategic priority. The objective of MEPI was to "democratise" the governments of certain allied States (Saudi Arabia, Bahrain, Egypt, Tunisia and Yemen) in parallel with the preparation of wars against the revolutionary states (Libya, Syria).

The idea that it is possible to "democratise" from the exterior, not only the institutions of a state, but the political practises of a People, is quite simply contradictory and grotesque. For the Trotskyists who run the NED, it is the old fantasy of "world revolution". The peoples, countries and histories do not matter, the revolution is for all, and the power is for the revolutionary elite. During the Bolshevik revolution, Leon Trotsky and his secretary were encouraged by the British to massacre their compatriots on a massive scale, thus weakening Russia. In the Greater Middle East, his US disciples followed in his footsteps – spouting extreme-left wing gibberish, they organised massive crimes in the service of imperialism.

On the ground, the MEPI programme was exclusively administered from Tunis or Abu Dhabi. The US embassies in Tunisia and the Emirates were built for the occasion – these are huge buildings, isolated from areas which may be used for demonstrations, hyper-secure and including underground installations which are much larger than the visible structures. The other US embassies in the region are asked to apply the directives they receive without knowing anything about the overall strategy. Washington has learned its lesson from the taking of the embassy in Teheran by students who were followers of Imam Khomeini. Its diplomats had been caught red-handed in acts of espionage – they were never taken hostage, despite what Washington propaganda claimed – and the documents seized enabled revolutionary Iran and the USSR to discover the whole of the US regional system.

Over a period of fifteen years, just as in George Orwell's nightmare, the United States spent more than $2 billion annually for the "promotion of democracy" (sic), knowing that their own constitution does not recognise popular sovereignty, the prerequisite for any real democracy – and despite the fact that the Bill of Rights has been suspended since 2001. The greater part of these budgets was spent by the United States Agency for International Development (USAID), then by the Bureau of Democracy, Human Rights and Labor at the State Department, and finally by the CIA and its "NGO", the National Endowment for Democracy (NED). The different appraisal reports demonstrate the impossibility of judging the impact of these programmes in terms of their official objective.

In sum, the current US version of "democracy" is not "The government of the People, by the People, for the People", according to Abraham Lincoln's definition, but a political régime servile to imperialism, which can only be measured once the "régime change" has taken place.

Having appointed itself to rule the post-Soviet world, Washington presented its plan for the "democratisation" of the Greater Middle East to its partners in the G8 Summit at Sea Island in June 2004. Although none of these partners were convinced that it is possible to export democracy to countries which are all so different from one another, and where, often, the population is massively illiterate, each of them nonetheless went along as they had 13 years before with "Desert Storm". Russia was on board, too, or seemed to be.

During this period, British Prime Minister Tony Blair systematically aligned himself with the US positions, to the extent that he was known, in his own country, as Washington's "little doggy". A spirit of revolt shook the Foreign Office, concerning both the appalling initiatives of George Bush and Ariel Sharon in Palestine, and the stupid and brutal behaviour of US forces in Iraq. This position was resumed by the ex-Minister for Foreign Affairs, David Owen. He explained to me that the United States were incapable of occupying a country – "We held the British Empire in India with a few thousand men. Our American friends are over-run in Iraq, despite their 170,000 soldiers and their mercenaries!" he exclaimed. 52 of Her Majesty's ex-ambassadors met with the Prime Minister and advised him to offer advice to the United States rather than blindly following them in their adventures.

At the Foreign Office, Sir James Craig, ex-ambassador to Syria and Saudi Arabia, presented a programme on the "engagement [of the United Kingdom] with the Muslim world". Officially, the aim was to sponsor a variety of different actions, but in reality, it was to set up a vast operation with the Muslim Brotherhood. An agent of MI6, Angus McKee, was tasked with convincing the members of the government of the relevance of this policy. Another agent, Mockbul Ali, supervised relations between the Foreign Office and the Brotherhood members who lived in the United Kingdom.

Sir James Craig's idea was to run a repeat of the "Arab Revolt of 1915". At that time, the Foreign Office entrusted Lawrence of Arabia with the responsibility of unifying the Arabs against the Ottoman Empire. They all fought in this adventure against the Turkish yoke, but in the end, none of them gained the freedom for which they had hoped – the British Empire simply replaced the Sultan. This time, the "Arab Spring" was to be directed against Iran. Just as in 1915, London would employ a group that was hated by everyone, so that this group would depend upon the support of London and be unable to betray it. The group used in 1915 was the Wahhabites, now it was to be the Muslim Brotherhood.

At the end of 2004, Tony Blair therefore proposed to George Bush Jr. a plan for the overthrow of secular Arab governments, and their replacement by the Muslim Brotherhood. The Prime Minister exposed part of his project on 1 August 2006, at the World Affairs Council in Los Angeles. In it, he defined the Anglo-Saxon strategy – "We made the mistake of believing that by fighting both the religionists of al-Qaeda and the secularists of Saddam Hussein, we could bring democracy. We must therefore now support the "moderates" [in fact, the Muslim Brotherhood] against the "extremists" [in fact, the Iranians, the secular Syrians, and the Lebanese Hezbollah], he proposed.

The West was therefore opting to ignore the religionist/secularist opposition which was eating away at the Muslim world, and to concentrate only on the conflict between the "moderate" nationalists who were ready to collaborate with imperialism and the "extreme" nationalist who refused to do so.

All that sounds fine, but it makes no sense when we remember that the Muslim Brotherhood had been created by the Anglo-Saxons, that al-Qaeda is one of the branches they used against the Soviets, and that Saddam Hussein was an ex-agent of the CIA. And yet this was the line that prevailed – the word games going so far as to describe the jihadists in Syria as "moderate".

During this period, the Westminster Foundation, a British "NGO" of the "Five Eyes" – the military alliance between Australia, Canada, the United States, New Zealand and the United Kingdom – and thus the equivalent of the US NED – organised many meetings, mainly with the Egyptian and Syrian Brotherhood. In Cairo, 2006, notably, it organised a large conference of parliamentarians and members of the Brotherhood.

Progressively, the British plan was put into practise by the United States.

Liz Cheney created the "Iran and Syria Policy and Operations Group" within the National Security Council. This very secret network installed itself successively in the State Department, the Defense Department and the offices of her father, Vice-President Dick Cheney. Notable members included the assistant National Security Advisor, James F. Jeffrey, and President Bush's special advisor, Elliott Abrams. With a budget of $80 million, this "Group" identified and corrupted people who would play a major role in Lebanon, (2006 and 2008), in Iran, (2009), and in Syria, (2012). In a speech before the Foreign Policy Association, Liz Cheney compared this to the work she had done with Lech Wałęsa to prepare for the régime change in Poland in the 1980's. She was considered in Washington as the "Tsar" of the Greater Middle East. In Iran, she created separatist groups in Baluchestan, and organised a gigantic terrorist campaign with a post-Marxist cult, the People's Mujahedin Organization of Iran.

In 2007, this Group was dissolved during the scandal of the "Office of Special Plans", which was tasked with inventing a story to justify the invasion of Iraq. Under the direction of Elliott Abrams, the members of the Group were incorporated into another even more secret structure, responsible for implementing the "Global Democracy Strategy". This strategy had been created years before by President Bill Clinton. It worked not only to implement the British plan for the Greater Middle East, but also to overthrow President Manuel Zelaya in Honduras, to plot various attempts for a coup d'état in Venezuela, and to attempt operations in Myanmar. Unfortunately, we know little more about their activities.

It seems that Elliott Abrams followed the logic of the Wolfowitz doctrine by promoting the idea of a division of the world in two – on one side a stable zone, dominated by the United States, and on the other, a vast stateless zone where the Empire could acquire raw materials – a theory developed in the Pentagon by Admiral Arthur Cebrowski, then popularized by his assistant, Thomas Barnett. In order to ensure that no Third World state could one day dare to compete with its ex-colonisers, it would be necessary to destroy entire regions of the globe and drag the populations back to the era when Man was a wolf for Man.

Direction – the "Arab Spring"!

Let's take a step back. To begin with, Washington was preparing the next Syrian government on the model of what had been planned for Iraq. In Brussels, January 2004, an arms dealer, Farid Ghadry, organised the founding congress for a democratic Syrian Coalition. Unfortunately, a number of ambitious characters showed up to push and shove without being able to select a leader. There would therefore be no Syrian equivalent to the role played by Ahmed Chalabi in Iraq.

The Anglo-Saxon plan found its first concrete application in the regional tour by Secretary of State Colin Powell, followed by the summit of the Arab League in Tunis (May 2004). The member states adopted an Arab Charter on Human Rights (ACHR), even though everyone was aware that many of the signatory nations would not respect it. Then the General Secretary of the League and the Tunisian President proposed the next element in their "democratic" toolkit – the adoption of a Declaration which would authorise the use of force to oblige certain recalcitrant states to apply the resolutions of the League. Immediately, Lebanon (Emile Lahoud) and Syria (Bashar al-Assad) intervened. The two Presidents had recognised the rhetoric of Colin Powell, according to which "democracy" was imposed from the outside, and saw in the text a way of justifying US aggression, while the real violators of Human Rights – like Saudi Arabia – would get a free pass. After several disputes, the Tunis Declaration was edited.

While the Arab Spring project was being progressively assembled, the project for war against the states of the Greater Middle East who resisted the Empire continued.

A "diplomat", Jeffrey Feltman, who had been schooled in Iraq with the Coalition Provisional Authority, and could therefore count on the support of the 11 September men, was nominated in Beirut. He was tasked with organising an uprising against the Syrian peacekeepers, who had ended the Lebanese civil war – thus provoking a bloody repression and justifying an invasion by the Marines to re-establish peace. In this way, Washington hoped to kill two birds with one stone and seize both Lebanon and Syria.

In his State of the Union address on 2 February 2005, President Bush mentioned the Syrian Accountability Act, threatening Syria because of its support for the Lebanese Resistance to Israeli expansionism. On 7 February, the Syrian ambassador in Washington, Imad Mustafa, was summoned to the State Department, where he was notified that his government had no more than 48 hours to break off relations with Hezbollah. On 14 February, a gigantic bomb attack in Beirut killed ex-Prime Minister Rafic Hariri. In the hours that followed, a world-wide Press campaign accused Presidents Emile Lahoud and Bashar al-Assad of having ordered the murder, and called for "régime change" in Damascus.

For many years, it was said that the attack had been committed with the use of a small truck crammed with explosives. However, Hezbollah broadcast hacked videos taken by an Israeli surveillance drone which had been filming Rafic Hariri and the crime scene in the days before the attack. As I published in the Russian magazine Odnako, the operation was a joint action between Israel, the United States, and Germany, with the use of a new weapon developed from nanotechnology and using particles of enriched uranium. In order to disprove my article, the United Nations reconstructed the attack at great cost in France, but since they were unable to prove anything at all, they never revealed their conclusions.

But no matter – during this time, on the day after the attack, the teams of the Centre for Applied Nonviolent Action and Strategies organised a sit-in and other demonstrations in Beirut. This Serbian organisation was the armed wing of the Albert Einstein Institution, the AEI, itself created by NATO and the NED, under the direction of Gene Sharp. It also worked with the head of the psychological unit of the Israeli army, Reuven Gal. The AEI has been manipulating crowds to overthrow political régimes under the cover of "colour revolutions" since 1989. It organised the attempted coup d'état by the liberal economic reformer President Zhao Ziyang in China, which was suppressed on Tienanmen Square (and there too, the facts were totally different from those reported by the Western medias[36]) – and also the "revolutions" in Lithuania, Kosovo, Iraq, Georgia, etc.

---

[36] See "L'échec de la Première 'Révolution Colorée': Tienanmen, 20 ans après," (The failure of the first color revolution': Tienanmen, 20 years after) by Domenico Losurdo, http://www.voltairenet.org/article160446.html. Reviews *The Tienanmen Papers,* a book condemning the suppression of the protests, which inadvertently glorifies accounts of violent, organised attacks on the soldiers and police, reminiscent of the Syrian insurgency since 2011.

In Beirut, it was to be the "Cedar Revolution", directed by Eli Khoury (Quantum Communications), a guest of President Bush two years later.

Gene Sharp disputed my investigation of his links to NATO and the NED when the President of the Bolivarian Republic of Venezuela, Hugo Chávez, referred to them at length. Unfortunately, and contrary to his denials, Sharp had indeed worked for NATO and been sponsored by the NED, and had indeed been present during the crises in the countries I mentioned. Moreover, the Russian Press confirmed all these points, one by one, after which this "philosopher" was forbidden to enter certain States.

The principle of "colour revolutions" comes from a study prepared for NATO by Gene Sharp in 1985 – "Making Europe Unconquerable". The author demonstrated the impossibility of installing a new régime without a minimum of support from the population. It was, however, possible to topple a régime simply by giving the impression that it had lost its popular legitimacy. On that principle, the CIA had worked out ways of manipulating crowds, organising demonstrations and making believe that a real revolution was taking place, while specialised teams took power. Since the fall of Ceausescu in 1989, Gene Sharp and the CIA had put this scenario into practise in numerous countries, often with success. However, a Revolution aims at changing society, while a "colour revolution" seeks only to change the leader and his team. Revolutions can take a decade, while régime changes can be operated in a few weeks. And above all, since colour revolutions are no more than staged productions intended to mask the coup d'état, the governments set up never last long.

Jeffrey Feltman coordinated the campaign against Presidents Lahoud and al-Assad. The Lebanese President's four main collaborators on national security – Mustafa Hamdane (chief of the Presidential Guard), Jamil Sayyed (head of general security), Ibrahim El-Haj (director of the internal security forces) and Raymond Azar (head of Military Intelligence) – were arrested and incarcerated by the United Nations. They would only be released four years later. Their imprisonment made it easier for Israel to attack Lebanon in the summer of 2006. An international committee of inquiry was set up under the auspices of the United Nations. Its two working languages were English and Hebrew, and it was headed up by two German killers: ex-magistrate Detlev Mehlis, who had already worked for the CIA and the Mossad against Libya, and police commissioner Gerhard Lehmann, implicated in the scandal of the CIA's secret prisons. A special UN Tribunal for Lebanon was set up by the Security Council and the Lebanese Prime Minister, without the approval of either the Lebanese government or the Lebanese Parliament. It was set up nonetheless, and was presided over by Italian judge Antonio Cassese, who was also being paid by the People's Mujahedin Organization of Iran, a terrorist organisation financed by the CIA to work against the Islamic Republic of Iran. Witnesses claimed to have taken part in the murder under the orders of Bashar al-Assad, but they fled once this lie was unmasked and it became known that they had been paid by the victim's son, Saad Hariri,[37] and Rifaat al-Assad, uncle of the Syrian head of state.

In any case, although the whole operation of the "Cedar Revolution", the National Enquiry Commission and the Special United Nations Tribunal was eventually exposed, Jeffrey Feltman managed to convince the Security Council that the Lebanese and Syrian Presidents had ordered the assassination of the ex-Prime Minister of Lebanon.

The initial CIA plan was designed:

▶ 1. to kill Rafic Hariri and blame the Lebanese and Syrian Presidents for the murder;

▶ 2. to organise a "colour revolution" with Gene Sharp's crew – the Cedar Revolution;

▶ 3. to provoke the repression of this revolution by the Syrian Peace Force in Lebanon;

▶ 4. to justify a landing by the US Marines – who would not only return order to Beirut, but also attack Damascus.

But in reaction to the anti-Syrian demonstrations, President Bashar al-Assad, who had already begun the withdrawal of his troops several months earlier, suddenly decided to withdraw them all, which pulled the rug out from under the feet of the CIA.

---

[37] Editor's note. The great paradox here is the suspicion that the son Saad Hariri may have cemented his political career by cooperating in or at least capitalizing on the murder of his father, the statesman Rafic Hariri; but as will be seen, Saad may have been the seed of a different father.

Considering that Damascus had abandoned Lebanon, Jeffrey Feltman grabbed the country for himself. He brought back General Michel Aoun, who bore a heavy responsibility for his role in the civil war (1975-90) and had exiled himself to France. Allying himself with all those who were financed by Saudi Arabia, Israel and the United States, Aoun founded the "March 14 Alliance" against the Resistance movement Hezbollah. But to his surprise, after having lived for a few months in his country, he realised that things were not what they seemed, and he allied himself with the Resistance. He signed a Document of Mutual Agreement with Hezbollah, on 6 February 2006.

Seeking to unify the military projects against the seven states in the region which were resisting them, and the subversive projects of the "Arab Springs", Washington and London organised various contacts between the Lebanese Cedar Revolution, the Syrian opposition and the Muslim Brotherhood, while at the same time planning a second attempt at invasion. This time, Israel would directly attack Lebanon on one pretext or another, and would crush Hezbollah. Syria would come to the aid of the Resistance, and the Marines could finally land. The United States would then hand power to the Brotherhood and other allies of Saudi Arabia in "liberated" Beirut and Damascus. This latest version of the perennial scheme against Syria was dubbed "Operation Blue Jasmine".

With this aim, Walid Jumblatt, the Vice-President of the Socialist International and leader of the faction of Lebanese Druzes favourable to Washington, received a delegation of the Muslim Brotherhood in May, at his palace in Mokhtara. The next meeting was the "National Salvation Front of Syria" in London, on 4 and 5 June. There were only 43 participants at this "important" encounter – from which both Walid Jumblatt and Saad Hariri were absent, despite having been announced. In fact, this Front was no more than a masquerade, hiding the Muslim Brotherhood behind Syrian ex-Vice President, Abdel Halim Khaddam.

The United States equipped Israel so that they could invade Lebanon in the months to come.

The war against Lebanon

However, in Lebanon, the friends of President Lahoud and his four generals were attempting on their own to throw some light on the assassination of Rafic Hariri. Military Intelligence managed to arrest a retired gendarme, Mahmud Rafeh, who admitted that he directed an espionage and assassination network for the Israeli Mossad. It turned out that this man was an ex-collaborator with Tsahal, the Israeli Army, when they occupied Lebanon. Step by step, light was thrown on the implication of his cell in many assassinations and attempted assassinations that had occurred over the last four years, and which had been wrongly attributed to Syria.

Lebanon demanded that the Security Council condemn the perpetual interference by Israel. The Hebrew state indeed invaded both Lebanese air space and territorial waters several times a day in order to spy on Hezbollah. It also spied on mobile telecommunications networks, and ordered the assassination of various political leaders. The United States, France and the United Kingdom didn't know what to say.

By coincidence, at the same time, an Israeli patrol scouting on Lebanese territory fell into an ambush laid by Hezbollah. Eight soldiers were killed and two others captured. In international law, any People, part of whose territory is occupied, may legally fight the enemy army, including on the territory of the aggressor state. The UN therefore does not consider that the prisoners were "kidnapped", but "captured" in the context of a non-governmental military action. Hezbollah intended to use these prisoners as bargaining chips for its soldiers held in Israel. But seen from Tel-Aviv's point of view, there was not a minute to lose. The war ordered by Washington had to kick off before the Lebanese Military Intelligence discovered the truth about the assassination of Rafic Hariri, in other words, about the previous attempt at war. Liz and Dick Cheney gave their approval, and Israel once again invaded Lebanon.

The ambassador of the United States for NATO, Victoria Nuland-Kagan (of the Project for a New American Century), beat the drums of war and mobilised the Allies, but after 34 days of fighting, Israel was forced to retreat. The Security Council imposed a cease-fire, thus allowing them to save face. While the international diplomatic community, with the exception of Damascus, counted a victory for Israel as a foregone conclusion, on the ground, a few hundred rebels managed to rout their ultra-modern, Pentagon-supported army. These exceptional combatants were placed under the command of Sayyed[38] Hassan Nasrallah and under the supervision of the Syrian Minister for Defence, General Hassan Tourekmani, who was secretly present on the battlefields.

Contrary to a wide-spread idea, Iran hardly had the time to get involved in this war, and had planned to offer political asylum to the leaders of Hezbollah. But after the cease-fire, President Mahmud Ahmadinejad invested heavily in the Lebanese Resistance, bringing their inventory of missiles up to 400.

The 11 September men who had until then been victorious in the United States, Afghanistan, and against Saddam Hussein, had just met defeat in Lebanon, while the deposed Ba'athists began the resistance in Iraq. Hezbollah's victory called into question the illegitimate power of the US "continuity of government".

The Baker-Hamilton Commission

In Iraq, things went from bad to worse. The Provisional Government which had succeeded the Provisional Authority was unable to stabilise the country. Once the "Shock and Awe" of the Allied bombings had worn off, the population woke up and became aware of the pillage and the destruction organised by the Provisional Authority. From the very first day, the United States had burned the archives and the national library, first pillaging the national museums whose treasures had not been hidden in time. They had methodically privatised, for their own profit, the socialist economy of the country, with the assistance of "their" specialists, like Bulgarian ex-President Petar Stoyanov, or Russian ex-Prime Minister Yegor Gaidar.

Everywhere, the soldiers demobilised by the US occupying forces reorganised and revolted against them. In order to escape the wrath of the Iraqis, US ambassador John Negroponte decided to shatter their unity and trick them into turning on one another. With the support of his old friend Elliot Abrams, and that of Liz Cheney in Washington, he created a Sunni group tasked with attacking the Shiites, and a Shiite group tasked with massacring Sunnis, under the aegis of the Shiite-dominated Iraqi puppet government. Negroponte had already become the US Director of National Intelligence when the civil war began. The road to Hell began with the colossal attack

---

[38] Sayyed is an Islamic honorary title for descendants of the Prophet Mohamed.

against the Shiite al-Askari mosque in Samarra, on 22 February 2006, which caused more than a thousand deaths. Although the attack was never claimed, it is generally attributed to the Islamic Emirate in Iraq, or future Daesh. Despite the calls for calm from the grand ayatollah Ali al-Sistani and the Shiite leader Muqtada al-Sadr, the slaughter was followed, tit for tat, by numerous attacks and lynchings, leading to the deaths of 3,000 Sunnis.

In concrete terms, this war could be summarised as follows – President Saddam Hussein was overthrown under false pretences – the country was methodically pillaged by the men responsible for the coup d'état of 11 September – and despite the investment of 170,000 GI's and several trillions of dollars, Iraq was bogged down in a terrible civil war.

The ruling class in Washington was divided, according to whether they had got a piece of the cake or whether they had to pay for it. Finally, Congress decided on the creation of a bipartisan commission tasked with finding a way out of the Iraqi adventure. It was co-presided by two personalities considered as neutral by both groups – Republican James Baker and Democrat Lee Hamilton. Baker had been Secretary of State, then advisor to The Carlyle Group, an investment company which handled the wealth of the Bush and Bin Laden families. Hamilton had been the accountant for the oil reserves of the Middle East, then Vice-President of the 9/11 Commission.

For almost a year, the Baker-Hamilton Commission examined not only Iraq, but all US policies concerning the Middle East, and in particular, Lebanon, Syria and Iran. On 6 December, 2006, it reached the conclusion that the project for successive wars against the states that resist Washington would have to be abandoned, and that, on the contrary, it would be wiser to negotiate a return to peace with Syria and Iran.

During the work of the Commission, Cheney and Rumsfeld brought pressure to bear on their military in order to hasten the war against Iran and its Shiite allies. They tried to start a war several times before the report was issued. A number of generals revolted, breaking the customary silence of military discipline, accused Rumsfeld of not being up to the situation, and publicly called for his resignation. This move by the military met with a clear show of support from the public, who were well aware of the disastrous situation in Iraq.

Finally, during his defeat in the mid-term elections, President George Bush Jr. decided to retire the interminable Rumsfeld, (74), and to replace him with a member of the Baker-Hamilton Commission. But since Baker wanted to retain his status as a "neutral sage", the post was given to Republican Robert Gates, ex-Director of the CIA.

For the whole of 2007, the 11 September men tried more dirty tricks. Discreetly, the Spanish, French and Italian contingents of the UN Peacekeeping Forces between Israel and Lebanon were brought under NATO command. After the assassination of Rafic Hariri and the Israeli war, a third round was being prepared in Beirut. At the same time, six atomic bombs were illegally moved from their silos at Minot AFB in North Dakota to Barksdale AFB in Alabama, in preparation to be sent onwards to the Middle East. At the last moment, the operation was cancelled. A spy satellite which was surveying the Middle East self-destructed. The debris fell in Peru.

Finally, the Director of National Intelligence, Vice-Admiral John Michael McConnell, published a confidential document stating that Iran had closed down its civilian nuclear programme several years before – at least four years earlier. By doing so, he prevented Dick Cheney from once again waving the "weapons of mass destruction" flag, which had enabled him to justify the attack on Iraq. The Generals were rebelling against the Bush administration, and they let it be known. Admiral William Fallon and Gen. James Mattis organised themselves around a prestigious retiree, Gen. Brent Scowcroft, ex-National Security advisor to Bush Sr.

The war against the Shiites will not be held in Lebanon

Admiral Fallon, the chief of Central Command – supervisor of the wars in Afghanistan and Iraq – was a Vietnam veteran. He was fully aware that his troops were exhausted, and could not fight a counter-guerrilla campaign against the Iraqi Resistance at the same time as a war against Iran. Using the networks he had developed during his career, he made contact with Iranian personalities and negotiated with the Islamic Republic in the presence of Russian and Chinese representatives. On 2 March, 2008, he met secretly with President Mahmud Ahmadinejad in Baghdad. The two men managed to find common ground. Iran said it was ready to withdraw its commandos from the sensitive areas of the Greater Middle East (Afghanistan and

Iraq, Bahrain and Lebanon, etc.) if the United States would do the same.

Furious, Dick Cheney disowned the Admiral. Betrayed by his own side, Fallon resigned, while Scowcroft took his defence. Teheran reacted by delivering massive supplies of arms to the Resistance movements in Iraq, Lebanon and Palestine.

The Commander of the US forces in Iraq, General David Petraeus, was overjoyed. He replaced Admiral Fallon as head of CentCom and inundated the Press with his version of the events in Iraq. He confirmed to anyone who would listen that the increase in manpower ("the surge") had enabled him to defeat the Resistance, and that things were on the point of being normalised.

The reality was quite different. John Negroponte's mercenaries had managed to set the Shiites against the Sunnis and vice-versa. However, although some armed groups were fighting one another, the population was not really taking part in the civil war. Little by little, people began to realise that they were the victims of manipulation. Tens of thousands of young unemployed people joined the Resistance against the Occupier.

General Petraeus, advised by David Kilcullen, an Australian expert, decided to buy peace by paying 80,000 Iraqi nationalists $10 a day. The great majority of anti-US operations therefore ceased, although it was obvious that once the payments dried up, the 80,000 "collaborators" who were working with the occupation forces would once again turn against them, but this time with the weapons that the Pentagon had just delivered. But no worries, Petraeus just wanted to gain a little time – the time to sign some very self-serving contracts for the oil-fields, and to obtain legal immunity for his troops, and the permanence of his military bases.

Today, Petraeus is presented as one of the world's leading counter-terrorist experts, which is, at the very least, something of an exaggeration. He is a showboat soldier who built his career by serving as a liaison officer between the Pentagon and Congress, not by serving on the battlefield. Moreover, he spent most of his time in Iraq abusing little girls rather than working to resolve anything at all.

The Secretary for Defense, Robert Gates, pleaded for a one-year truce between the two groups which divided the Pentagon, and from there, the suspension of US interventions in the world.

The 11 September men put up with this, but did not give up. Since they could not use the US armies, they turned to the British and the Israelis. The latter were ready to take their revenge on Hezbollah and Syria, and also to launch a raid on Iran, as they had done in 1981 with their raid on an Iraqi nuclear reactor (Operation Opera).

However, their bombers do not have enough range. London therefore proposed to give them the use of its airfields in Georgia, which was closer to the target. President Mikheil Saakashvili agreed to rent two military bases to Israel. The British placed one of its citizens in his government, and the Israelis placed one of theirs, David Kezerashvili, as Minister for Defence.

Meanwhile, in Lebanon, Prime Minister Fouad Siniora attempted to cut Hezbollah's communication lines, and also block transports between Hezbollah and Iran, in order to facilitate the next Israeli attack against his country. Siniora was the ex-accountant for the Hariri family, and, notoriously, a secret agent for the Jordanian Intelligence services. He gave instructions to cut the telephone land-lines that had been set up by Hezbollah with the help of Iranian engineers. The Resistance would therefore be obliged to use either the state-run corded telephone network, or one of three mobile networks, all of which were controlled by the Israeli enemy. Besides this, it forbade Hezbollah to use the runway that Beirut airport kept available for its air bridge with Teheran. Many aircraft flew the air bridge in rotation, sending young Lebanese for training with the Revolutionary Guards and the Basij militia. In return, these organisations sent quantities of weapons, including innumerable missiles.

Hassan Nasrallah, the General Secretary of Hezbollah, demanded that the Prime Minister cancel these orders, which he called a "declaration of war". Siniora refused, while preparations continued for a new war against Lebanon, Syria and Iran. On 7 May 2008, Hezbollah occupied the buildings used by the Power structure and the private homes of officials. Within a few hours, the security services of the state were disarmed, and Hezbollah had triumphed. More discreetly, the elite troops of the Party of God attacked a bunker located under the ex-headquarters of the Television of the Future (property of the Hariri family, of the Future Party). The bunker sheltered the centre of operations for British, US, Israeli and Jordanian Forces. The foreign officers managed to escape by way of a tunnel and reach the beach, where pneumatic dinghies took them off-shore to be collected by a US ship. Having thus protected the Resistance, Hezbollah withdrew.

This lightning victory was to lead to the Doha agreement. The March 14 Alliance, centred around the Hariri family, negotiated the continuation of its place in government. Hezbollah couldn't care less, however, and demanded all latitude for the defence of the country.

While the destruction of Hezbollah was postponed, the destruction of Iran was under way.

The aborted war against Iran

In the Caucasus, persuaded that his concessions to the West would protect him, President Saakashvili took the initiative and attacked South Ossetia and Abkhazia. These two states had been joined with Georgia during the Soviet era – when the USSR was breaking down, they had declared their independence, but were never recognised by the international community. Since most Ossetians and Abkhazians also have Russian nationality, President Dmitry Medvedev authorised an intervention by his troops. His Prime Minister, Vladimir Putin, took command of the operations. To everyone's surprise, he started by bombing the two military bases rented to Israel, thereby grounding their aircraft, then attacked the Georgian army.

The Western medias refused to mention either the presence of Israel or the Iranian issue. They assured us that the Russian army was totally obsolete. According to them, Russia only won the engagement because Georgia was also under-equipped. Maybe. Maybe not. Russia, which everyone believed to be devastated since the collapse of the USSR and the pillage of the Yeltsin era, was in fact beginning to recover.

Since neither of the US parties involved had any interest in revealing what was going on, Washington asked its French agent, Nicolas Sarkozy, to "negotiate" peace. In reality, there was nothing to negotiate – Georgia was wrong, and it lost. Israel was unable to explain its presence.

Sarkozy zoomed off to Moscow to meet with President Medvedev. On his way from the airport to the Kremlin, he noticed a massive poster campaign for the magazine *Profile*. Since his own portrait was on the cover, he asked his ambassador to find out what it was all about. It turned out to be the publication of a study I had made, based on the family connections between President Sarkozy and one of the three founders of the CIA. When he arrived at the Kremlin, Sarkozy was received by his opposite number, Medvedev. But hardly had the two men sat down when the door opened again, and Prime Minister Vladimir Putin walked in. As soon as Sarkozy began to list his conditions, Putin, without a word, placed a copy of the magazine before him on the table, turning the cover towards their guest – as Sarkozy would recount later on. Finally, it was Sarkozy who accepted the Russian conditions, which sparked the anger of his partners from Central Europe.

State terror

During his two terms, George W. Bush terrified the Muslim world. Not only did he support the balkanization of the borders of the Middle East so that no state with more than 10 million citizens would be left, not only did he attack Afghanistan and Iraq, killing at least 3 million innocents, but he also submitted at least 80,000 Muslims to torture.

Contrary to what is shown by Hollywood films and TV series, torture has never been an effective means of gathering intelligence. However, it is a method that has been used by governments from time immemorial – because it is dissuasive.

During Antiquity and the Middle Ages, torture was not practised on the pretext of seeking information, but to force the condemned to sign prepared confessions. During the Second World War, the Nazis used torture on a massive scale, but this technique only ever provided incidental information. The real interrogators, as Hanns Scharff had instructed, did not use violence, and yet they gathered all sorts of useful and trustworthy information. The torturers terrorised the populations, which tightened their grip on power, but also led to the growth of the Resistance which finally defeated them.

Vice-President Dick Cheney organised a dozen meetings at the White House in order to decide what techniques should be used against Muslims. National Security Advisor Condoleeza Rice, Secretary of Defense Donald Rumsfeld, Secretary of State Colin Powell, Public Prosecutor John Aschcroft and Director of the CIA,

George Tenet all participated, and gave their opinions on experiments which were carried out before their eyes.

Dictators who sink to this depth are very rare – not even Chancellor Hitler did it. John Ashcroft finally refused to attend these meetings, and moaned, "History will not forgive us for what we have done".

Although Western public opinion has heard about Guantánamo, Abu Ghraib in Iraq and the CIA's secret prisons, it is not been informed about the Navy prisons in the holds of warships sailing in international waters. 17 of these floating prisons have been identified – USS Bataan, USS Peleliu, USS Ashland, USNS Stockham, USNS Watson, USNS Watkins, USNS Sister, USNS Charlton, USNS Pomeroy, USNS Red Cloud, USNS Soderman, USNS Dahl, MV PFC William B Baugh, MV Alex Bonnyman, MV Franklin J Phillips, MV Louis J Huage Jr, MV James Anderson Jr.. According to the British association Reprieve, more than 80,000 people had been taken from the Greater Middle East and tortured in these prisons, before being released and sent back to their countries.

It should therefore come as no surprise that if, after learning these facts, some of those close to the victims should manifest hatred of the West and sign up, without thinking, to any group which claims to be in revolt against it.

Colonel Lawrence Wilkerson, Director of Colin Powell's Cabinet, confirmed in a written witness statement during a trial in Guantánamo that the administration knew perfectly well that most of the individuals imprisoned there were in no way connected to terrorist activities.

As far as torture was concerned, the six "democratic" leaders mentioned above decided to test the theories of the ex-President of the American Psychological Association, Professor Martin Seligman, concerning the possibility, not of obtaining intelligence, but of behaviour modification.

He based himself

► on a study of Chinese torture during the Korean war, by Professor Albert D. Biderman from the Rand Corporation,

► on the practices of the CIA during the Cold War at the Political Warfare Cadres Academy (Taiwan) and the School of the Americas (Panama) – as exposed in the KUBARK manuals,

► on the experiments with mental manipulation in the CIA's MK-Ultra Project,

► on the racial profiling in the book *The Arab Mind*, by Professor Raphael Patai.

Seligman had designed a method aimed at breaking down the personality of individuals – the "learned helplessness" theory– and creating a new one for them.

No Western media picked up on the information that I published about this subject in Russia, in 2009. We had to wait until US psychologists translated my article, immediately denied by Professor Seligman, until their association (APA) opened an enquiry, and especially, until Senator Diane Feinstein published a report about 119 CIA prisoners, for the scandal to surface.

In passing, Diane Feinstein established that, apart from the screams of the victims, the United States had never collected even one comment linking the events of 11 September to al-Qaeda (of course, no such link existed). She also implicated two of Seligman's students who had showed a rare degree of sadism during the "enhanced interrogations", Bruce Jensen and the Mormon bishop, James Mitchell.

The Obama Presidency

It was in this context that the sub-prime crisis hit, followed by the financial crash that it provoked. On 15 September 2008, the Lehman Brothers bank collapsed. It had a turnover of $46.7 billion annually. The counter-shock affected the entire global financial system. In truth, this collapse and those which followed had little connection with real economic activity, but they disorganised the whole banking sector. They also provided the occasion for the Bush and Obama administrations to plunder the National Treasury and bail out their sponsors.

The United States had absolutely no choice but to drastically reduce their lifestyle and make some gigantic budget reductions. The wars would have to wait.

It was at that point that George W. Bush ended his two terms as President, and the Democratic candidate, Barack Obama, was elected. While the international Press thought that President Bush was too stupid to run things, and that his VP ran the show from the wings, it would not admit that Dick Cheney was not only the Vice-President, but also a member of the deep state grouping who had organised the coup d'état of 11 September. They therefore pretended to believe that power resided in the White House, and that Obama would be a real President.

The US mentality has no problem with the idea of "wiping the slate clean". So, when an entrepreneur goes bankrupt, he simply files for bankruptcy without paying his creditors. While in Europe, once judged, he is generally sentenced and forbidden from directing other companies, in the United States, he can immediately create another business and carry on as if nothing had happened. In the same way, at each Presidential election – until Donald Trump – the new President did not present himself as the accountant of the crimes committed by his predecessors. Barack Obama excelled in this register. He was able to keep a straight face while promising to unilaterally reduce nuclear arsenals and lead us to world peace, sparking explosions of applause and receiving, as a preventative measure, the Nobel Peace Prize. In the same register, the Atlantist propaganda celebrated the colour of his skin as the sign that racism was now null and void, and that equality had triumphed. In reality, however, white supremacist associations proliferated during Obama's terms of office, and policemen got into the habit of murdering African-Americans without any consequences.

Barack Obama is the son of a US mother and a Kenyan father. He was raised by his mother's second husband, the Indonesian Lolo Soetoro, then by his maternal grandmother, Madelyn Dunham. His father and father-in-law were students at the East–West Center in Hawaii, the US equivalent of the Russian Peoples' Friendship University of Russia (or Patrice Lumumba University). His mother and his father-in-law worked for the CIA in Indonesia at the time of the coup d'état by Suharto. His maternal grandmother handled the accounts of the CIA for the Far East, at the Bank of Hawaii in Honolulu. Considered as a foreigner by the US administration, Obama was awarded a Fulbright scholarship. Elected as senator for Illinois, he made a tour of Africa for the CIA, under cover of his parliamentary responsibility. The launch of his Presidential electoral campaign was financed by the Iraqi-British billionaire Sir Nadhmi Auchi, close to Prime Minister Tony Blair and MI6. By financing Obama, in all probability, Auchi acted on behalf of the Crown of

England. Once he had become President, Barack Obama's first administration included numerous members of the highly secret Pilgrim Society, the Anglo-American association headed by Queen Elizabeth II.

It also appears that, in all probability, Barack Obama is not a US citizen from Hawaii, but a subject of the British Crown from Kenya, which might have prevented him from running for the Presidency in accordance with the Constitution. In any case, his grandmother gave testimony about having been present at his birth in Kenya, although it is possible that she mixed him up with another of her grandchildren. The registers in Hawaii have no record of his birth certificate, but they may possibly have been poorly filed. The Secretary of State had awarded him a scholarship as a foreign student, but he may have falsified his declaration in order to obtain it. Later on, the White House Press service published a copy of his birth certificate, but it turned out to be a forgery. A marginal movement developed contesting his legitimacy (they were mocked as "birthers", after the 9/11 dissidents who were scorned as "truthers"). It was financed by the New York entrepreneur, Donald Trump.

The Colour Revolution in Iran

Since it was now essential for the USA to spend with caution, the idea of a great war against Iran was abandoned – but not the target. It would be war on the cheap, by using intrigue, inciting divisions and fanaticism. Specifically, to overcome the Iranian adversary in the person of the Revolutionary Guard, President Mahmud Ahmadinejad and Guide Ali Khamenei, the CIA organised a colour revolution relying on the personalities selected by Liz Cheney in 2006-08, namely Ayatollah Rafsanjani's second son, Mehdi, and Sayyed Mohammad Khatami.

The CIA asked the Allies to set up Persian-language satellite channels to compete with Iranian national TV. Although Iran produced quality fiction, its range of decors and costumes was very poor. In contrast, the movies proposed by Hollywood are flashy and hugely spectacular. Aware of the prudery of the Iranian culture, the Muslim Brotherhood swamped the country with full versions of the most shocking films and series from Hollywood, via MBC Persia[39],

---

[39] Saudi-owned MBC Persia was founded in London in 1991 as the first free satellite TV service in the Middle East. There is a worldwide diaspora of about

although they censored sex scenes on MBC in Arabic. Within a few months, the Allies created 70 TV channels in Persian, a language that is spoken only in Iran and Afghanistan. Even South Korea created a Persian TV channel.

While the Iranian masses identified with the anti-Imperialist Revolution of Imam Ruhollah Khomeini, they were in disagreement about its consequences. A part of the bazaar, in other words, the business people of Teheran and Ispahan, had been seriously affected by the closure of the international markets which followed the attempts to export the Revolution. Besides, this social class, used to their journeys to the West, was suffering from the strict sexual morality currently applied in Iran, and was dreaming of a "May '68".

For the last thirty years, the CIA had been trying to isolate the Revolution, while at the same time, doing business with the Iranian ruling class. During the years 1983 -1986, Israel and the US deep state discovered a way around the Congressional embargo on the sale of arms to Nicaragua (the "Iran-Contras" affair). Elliot Abrams and Colonel Oliver North at the NSA contacted the Speaker of the Parliament, Ayatollah Rafsanjani, via a deputy, Sheikh Hassan Rouhani, who was already working at that time with Paul Wolfowitz and Robert Gates. Israel put together a system for selling arms to the Nicaraguan counter-Revolutionaries (also known as terrorist death squads), who were secretly financed by the CIA, mainly with its profits from drug trafficking. Without scruples, Rafsanjani trampled on Imam Khomeini's revolutionary ideal, came to the aid of Israel, the United States, and the Latin-American counter-Revolutionaries, and managed to pile up the biggest fortune in Iran.

But in 2009, Rafsanjani refused to implicate himself directly in a new operation against his own country. Prudently preferring to hedge his bets, he chose his own son Mehdi to act as the go-between. Ex-President Khatami announced that he would run against Mahmud Ahmadinejad, a Revolutionary Guard who had relaunched Khomeini's movement, but then, claiming that he had been attacked in the street, Khatami deferred in favour of his ex-Prime Minister, Mir-Hossein Mousavi. Khatami then flew to the United States where

---

4 million Iranians, of which about half are in North America and Europe, and half in other Middle Eastern countries. Many of them left Iran after the 1979 Revolution.

he met with billionaire George Soros in order to organise the coup d'état.

As soon as Mahmud Ahmadinejad's victory (62,63% of the votes) was announced on 13 June, the NED claimed that the ballots had been manipulated. The partisans of Mousavi (33,75% of the votes) took to the streets. This was followed by several days of extreme confusion. Despite the support that Ayatollah Rafsanjani publicly offered the demonstrators, the Power structure held firm. Within a few weeks, the "Green Revolution" had come to resemble a class conflict – the urban bourgeoisie against the rest of the country.

The following year, Mahmud Ahmadinejad took revenge on behalf of his People for this attempted coup d'état. He first organised the most massive popular demonstration in Iranian history, in support of the Revolution. Then, at the podium of the United Nations General Assembly, he denounced the "clash of civilisations" meme of Bernard Lewis and Samuel Huntington – two ex-members of the US National Security Council. If there is a conflict which involves all humanity, he continued, it is not between religions, but between the materialism of capitalism and the consumer society on one hand, and on the other, the spiritual values of the Revolution, which are justice and heroism. He asked the awkward questions about the events of 11 September in the United States. He avoided the question of the religion claimed by Osama Bin Laden, but noted the personal business relations which linked the bin Laden family to George W. Bush – connections which I had revealed in 2001 in the Mexican weekly magazine Proceso, and which were mentioned in Congress by Representative Cynthia McKinney. Having shown that the version of 9/11 cobbled together by the Bush administration had served to justify wars against Afghanistan and Iraq, yet withholding judgment on the issue, Ahmadinejad renewed my demand, in the name of the Iranian people, for the creation of an International Commission of Enquiry. This caused an earthquake in Washington.

On the same day, the National Security Council called an emergency meeting. The very next morning, President Barack Obama rushed to the BBC Persian radio channel to calm things down, while the Iranian Press talked about my relations with Mahmud Ahmadinejad – the diplomats were extremely busy. The interview with the Anglo-Iranian journalists was organised by the person responsible for strategic communication for the White House, Ben Rhodes, a man who had worked on the 9/11 Commission Report under President Bush. Obama accused his Iranian opposite number of using hate speech at the United Nations podium, but anyone who has the opportunity to read the text of his speech will see that this accusation is false. The important thing was to put out the fire before it spread. In the end, not only was the Iran War avoided, but the United States ceased all direct attacks in exchange for Iran's silence.

"Leading from behind"

According to one of Obama's advisors, his administration, aware of the relative decline of the United States compared with China, and the hostility that the US provokes in the world, thought up a new form of leadership – leading from behind. "The defense of our interests and the spreading of our ideas now requires discretion and modesty as well as our military power", he said. In other words, even if it wasn't a very "John Wayne attitude", and contrary to his predecessors, Barack Obama would not deploy US troops in new conflicts, but would influence his allies to do his dirty work for him. In order to succeed, this method would require the US to convey the impression of shocked surprise at each new "spontaneously" generated event, and then encourage its allies to react first.

Proposed at the end of 2004 by the British, the project for the overthrow of the secular Arab governments in favour of the "moderate" anti-imperialists – the Muslim Brotherhood – would be the first application of this new method for ruling the world.

In November 2010, Washington pressed Paris to sign the Lancaster House Treaties with London – the plan for the attacks on Libya and Syria. As in 2005, an ultimatum was addressed to Syria. The European Union notified Damascus that if it did not immediately sign an association agreement, war would ensue. President Bashar al-Assad flew discreetly to Europe, where the EU asked him to liberalise his economy to the detriment of his people, and demanded that he accept the loss of the Golan Heights and normalise relations with Israel. Of course, the Syrian declined. It was to be war.

The Ivory Coast test

Although the Pentagon did not question the military capabilities of the United Kingdom, to be on the safe side, it wanted to check what France could do before entrusting any mission to the Europeans. So it encouraged Paris to reconquer the Ivory Coast, whence it had been earlier expelled. Since the election of President Laurent Gbagbo in 2000, the country had been controlled by the Pentagon via the First Lady Simone Gbagbo and the Protestant missionaries, and by Israel via the Minister for the Interior, a pro-Israeli Lebanese refugee from the South Lebanese Army. The first part of Gbagbo's presidency was particularly violent. But, like many of those who collaborate with imperialism, with time the President began to realise that he could look after his own people rather than serve foreign interests. It was time to kick him out.

As soon as the Ivorian Presidential election results of 2010 were made public, France claimed that the ballot had been rigged against Alassane Ouattara, a personal friend of Nicolas Sarkozy. For a few days, the two candidates traded mutual accusations and argued over the Presidency. Paris was able to freeze the country's finances, with the result that the army and the police defected and rallied to Ouattara. Laurent Gbagbo was arrested and dragged before the International Criminal Court, the jurisdiction of choice for justifying Western imperialism. Oddly enough, the two companies which supported the French operation for "régime change", Bolloré and Bouygues, fell out with Nicolas Sarkozy, while the Pentagon praised France. As for the ICC, it was never able to prove the accusations against the deposed President.

Phase I – Tunisia

Straight-faced, Washington and London feigned great surprise at the uprising in Tunisia at the end of December 2010. The French, who were still trying to support Zine el-Abidine Ben Ali, realised too late that the Anglo-Saxons had ditched them. Yet the President had never failed his sponsors. He was a CIA agent, trained at the Senior Intelligence School at Fort Holabird, Maryland. He had faithfully obeyed the orders of Paris, Rome and Washington. But he had no contact with London, and was no longer suitable for the grand design of MI6.

In the streets, Gene Sharp's men came from the United States, Germany and Serbia to organise the "Jasmine Revolution". At the request of the head of AfriCom, General William Ward, Tunisian Chief of Staff General Rachid Ammar persuaded the President to take a leave of absence abroad, just long enough to restore order. So

Ben Ali left, just as Shah Reza Pahlevi had left Iran, believing that he was only taking a couple of weeks off. The international Press ran amuck, exposing the dictator's hidden fortune. Jeffrey Feltman was already in charge at the US embassy in Tunis, the CIA's regional base. It only remained for MI6 to bring Ben Ali's perennial opponent back from London, the Muslim Brother Rached Ghannouchi.

So the United Kingdom fulfilled its bargain of placing a "moderate" in power, at the same time steering Tunisia from the French sphere of influence towards its own.

Phase II – Egypt

Now it was Egypt's turn. Gene Sharp's men and the supposedly "non-governmental" NED took over Tahrir Square. It was the "Lotus Revolution". This time it was ambassador Frank Wisner (Nicolas Sarkozy's father-in-law) who came to inform President Hosni Mubarak that he was fired. Mubarak had no more to be ashamed of than did Ben Ali – apart from his refusal to transfer the Palestinians from Gaza to the Sinai desert – but he also had no part to play in the British plan. The international Press once again ran amuck, exposing the dictator's hidden fortune. Except that this time it was all a lie, because Hosni Mubarak was not a thief. But no matter, MI6 organised the return of the Muslim Brotherhood anyway. Completely bewildered, the French made no comment about any of it.

Phase III – Libya

So now it was time for Libya and Syria. "Senator" John McCain and "philosopher" Bernard-Henri Levy met together in Cairo with the men from the "NGO" NED, al-Qaeda, and the future leaders of both countries. Muslim Brother Mahmud Jibril, number 2 in Muammar Gaddafi's government, was suddenly crowned as head of the Libyan opposition in exile. Italian snipers, firing from the rooftops, killed demonstrators and policemen indiscriminately in Benghazi, provoking chaos, while al-Qaeda attacked military arsenals. In Geneva, the Muslim Brothers of the Libyan League for Human Rights denounced the régime's imaginary crimes, allegedly bombing its own people. There was talk of thousands of dead, but NATO would take care of killing them later. Immediately afterwards, the Security Council authorised a military intervention to protect the civilians, although only Al-Qaeda was threatening them.

In Libya, the African immigrant workers were the only ones who understood what was happening. They witnessed the mass arrival of Western special forces in Benghazi, and expected that the Westerners were about to overthrow the régime, as they had in the Ivory Coast. No one lifted a finger when, in the East of the country, the Muslim Brotherhood and the Senussi Order indulged in pogroms against black Africans. More than 800,000 immigrant workers fled Westward and out of the country, while the Atlantist Press pretended, straight-faced, that they were being terrorised by the "Gaddafi régime", which on the contrary was protecting them.

So far, everything was going well for the organisers. President Obama ordered the Allies to attack Tripoli, under the coordination of AfriCom, and with ground support from the forces of al-Qaeda.

This plan was unacceptable for General Carter Ham, the commander of AfriCom and one of the highest-ranking officers in the United States military. He refused to fight alongside men who had killed so many GI's in Afghanistan and Iraq. Suddenly, the White House had to put the whole system under the responsibility of another officer. They decided on the head of EuCom and Supreme Commander of NATO, Admiral James G. Stavridis. So much for the painstaking charade about not looking like a Western crusade on Muslim lands, by avoiding any hint of NATO involvement.

Phase IV - Syria

Despite the calls for uprising, Syria was not moving. A few statues of ex-President Hafez al-Assad were pushed over, but nothing more. The Muslim Brotherhood organised demonstrations on Fridays, at the time when the faithful left the mosques. Since the country is only two thirds Sunnite, they had to explain why these demonstrations "for democracy" were held only on Fridays, and only at the exits of Sunni mosques. Well, it must be because the "dictatorship" is "Alawite". No mention is made of the secular nature of the Ba'ath party and Syria's religious minorities (the Christians, the Druzes, the Twelver Shiites, etc.)

Finally, Israel organised the riots in Daraa, while on the Qatari and Saudi TV channels, MI6 broadcast the horror tale about the children who supposedly had their nails ripped out by the police.[40]

The role of MI6

During the whole of the "Arab Spring", MI6 specialised in war propaganda. A sensible division of labour, since the use of modern psychology to hoodwink your own population and obtain their support was an English invention, developed well before the USSR and the Third Reich. In 1914, London created the War Propaganda Bureau at Wellington House. One of its methods was to use artists, since images are direct and untrammelled by logic. In 1914, they also recruited the great writers of the day – Arthur Conan Doyle, H.G. Wells, Rudyard Kipling – to publish screeds ascribing imaginary crimes to the German enemy. Then they recruited the editors of their major newspapers to publish the imaginary tales served up by the writers.

When the United States picked up on the British method, in 1917, with the Committee on Public Information (CPI), they concentrated more on the mechanics of persuasion, with the help of star journalist Walter Lippmann and the inventor of modern publicity, Edward Bernays, the nephew of Sigmund Freud. But persuaded by the power of science, they forgot the aesthetics. This is how propaganda passed from the artistic orientation to "storytelling", systematically fabricated according to scientific rules.

Twenty 20 years on, the Nazis developed two new concepts. Joseph Goebbels held a daily briefing for the Minister of Information in which he defined the "elements of language" that the journalists were to use.[41] It was no longer simply a case of convincing people, but

---

[40] Editor's note – An accusation so shocking, with such a powerful effect on our imagination, the cruelty we project onto another (the leader they want to remove), that it has been used regularly, against the Afghani Talibans, then Muammar Gaddafi, before being applied to "Bashar". The visceral horror that it provokes is so intensely revolting that it prevents us from thinking, locking us into the emotional sphere, and demanding that we accept in advance all the crimes that may be needed to free the people from such tyrants.

[41] Meyssan, "Die Methoden der modernen militärischen Propaganda," http://www.voltairenet.org/article191805.html . The control of vocabulary foreshadows Orwell's "Newspeak" and the modern usage of memes, buzzwords, soundbites and "staying on message." Goebbels also greatly

changing their frame of reference or world view. This technique was systematised in 2003 by the White House and Downing Street, who created the "Office of Global Communications". The spokespersons of the President and the Prime Minister exchanged information every day by telephone conference. They distributed a daily e-mail to all their embassies and various administrations, "The Global Messenger", which specified the elements of language which were to be adopted.

Moreover, Goebbels recruited the citizenry to participate in the lie, thus identifying with it and making it doubly difficult to return to the truth. For example, after taking part in torchlight parades in his Hugo Boss uniform, a man could not question his Nazi beliefs without questioning himself, and rethinking his past and his vision of the future. Similarly today, Westerners who demonstrated in solidarity with the Libyans being crushed by the dictator Gaddafi's bombs, now have a hard time accepting the fact that the only bombs dropped there were by NATO "airstrikes". It's a human characteristic that, even when we are shown proof, we find it very hard to face the fact that we have been manipulated.

In 2010, MI6 did little more than simply invent stories which made it possible to give a continuous narration of events. For example, it invented a biography for Mohamed Bouazizi – the young man whose suicide sparked the demonstrations in Tunisia – and confabulated the circumstances of his death so as to transform it into a symbol of oppression. These lies helped to mask the role of the Muslim Brotherhood, the NED and Gene Sharp, making the events appear spontaneous – which to a certain extent they were, once the Tunisians fell for the fable.

MI6 also coordinated the work of the Atlanticist television channels in the Arabic language, as it was already coordinating those of the allied televisions in Persian. Its method is simple – every station quotes the others. So false information broadcast by one would be quoted by the others. Repetition is the most basic principle of

---

appreciated the use of images, and his favorite medium was the newsreel. "Goebbels believed that propaganda must be thoroughly learned and that thereafter more repetition was necessary to reinforce the learning." L. Doob in "Goebbels' Principles of Propaganda," *Public Opinion Quarterly*, 1950, scribd.com

conditioning, as was noted by Pavlov, as well as by Goebbels and Hitler.[42]

The spearhead of this propaganda machine is the Qatari station al-Jazeera. The channel was created in 1996 by brothers David and Jean Frydman, after the assassination of Yitzhak Rabin, with whom they were close. The idea was to set up a television service in the Arabic language where Arabs and Jews could discuss issues with each other peacefully, in spite of the war between them. Lacking the necessary personnel, the Frydman brothers turned to MI6, who happened to be thinking about setting up a news service in Saudi Arabia. After a few false starts, MI6 press-ganged almost the entire Arab service of the BBC in order to create the Qatari al-Jazeera. The format worked very well as long as the station allowed the expression of a wide gamut of opinions, challenging the monolithic dogmatism which typified Arab TV. Without a doubt, al-Jazeera became the most watched TV channel in the Arab world during the invasions of Afghanistan and Iraq, because it was the only outlet which mentioned US crimes. As we saw earlier, this apparently anti-US point of view was nothing revolutionary, but was simply that of MI6. In any case, the aura of al-Jazeera was such that most of the Arab TV stations requested either al-Jazeera, or else the BBC itself, to train their journalists. In a few years, MI6 had a roster of respectable correspondents in almost all the editorial offices of the Arab audio-visual world, including Libya and Syria.

Everything changed in 2005, when MI6 began preparing for the "Arab Spring". The editorial staff of al-Jazeera was placed under the supervision of Jtrack, the studio of Brother Mahmud Jibril – the future leader of the Libyan "revolution". He worked to give the channel a coherent tone, and furnished it with a spiritual guide, Sheikh Yusuf al-Qaradawi, the star of the Muslim Brotherhood. It was during this period that I organised the "Axis for Peace" conference in Brussels, which brought together more than 150 personalities from more than 40 countries. While al-Jazeera had agreed to sponsor the conference – as did TeleSur and Russia Today – I received, on the second day of the meeting, a panicky telephone

---

[42] Hitler in *Mein Kampf*: "Propaganda must confine itself to very few points, and repeat them endlessly" (wikiquote.org), translated from the original, 1925, p. 202. "Propaganda... hat sich auf wenig zu beschränken und dieses ewig zu wiederholen." (archive.org)

call from the channel's director, swearing that he was really sorry but that he was obliged to cancel his participation. Mahmud Jibril had apparently just looked at the list of participants and realised how important the meeting was. Within a few months, the Qatari editorial staff was purged and handed over to Brother Wadah Khanfar – who today directs the Sharq Forum in Tunis, the Muslim Brotherhood think tank.

At the beginning of the Arab Spring, MI6 set up a coordination center for the Atlantist and Western-oriented TV channels in Doha, Qatar. Al-Arabiya, al-Jazeera, BBC, CNN, France 24, and Sky joined up, along with small, CIA-created Arab-language stations. Together, they produced images of the revolutionaries pouring onto Green Square in Tripoli, which were broadcast for the first time by Sky, on the second day of the battle for the control of the Libyan capital. Careful examination of these images reveal that they were filmed in an open-air studio. Certain of the Square's buildings are not rendered in detail. Above all, the scaffolding that the Gaddafists had erected the week before the battle, in order to hang a huge portrait of the Guide, was absent. This was perhaps the first time in history that fiction film was broadcast and presented as live footage of combat operations. The effect on the Libyans was catastrophic. Persuaded that they had been invaded and had lost the war, many of them gave up resisting. The same trick was meant to be used in Syria at the start of 2012, but had to be cancelled due to the early Syrian reaction and the Russian intervention.

The coordination cell for the Atlantist and Gulf television stations used a system which had already proved itself during the invasion of Iraq. At that time, the CIA, MI6 and the Israeli Shin Beth coordinated the publication of their false information about the alleged implication of Saddam Hussein in the attacks of 11 September, or about the supposed capacity of Iraq to fire chemical missiles at the United States. Her Majesty's secret services had not hesitated to assassinate Doctor David Kelly, who was preparing to go public on the BBC about "Rockingham," the UK's data-twisting unit for the Iraqi WMD issue.[43]

---

[43] The day before his death, David Kelly told the Intelligence and Security Committee of Parliament about Operation Rockingham, a cell within the UK secret services tasked with crafting misleading information that Iraqi had WMDs.

MI6 installed Press units in Syria, at Baba Amr, in 2012, and in East Aleppo, in 2016. To do this, it placed Syrian collaborators, so-called "citizen journalists", who received foreign war correspondents. Not only did the Western media swallow any and all allegations made by these Syrians, but they never inquired about their political leanings. For example, Abu Saleh, who wangled his way into the post of freelance journalist for France 24 and al-Jazeera, was presented as a "democrat". And yet he had been a member of the Sharia Tribunal in Baba Amr, which condemned to death more than 50 civilians, Christians and Alawites, and had their throats cut.

The Syrian Observatory for Human Rights was set up by the two al-Abdeh brothers, (BaradaTV) plus Osama Ali Suleiman (under the pseudonym of "Rami Abdel Rahman"), before the beginning of the crisis in their Syrian homeland, but is actually a one-man show.[44] "Rami Abdel Rahman", in between managing his shop in Coventry, also puts out a daily report of military operations and casualties in the Syrian conflict from his living room, which he allegedly composes from the eye-witness accounts of his 230 correspondents on the ground. His bulletin, fed by Her Majesty's secret services, has been conveniently accepted as the unique source of war reporting for the Western Press. With each battle, "Abdel Rahman's Observatory" tallies the number of deaths on each side, even before the Syrian Arab Army has the count. Even the armies themselves need time to make an estimate, to find out whether their missing are dead or wounded. The accounts of this clairvoyant alleged "Observatory" are taken as Gospel by the TV channels that MI6 is working with, as well as by the agencies AFP, Associated Press and Reuters.

After the massacre in the Eastern Ghouta suburbs of Damascus, in summer 2013, MI6 outsourced communications between the armed groups to third party vendors. The first firm was the crisis management consultants Deloitte Touche Regester Larkin; soon after the work was given to Innovative Communications & Strategies (InCoStrat), another company created by Larkin director and MI6

---

[44] At first the SOHR was incorrectly registered, so that the latter of the three Muslim Brothers took the name for himself. Recently it has become public that far from being neutral, the SOHR, like the White Helmets, has been financed by the UK Foreign Office. https://www.mintpressnews.com/report-traces-neutral-syrian-war-observer-sohr-funding-to-uk-foreign-office/242096/

officer Colonel Paul Tilley.[45] The group deals with the conflicts in Syria as well as in Yemen. It produces videos touting the "democratic revolutions", and designs the logos for almost all the jihadist groups, often very meticulous work. For example, in the suburbs of Damascus, they filmed a parade of the Islamic Army, with four tanks and a few hundred extras who marched past the camera, then turned around and went by the camera again, several times, just as Mussolini's Blackshirts paraded before the King of Italy during the march on Rome.

Among the great successes of MI6 we should count the White Helmets, allegedly a humanitarian organisation occupied with Civil Defence in the jihadist-occupied areas. In reality, it is a unit linked to al-Qaeda whose task is the production of propaganda. It pretends to carry out "rescue missions" – all staged, directed and filmed like a movie. It sent its representatives to meet with politicians in the West, and was even a front-runner for the Nobel Peace Prize.[46] The organisation was founded by James Le Mesurier MBE, a top mercenary officer and MI6 agent honoured by Queen Elizabeth with the Order of the British Empire.[47] A documentary film about the White Helmets won an Oscar in Hollywood. But when al-Qaeda cut off the water supply to more than 5 million civilians in Damascus for a period of 42 days, the communiqué from the jihadists claiming responsibility for the crime was signed by several organisations … including the "humanitarians" of the White Helmets.

The Syrian state and Bashar al-Assad

The United States had succeeding in spreading chaos in Afghanistan, Iraq, Tunisia, Egypt, Libya, Yemen and Syria. However, three of these countries were slowly beginning to pick themselves up from the terrible blows they had been dealt. In practice, Washington had disorganised only the tribal populations (in Afghanistan, Eastern Iraq, Libya and Yemen), but not the states themselves.

---

[45] See https://www.linkedin.com/in/paul-tilley-mbe-2972056/ and "How the United Kingdom puts Jihadists on the map," http://www.voltairenet.org/article192256.html

[46] http://time.com/4522709/white-helmets-syria-nobel-peace-prize/

[47] Mesurier ran intel for the NATO war crimes operation in Pristina, Kosovo, then a unit that merged with Academi-Blackwater. From Blackwater to White Hatter, by any other name, a death squad capo.

The very notion of statehood had been invented with the ancient City-Kingdoms of Mesopotamia and the Levant. It was because the US feared national resistance that Washington had been corrupting President Saddam Hussein's régime for many years, and had then organised the de-Ba'athification of Iraq. And despite all the clichés about corruption in Syria, the US had never been able to buy the real leaders of the country.

Although the Syrians were taken in at the beginning of the war, and expected to see NATO invade their country and assassinate their President, by the start of 2012 they realised that it was all a production, a show. So they moved back to their homeland, which proved able to protect them. Astonishingly, the grocery stores of Syria were never empty, even when the fighting was at its worst. Although the choice was often limited, or lacking, it was always possible for parents to feed their children. In the same way, while the jihadists never stopped attacking the electric power stations and the water mains, electricity and water were still available for a few hours on most days. The state never abandoned its schools, its hospitals and its courts. It always paid all its civil service staff, including those who were working in enemy-occupied territory. It maintained its roads and even the public parks.

Behind this extraordinary permanence of the state was the national union between the Ba'athist Arabs, the anti-imperialists of the SSNP, the Syrian Social Nationalist Party, and the communists, all under the command of one man – President Bashar al-Assad.

The youngest son of President Hafez al-Assad was not attracted to politics, but to medicine. An ophthalmologist, he had studied in London, where he met his wife, Asma al-Akhras, a British-Syrian Sunni who worked in the City for JP Morgan. Everyone who knew him in the United Kingdom speaks of his kindly disposition and his sense of responsibilities. Son of a head of state, he refused to open a private surgery, considering that his position obliged him to serve others in a hospital setting. When his elder brother Bassel died at the wheel of his car, Bashar returned to Syria, where his father began to introduce him to politics. At the President's death in 2000, although nothing had been planned for this eventuality, his father's generals asked Bashar to accept the succession. The Syrian people confirmed this by referendum. And then, little more than a year after his investiture, the United States decided to wipe his region off the face of the earth. During the decade which followed, he was caught up by external questions, trying successively to prevent war, and then being obliged to prepare for it. Extremely popular in his own country and the whole of the Arab world, he was deeply destabilised when the Syrians turned their backs on him in mid-2011. Conscious that his departure would plunge the country into chaos, he decided to stay, despite the attempts to assassinate him.

Put to the test of adversity, finding in himself a courage and a tenacity of which he was probably unaware, al-Assad (in Arabic, the "Lion") slowly got back to his feet, progressively re-assembled his people behind him against the invaders, and was triumphantly, and legally, re-elected in June 2014.

In 2006, the Secretary General of the United Nations had created a Tribunal specially intended for his judgement. Thereafter, 116 states and 14 international institutions accused him of some truly odious crimes, and in 2012, demanded his departure. No other leader in our time has surmounted such enormous difficulties.

President Hugo Chávez Frías was the first, many years earlier, to see in this spindly, modest man the potential of embodying the Resistance against imperialism. Chavez had warmly designated Assad as his successor to stand up against the crimes of Washington and its allies on the world stage. And in the last five-year plan that he drew up for Venezuela, seeing the storm-clouds gathering, he called for all members of his administrations to support this distant country called Syria.

Bashar al-Assad is an extremely rational person, and will sweep aside intuitive remarks in order to concentrate on the facts alone. Some find this gives him a chilly appearance – but I believe, on the contrary, that he is a man of great sensitivity who takes care to protect himself from the main weakness of the Arab culture – emotion. Arabs in general, and he more than others, are passionate men. Arab poetry is composed using musical tonalities which the European languages do not possess. Arab culture is full of intense emotions, which are poor counsel in politics. He therefore restricts himself to looking only at the facts, and demands the same of his advisors and generals. This approach may not suffice to anticipate events far in advance, but it does give him an undeniable intellectual superiority over most people he meets.

While the Western powers present him as a dictator, I can bear witness to the fact that some of his ministers do not obey him, and that others misappropriate public funds for their own profit. Like all world leaders, therefore, he is regularly obliged to remove some of them from office.

After having celebrated him as a great democrat, the Western powers now present him as a new Hitler, torturing and eliminating his opponents en masse in an extermination camp, the prison at Saidnaya. The truth is astonishingly different. Before the war, Bashar al-Assad was practically the only Syrian who believed in the superiority of democracy over the third-world practices of the government he had inherited. However, for political institutions to be efficient, they need to be adapted and rooted in the History and the society of their countries. He therefore set himself to transforming his society as well as the Institutions. He created a vast middle class from nothing, and began to democratise political practice – the recognition of the plurality of parties and the end of the preeminence of the Ba'ath Party (of which he is still the Regional Secretary) – the organisation of para-administrative Commissions whose composition is representative of the diversity of opinion – and the liberalisation of the Press (but not the organs of public information), etc.

When the insurgency began, in 2011, President al-Assad did not react at all in the way that his supporter and his enemies expected. While the majority of his people had lost confidence in him, expecting the overthrow of the Republic by the Muslim Brotherhood, he decided to trust in his people. He did not impose exceptional powers for the police forces, as Western governments had done after the attacks of 9/11. On the contrary, he annulled the State of Emergency (resulting from the Israeli occupation of the Golan), dissolved the special courts, freed Internet communications (except for the Israeli sites), and forbade the armed forces to use their weapons if their deployment might endanger the innocent. Many Syrians regretted the lack of the uncompromising attitude of his father, Hafez al-Assad, and were convinced that Bashar had just committed a devastating error, and that the country was about to be crushed.

When the troubles developed into war, around the middle of 2012, and a multitude of jihadists from all Muslim populations, from Morocco to China, attacked his country, President Assad decided to move his troops back into Syria's major cities. The Western medias noted with delight that a growing part of the national territory was in the hands of the jihadists. They interpreted the withdrawal of the Republic to "Useful Syria" as the beginning of his defeat. In reality, Bashar al-Assad had chosen to defend his people rather than his territory. The populations from the countryside found refuge in the cities, under the protection of the army, and almost no one migrated to the desert regions which were occupied by the jihadists.

During his speech on 12 December 2012, President Assad set the conditions for the restoration of the country's unity. He emphasized the need for a new constitution, to be put to a referendum and adopted by a majority – and to elect all the nation's political representatives democratically, including himself as President of the Republic. That is what he did in 2014, and he is ready to do so again.

The rapprochement between Washington and Teheran

Apart from their severe illiteracy in Syrian History, and their dismal misunderstanding of the personality of President al-Assad, the Anglo-Saxons also had to deal with the unexpected reactions of several other international players. Starting with Iran.

The conflict between Washington and Teheran dated from the megalomania of Shah Reza Pahlavi. The Shah was the son of a military commander who seized power after WWI; then, because he had sympathized with Germany, Britain replaced him with his son after WWII. The young Shah became the faithful ally of the Anglo-Saxons, allowing them to dismiss his Prime Minister, the nationalist Mohammed Mossadegh, and replace him with ex-Nazi General Fazlollah Zahedi. In October 1971, he organised wildly extravagant festivities for the 2,500th anniversary of the Foundation of the Imperial State of Iran, or Persian monarchy, and began to believe that he could act alone. The terror imposed by his political police, the Savak, and the persistent under-development of his country, led to a generalised insurrection. President Carter's National Security Advisor, Zbigniew Brzeziński, persuaded the Shah to leave Iran for a short time (the same trick was used during the Arab Spring against Tunisian President Zine el-Abidine Ben Ali), and in his absence, organised the return of an exiled historical opponent, the Ayatollah Ruhollah Khomeini. US experts believed that this old man, then aged 76, together with the whole of the high clergy, only wanted to overthrow the monarchy because they hoped to regain the lands that had been confiscated by the Shah. Imagine the experts' astonishment when, on the very day he returned, 1 February 1979, Khomeini went straight to the Behesht-e Zahra cemetery to honour the memory of the victims of the régime and, before a gigantic crowd, called on the army to defend the country against the Anglo-Saxons.

The Revolution that he led until his death in 1989 had been prepared by a young philosopher, Ali Shariati – a translator for Che Guevara, and a personal friend of Frantz Fanon, Jean-Paul Sartre and Simone de Beauvoir. Profoundly mystical, this unconventional thinker reinterpreted Islam as a theology of Liberation. He called upon his compatriots to test its principles and only retain those which gave them the strength to struggle against imperialism. He was assassinated by the Savak in London, seven months before the return of the Ayatollah to Iran.

For his part, Ayatollah Khomeini reinterpreted Shiism, which until then had been little more than a lamentation on the martyrdom of Ali and Hussein (early Caliphs who were members of the Prophet Mohamed's family). He called on his disciples to weep less and, on the contrary, to imitate those early leaders' sacrifices for the liberation of their people. Under his influence, Shiism, once a religion of submission, became the religion of the Revolution. Instantly, Iran was a source of panic for all UK and US interests throughout the Muslim world. The West took note only of the rigid and restrictive aspects of this change in the lives of Iranians, ignoring any positive features for Iran's development.

The Anglo-Saxons attempted to crush the movement before it contaminated the region. They encouraged Sunni Saudi Arabia to make a religious attack on Shiite Iran, and for Iraq to attack them militarily. Once this war began, they helped it to last as long as possible, in order also to weaken their Iraqi ally. This eight-year war took more than a million victims. During its final year, Iraq fired missiles into Iranian cities, provoking very heavy damage. Iran replied in kind, killing many Iraqis. The Ayatollah Khomeini then intervened, ruling that weapons of mass destruction were contrary to his vision of Islam. The Iranian forces therefore stopped using them – which extended the war and multiplied their losses – and halted their military research into chemical, biological and nuclear weapons. These programmes were never resumed.

According to Khomeini, in the expression "Islamic Republic", it was necessary to understand the word "Republic" as defined by Plato, a concept he had taught all his life. Consequently, the régime was to be placed under the supreme authority of a virtuous sage, the Guide of the Revolution – in this case Khomeini himself. The word "Islamic" should be understood both as "Muslim" and as "fighting for Justice". Indeed, even if he or she is not a Muslim, the person who fights for Justice follows the example of the martyrs Ali and Hussein, and serves God.

On the death of Ayatollah Khomeini, the high clergy showed their true colors. They had earlier excommunicated him, and after his ascent to power, they continued to hate him, while pretending that they had joined him, in order to profit from his immense popular support. They now tried to turn the situation to their advantage. There followed a period of approximately fifteen years during which Iran licked her wounds and played almost no role on the international stage. But in 2005, Khomeini disciple Mahmud Ahmadinejad was elected President, and relaunched the Revolution. He placed his country at the service of all the Revolutionary movements in the region, notably those who were fighting against the Jewish colony installed by the Anglo-Saxons in Palestine. Considering that its proclamation of independence in 1948, (like that of Rhodesia in 1965), did not alter its colonial character, Ahmadinejad also supported the secular PLO, the Sunni Hamas and the Shiite Hezbollah.

During his two terms in office, he became friends with his Venezuelan and Syrian counterparts, Hugo Chávez Frías and Bashar al-Assad, and also with the Secretary General of Hezbollah, Hassan Nasrallah.

The United States, the United Kingdom and Israel reacted by organising a long propaganda campaign against him, of which the first episode was the deceitful translation of one of his speeches. Reuters falsely translated him as saying that he wanted to "wipe Israel off the map", which was clearly contrary both to his words and to his intentions.[48]

---

[48] One can never repeat often enough that the Iranian President never pronounced the words "Israel must be wiped off the map". This is one of the greatest operations of contemporary propaganda. The exact words he used

Then the three powers accused Iran of pursuing nuclear research in order to attain this military goal which was nothing but the fruit of their own imagination. This was obviously an idiotic interpretation, in view of Ayatollah Khomeini's *fatwa* and Iran's history. And yet for ten years, the Westerners continually denounced an imaginary "Iranian military nuclear threat".

Facing the most Draconian sanctions blockade ever forced on any state in the modern era, Ahmadinejad industrialised his country by leaps and bounds – a country whose economy, until that time, had been based exclusively on its oil revenue. Simultaneously, Iran reached an agreement with the Emirate of Dubai, whose rapidly growing port enabled Iran to avoid international sanctions.

After their successive failures to start an open war and a colour revolution, the United States tried a new approach. During the last few months of the Ahmadinejad presidency, the Supreme Leader and successor to Khomeini, Ayatollah Ali Khamenei, had authorised certain members of the opposition to talk with the United States. Secret negotiations began in Oman, in March 2013. The US delegation was led by Assistant Secretary of State William Burns, and National Security Advisor to the Vice-President, Jake Sullivan. The negotiator for nuclear questions, Wendy Sherman, participated in the final meeting. However, we do not know who represented Iran. During these negotiations, the Supreme Leader asked everyone present to cease any activities which could be perceived as a provocation by Washington.

Back in Washington, the US delegation reported to President Obama that Ahmadinejad's candidate would be swept aside in the Presidential election, and that their old friend Sheikh Hassan Rouhani would be elected. According to plan, the outgoing President's Chief of Staff, Esfandiar Rahim Mashaei, was accused of not being a real Muslim, and was blocked from running for President. Rouhani was elected, to the great delight of his friend Elliot Abrams, who had been successively the man for Reagan's

---

("The régime which occupies Jerusalem must be erased from the page of time"), were taken from a speech by Imam Khomeini, in the context of a regime change like those in the USSR and South Africa. This has been confirmed by the New York Times, the Guardian and Israeli sources such as MEMRI.

Iran-Contras affair, for Bush Jr.'s programme to democratise the world, and for Obama's colour revolution.

Making the best out of a bad deal, Ayatollah Khamenei authorised the new President to negotiate with Washington or the lifting of sanctions. The announcement of the official negotiations caused panic in Israel and Saudi Arabia. A provisional agreement was signed on 24 November 2013. Then, for a year and a half, the two sides negotiated in secret about the way in which they were going to share the Middle East. President Rouhani's ambition was to reclaim the role of regional policeman that Washington had once entrusted to Shah Reza Pahlavi. Besides this, he negotiated with Austrian President Hans Fisher to connect Iran to the Nabucco pipeline. In this way, the Europeans would be able to buy Iranian instead of Russian gas. This was an enormous 8,5 billion dollar contract, generating a lot of under-the-table bribes.

The final agreement on the military nuclear programme – which had not existed for 26 years – was officially signed on 14 July 2015. It was a disaster for Iran, which was obliged to dismantle its university programmes in nuclear physics and a part of its civilian installations. No matter, the event was saluted by a joyous crowd in Teheran and Ispahan, where the population awaited the lifting of the sanctions which were suffocating their country. But the sanctions were not lifted. First of all, Washington organised a trial in its own courts, accusing Teheran of being behind the attacks of 11 September – while simultaneously persisting in blaming al-Qaeda. As a protective measure, since the trial which just kept dragging on, a judge blocked the release of $150 billion of Iranian assets which had been frozen by the sanctions. Secondly, the State Department used missile tests by the Iranian army as a pretext for prolonging the sanctions. This was based on a United Nations resolution against the construction of missiles with nuclear war-heads, not conventional ones, while Iran had agreed not to pursue a nuclear programme for ten years.

Finally, although the Rouhani clan certainly enjoyed plenty of personal advantages from the agreement, the Iranian people had been cheated.

In January 2018, there were demonstrations against the high cost of living in the Khorasan region, on the Afghan border. At first, the police sympathized with the peasants, and the protests quickly spread to a third of the country, and took an anti-government turn. Heavy repression was then visited on the people. Persuaded that the "colour revolution" of 2009 was starting up again, the West gave its unconditional support to the demonstrators. However, unlike the movements of 2009, this time it was the country people who were denouncing the bourgeoisie of Teheran and Ispahan. Finally, President Rouhani put his predecessor, Mahmud Ahmadinejad, under house arrest. The Western Press made no mention of this and changed the subject.

In the Western imagination, Iran is an absolute enemy. And yet it was the men of the Rafsanjani clan who participated alongside Israel in the Iran-Contras operation against the Revolutionaries of Central America, and the same men who sent the Guardians of the Revolution to die alongside the United States and Saudi Arabia in Bosnia-Herzegovina, and once again, it is they who secretly manage, with the Israeli state, the company EAPC, which has the Eliat-Ashkelon pipeline.

The Israeli-Saudi tandem

Washington played with the power rivalries in Iran while controlling the way in which Teheran and Tel-Aviv should supervise the Arabs on its behalf – a situation which was all the more improbable since for close to 70 years, the Arabs, and then the Iranians, had openly refused to speak to the Israelis as long as they refused to recognise the inalienable rights of the Palestinian people, and also because since 1978, Iran and Israel had been provoking one another.

Israel is a colony created by British Prime Minister David Lloyd George and US President Woodrow Wilson in 1917, in the wake of the Sykes-Picot-Sazonov agreements (Great Britain, France, Russia). In 1948, although it was about to be recognised by the international community, this colony seceded from the United Kingdom and proclaimed itself independent. The Arab and Muslim countries attempted to oppose this, but as yet had practically no armies, and were easily repelled.

David Ben Gurion, the Commander-in-Chief of the Jewish army (Tsahal), and the founding fathers of Israel, terrorised and expelled a large majority of the native population. This is remembered by the Arabs as the "Nakba" or Catastrophe. Conceiving of themselves as a colony of European Jews awash in an ocean of hostile Arabs, the Zionists imagined a defense policy based on the creation of neutral zones on their frontiers, but in "enemy" territory, which of course strategically "extended" their own territory. Concerning their foreign policy, they adopted the "Periphery Doctrine" according to which they attempted to unify the non-Arab actors in the region (Iran, Turkey, Ethiopia) against the Arab countries. Besides this, they sought to conclude new alliances, which, since there was nothing better on the menu, drew them closer to colonial France (during the Algerian war), and then to apartheid South Africa.

With the development of missile technology, it became less important to occupy buffer zones on neighbouring lands, such as the Egyptian Sinai, South Lebanon and the Syrian Golan. After having made peace with Egypt, Israel withdrew from Lebanon in 2000 (excepting the Shebaa farms), but not from Syria. Indeed, the Golan plateau, apart from being an important water source, is also a strategic promontory. Simultaneously, Israel promoted the creation of two new states which enabled it to take its two powerful neighbours, Syria and Egypt, in a stranglehold – in 2003, it helped to create Iraqi Kurdistan around the Barzani family, who had been working for Mossad since the Cold War – and in 2011, Israel helped to create Southern Sudan.

Progressively, Israel – that is to say the State of the Jewish army – acquired a military expertise which they sometimes rented out to the highest bidder, and sometimes offered for use by Anglo-Saxon parents. It received US-French nuclear technology during the 1950's, and tested the atomic bomb in South Africa. It developed a chemical and biological arsenal, going so far as to carry out research on selective weapons which would kill only black people and Arabs (programme by Dr. Wouter Basson).

Israel is probably the only state in the world to have signed neither the Biological Weapons Convention, nor the Treaty on the Non-Proliferation of Nuclear Weapons. It shelters the arsenal of the United States in the Near East (sites 51, 53, 54, 55 & 56), and participates in many US operations, not only in the Near East, but around the world. Thus, most recently, Israel took charge of Security for the Olympic Games in Rio de Janeiro (2016). The Hebrew state coordinated all the security forces in the country, and was therefore able to supervise the demonstrations against President Dilma Rousseff. The Parliament impeached and dismissed her, sparking a hurricane of Israeli flags, and the Lebanese Michel Temer took her place.

Over the last few years, a fracture has appeared in the Arab world between the monarchies and the republics – the ruling families seem increasingly illegitimate, considering the differences between their life-style and that of their populations. Israel has therefore given up the "Periphery Doctrine" in order to draw closer to the most powerful Arab monarchy, Saudi Arabia. Step by step, Israel has solicited the Saudis for help facing their common adversary, Iran. Riyadh paid for the Israeli aggression against the faction of Hamas which is linked to Teheran, at Christmas 2008, known as Operation Cast Lead. This operation was supervised by NATO by virtue of the cooperation agreement signed on 2 December 2008.

A decisive step was taken in November 2013, after the election of the new Iranian President, and with the revelations about the secret negotiations that Rouhani had been pursuing with Washington for six months. There was no time to lose – Teheran wanted to re-occupy its old post as the "the policeman of the Middle East".

The US "Continuity of Government" – via Jeffrey Feltman at the UN – organised a meeting in Abu Dhabi for the Foreign Ministers of 29 of the 57 member-states of the Organisation of Islamic Cooperation. The "Continuity of Government" was represented by the Norwegian Terje Rød-Larsen, and the Obama administration by ambassador Martin Indyk (with close ties to Qatar). The Israeli President, Shimon Peres, spoke at length to the participants by video-conference, and was applauded. The Israelo-Arab conflict, at that time 65 years old, had just ended, leaving the Palestinians to their fate.

Negotiations therefore began, not to bring Tel-Aviv and Riyadh closer together – that job had already been done – but to elaborate a common strategy. Top-level delegations met five times, in India, Italy and the Czech Republic. The Israeli side was steered by Dore Gold, Central Director of the Ministry for Foreign Affairs, and for Saudi Arabia by General Anwar Eshki, ex-assistant of Prince Bandar Ben Sultan.

An agreement was concluded

At the political level –

▶ to "democratise" the Gulf states, in other words, to associate the People with the management of their country while safeguarding the monarchy and the Wahhabi way of life;

▶ to change the political system in Iran (rather than making war against Iran);

▶ to create an independent Kurdistan on the basis of the current Iraqi Kurdistan, augmented by a Syrian Kurdistan still to be created, in such a way as to weaken Iran, Turkey and Iraq.

At the economic level –

▶ to exploit the Rub'al-Khali oil field and organise a federation between Saudi Arabia, Yemen, and perhaps even Oman and the United Arab Emirates;

▶ to exploit the oil fields of Ogaden, under Ethiopian control, to secure the port of Aden in Yemen, and to build a bridge linking Djibouti and Yemen.

Given these conditions, President Obama's National Security Doctrine, published on 6 February 2015, specifies – "Long-term stability [in the Middle East and North Africa] requires more than the use and presence of US military force. It demands that the partners involved must be capable of defending themselves. That is why we are investing in the capacity of Israel, Jordan and our partners in the Gulf to discourage aggression while maintaining our unwavering engagement to the security of Israel, including by its qualitative military advancement".

So the Pentagon's strategy consisted of creating a modern version of the Baghdad Pact – an Arab NATO.

In this way, the US could withdraw its military forces from the Middle East and North Africa, and reposition them in the Far East (the "pivot" to Asia).

The Pentagon's idea envisages a "Common Arab Defence Force", composed of the Gulf States and Jordan, and placed under Israeli command. To return to the example of the Baghdad Pact, we remember that it was created by the United Kingdom with its old colonies. However, after three years, its military Staff was placed under command of the Pentagon, even though the United States had never participated in the Pact.

According to the Stockholm International Peace Research Institute, Saudi Arabia had prepared for the creation of this "Common Arab Defence Force" by increasing its military budget in 2014 by $13 billion (+17%). In order to overcome the reluctance of Egypt, the Gulf Cooperation Council offered Egypt $12 billion for its investment projects. Finally, the Arab League announced the creation of the Common Arab Defence Force during the summit conference at Sharm el-Sheikh, on 1 April 2015. Officially, its intention was to apply the Arab Defence Treaty of 1950 to fight terrorism – sixty-five years late.

In application of the Israelo-Saudi agreement, and in view of the Yemeni refusal to share the oil fields of Rub'al-Khali with the Saudis, and contrary to all expectations, a common Israelo-Arab military staff was assembled in Somaliland to attack Yemen.

Somaliland, which proclaimed its independence in 1960, was first annexed to Somalia after a coup d'état in 1969. It proclaimed its independence for the second time in 1991, before being annexed once by Somalia in 1994, and then proclaimed its independence for the third time in 2002. During its first two independences, Israel was the first state to recognise Somaliland. Today it is not recognised by any state, but since 2010, it has become an Israeli base controlling the Bab el-Mandeb straits, which link the Suez Canal and the Red Sea to the Gulf of Aden and the Indian Ocean.

Although Tel-Aviv and Riyadh were both fighting the war against Yemen, their diplomatic relations had still not been officially established. Prince Walid Ben Talal (owner of the fifth largest world fortune with Citigroup, Mövenpick, Four Seasons) was the first Saudi ambassador in Tel-Aviv. On the side, he has been financing the TV channels of the Muslim Brotherhood since the 1980's. Meanwhile, diplomatic relations between the Gulf Cooperation Council and Israel were enabled via Abu Dhabi, where Dore Gold was setting up an official representation for the Hebrew state with the International Renewable Energy Agency (Irena). Curiously enough, Israel is the only state which has a permanent representation with this tiny UN agency.

In May 2015, Saudi Arabia used several tactical atomic bombs in Yemen. They had probably been bought from Israel – in private, by the royal family. One should not forget that Saudi Arabia is the private property of the Saud family, much like the former Congo of

King Leopold II. This transfer of weapons irritated the Obama administration, and in particular Secretary of State John Kerry, who reminded Arabia that it must also respect the Non-Proliferation Treaty. Unfortunately, the sale did not violate the Treaty, which had not foreseen the possibility of a private market for this type of weapon. The sale by Israel did not violate the Treaty either, because the Hebrew state had never signed it.

In any case, the strategic regional balance was upset. While the West persisted in accusing Iran of seeking to re-start its research on the atom, a second nuclear power had been born. In reality, however, since tactical nuclear bombs are much more difficult to maintain than strategic bombs, and since the Saudis do not have the adequate scientific personnel, Arabia remains dependent on Israeli engineers, and therefore can not plan to use these bombs against Tel-Aviv.

Contrary to its public declarations, not only did Washington not disapprove of the acquisition of the bomb by the Sauds, but it also authorised Israel to move into permanent offices in NATO headquarters – next to Turkey's offices – on 4 May 2016.

Still in 2016, Saudi Arabia and Egypt concocted a plan which would allow Riyadh to accept the Camp David peace agreements long after their initial signing – the agreement that Anwar el-Sadat and Menachem Begin had concluded to the detriment of the Palestinians. Cairo announced that it would give back to Riyadh the islands of Tiran and Sanafir (in the inlet of the Red Sea which separates the Sinai from Arabia). Straight-faced, the Egyptian administration affirmed that these territories were historically Saudi, and had been lent to Egypt many years ago. In reality, the islands have been Egyptian since the Convention of London in 1840. In any case, by accepting them, Arabia would be obliged to respect the free circulation of Israeli ships in this part of the sea, as agreed at Camp David, thereby recognising the said agreements, and also institute diplomatic relations with Tel-Aviv. Egyptian nationalists – probably supported in secret by President al-Sisi – opposed the transfer, which was held up for months by a tribunal, but Sisi eventually signed the deal in June 2017.

Also in 2017, President Donald Trump tasked his Jewish son-in-law, Jared Kushner, with reforming Saudi Arabia and finding a solution for the Israeli-Palestinian conflict. The young man was given total latitude and was not expected to report to the Secretary of State, who knew nothing about these initiatives. Contrary to the rules of US diplomacy, no account of these negotiations was recorded.

Kushner managed to convince King Salman that Washington would support a change from the system of Adelphic succession (from brother to brother) to filial succession (from father to son). The Trump administration would aid the King's beloved son, Crown Prince Mohammad Bin Salman Al Saud (nicknamed MBS), to accede to the throne if Riyadh would agree to cease its support for the Muslim Brotherhood.

On 22 May, Donald Trump journeyed to Riyadh to meet the heads of State and governments of the Muslim world. He demanded that they cease all support for terrorists. Only Qatar refused. Turkey and Sheikh Rouhani's Iran, who were absent from the meeting, sided with Doha. Immediately, Saudi Arabia and its allies attempted to suffocate Qatar by closing their frontiers and denying their air and maritime routes to the aircraft and ships going to and from to the little State.

On 4 November, King Salman organised a palace coup. He ordered the arrest, by US mercenaries of Academi, of 1,300 Princes and personalities from other clans, demanding that each of them hand over the greater part of their fortunes to the kingdom. Within three days, he had gathered $800 billion. The kingdom's finances, which had been in the red since the drop in the price of oil, were suddenly very comfortably back in the black. In the West, stupefied, we contemplated the disappearance of large numbers of the richest men on the planet. Yet no one complained when old men were assassinated or hung by their feet and tortured until they gave up their bank details. On the contrary, the Press celebrated the supposed merits of MBS, the new strong man of Saudi Arabia.

In passing, the palace coup included the arrest of the Lebanese Prime Minister, Saad Hariri. Passed off as the biological son of Rafic Hariri, he is in reality a bastard son of the Fadh clan, and as such, had to be submitted to the same treatment as his biological half-brothers. However, his political adversary in Lebanon, Sayyed Hassan Nasrallah, Secretary General of Hezbollah, contested the detention of Hariri and Saudi interference into Lebanese political life. Since Saad Hariri enjoyed triple nationality (French-Lebanese-Saudi), French President Emmanuel Macron demanded his liberation. He was shown the door. Lebanese President Michel Aoun refused to accept the resignation of his Prime Minister being announced from Riyadh, and demanded Hariri's return to Beirut. *Considering that, of course, diplomatic immunity can not be granted in any of these countries to a multi-national,* but that arresting a sitting Prime Minister is an act of war, he prepared referrals to the Permanent Court of Arbitration in the Hague and the UN Security Council. MBS surrendered and Saad Hariri was freed. This episode reversed the alliances in Lebanon, and Hariri's Future Movement moved away from Saudi Arabia and drew closer to Hezbollah and President Aoun's Free Patriotic Movement.

Simultaneously, Jared Kushner was attempting to solve the Palestinian conundrum. He noted that the Palestinians no longer have leaders to continue their struggle. The PLO has discredited itself by successively attempting to create a Palestinian State in Jordan, Lebanon and Tunisia. Hamas has also discredited itself by participating openly in the war against Syria, and by carrying out operations alongside Al-Qaeda and Mossad. Only the FPLP (Popular Front for the Liberation of Palestine) can still lay valid claim to an egalitarian Palestine for both Jews and Arabs, but it has a minimal audience. Kushner therefore envisaged halting the daily nibbling away of Palestinian territory by Israel, and recognising – at last – clear frontiers for the Hebrew State. He proposed to base his plan on the reality of the current sharing of the territory. President Trump announced that "Jerusalem" (West Jerusalem, or the whole city) is the capital of Israel, and prepared to announce that only the neighbourhood quarter of Abu Dis, still inhabited by the Palestinians in Jerusalem-East, may become the *capital* of Palestine. This caused an immediate and general international outcry. The US ambassador to the Security Council had to use her veto to prevent the condemnation of her country, but the General Assembly of the UN pronounced against the declaration of President Trump. So the war must continue. Humiliated, the United States cut off part of their financial aid to the UNRWA (United Nations Relief and Works Agency for Palestine Refugees), the United Nations agency for support for Palestinian refugees.

Qatar's opportunism

Another regional uncertainty – Qatar. Small, wealthy, and ambitious.

Shortly after Qatar's declaration of independence from the United Kingdom, in 1971, Prince Khalifa al-Thani overthrew the puppet ruler that the English had placed in power. Relying on French support, he surrounded himself with his family and set up a social régime. Conscious of the treasure that was there underground, he decided not to cause trouble for his community, and managed his wealth like a good father. Nevertheless, in 1995, he was overthrown by his son, Prince Hamad ben Khalifa and his cousin and evil genius, Prince Hamad ben Jassem. The betrayed sovereign settled in exile in Switzerland, under the protection of Capitaine Paul Barril, ex-head of security for President François Mitterrand.

The new tandem was unable to resist the lure of lucre, and entrusted the exploitation of the gas fields to ExxonMobil, the Rockefeller company. The multinational built gigantic infrastructures, and paid enormous royalty sums to the Emirate, which became the fourth world exporter of gas. In practice, the micro-state had handed over its foreign policy to the Rockefellers, while the princely family did everything it could to waste this incredible and universally unprecedented influx of cash as fast as possible.

In 1996, Emir Hamad accepted the proposal of the Frydman brothers and approved the creation of the pan-Arab TV channel al-Jazeera, which made a place for itself in the Arab-Israeli dialogue engaged by Yitzhak Rabin and Yasser Arafat. In 2003, the US troops based in Saudi Arabia (Prince Sultan Air Base) bought a concession on part of the Qatari desert (al-Udeid Air Base). The Emirate became the headquarters of CentCom during the war against Iraq. In 2005, the Emir and his television channel Al Jazeera joined the Anglo-Saxon programme for the preparation of the "Arab Spring". In 2006, he visited the Palestinian territories and launched a vast programme of rebuilding, including numerous Wahhabi mosques. In 2007, he was seen out and about in New York with the Israeli Prime Minister, Tzipi Livni.

Everything can be bought, everything can be sold. However, this kind of behaviour is not without certain risks. One morning, the Emir was awakened by Marines in his bedroom. They declared that they were there to protect him from a non-existent attempted coup d'état. The message was clear – from now on, the Emir was the hostage of his guests.

Qatar, with Saudi Arabia and the Emirate of Sharjah (UAE) is one of the three Wahhabi states. In theory, they are bound to show their respect for the King of Arabia, the Guardian of the Holy Places. In practice, he was tough competition. Doha's sudden prosperity had upset the balance of the Gulf region.

Backed by London, Washington and Tel-Aviv, the Hamad Princes paid huge amounts of money to acquire international respectability. They invested overseas, not for future revenue, but to extend their influence. In 2004, they participated in negotiations which ended with an agreement to create South Sudan. In 2008, Emir Hamad al-Thani sponsored the Doha agreement between the Saudis (represented by Saad Hariri) and Hezbollah, and then inaugurated the new Lebanese President. He also consolidated personal relationships with Nicolas Sarkozy and his wife Carla Bruni.

From the very start of the Arab Spring, on the first day of the first events in Tunisia, at the end of 2010, al-Jazeera took the side of the crowd, and called for the overthrow of Zine el-Abidine Ben Ali. The TV channel, which at that time enjoyed a very favourable image in the Arab world, also promoted "régime changes" in Egypt, Libya, Yemen and Syria. Unhesitatingly, it claimed to be on the side of democracy. And yet the Emirate is a dictatorship which practices slavery, never holds elections, and imprisons its political opponents, including the poet Mohammed al-Ajami.

In 2011, Qatar raised an army of 5,000 mercenaries to be its Special Forces. He sent them to Libya. The Emir hoped to overthrow Muammar Gaddafi during the month of Ramadan, just as, long ago, the prophet Muhammad had vanquished the Quraysh at the battle of Badr. His men, all dressed in black, wore face masks to hide their origins. They participated in the taking of Tripoli, together with NATO troops. In May 2012, the Emir failed to organise a colour revolution in Kuwait. However, the rigged election of Mohamed Morsi in Egypt was a benediction for him. He believed he would now be able to buy the Suez Canal and seek rapprochement with Turkey. Following the attack on Saudi Prince Bandar Bin Sultan, on 26 July 2012, Qatar pitched in at supervising the Muslim Brotherhood and their numerous jihadist groups. Developing his ambitions, the Emir incorporated units from the Tunisian army into his Forces. In 2013, he financed the Likud party electoral campaign of Benjamin Netanyahu ($3 million) and the Yisrael Beiteinu party of Avigdor Lieberman ($1.5 million).

In June 2013, Moscow informed Washington that Qatar was speculating against it on the Stock Market. Without hesitation,

President Obama ordered the Emir to hand power over to his son Tamim. Prime Minister Hamad Ben Jassem was thrown out, along with his master, Emir Hamad al-Thani. The Emir also had to give up the directorship of the Qatar Investment Authority. He withdrew by investing in the Brookings Institution, the most prestigious think tank in the United States, which became a mouthpiece for Qatar and the Muslim Brotherhood.[49] At the same moment, the Egyptian army ousted Mohamed Morsi. The tide was turning.

Saudi Arabia took over from Qatar as Egypt's sponsor. The rivalry between the two Wahhabi states turned into a secret war. They organised terrorist attacks against one another. The balance of power quickly turned to the advantage of Riyadh, and Doha submitted.

The new Emir, Tamim ben Hamad, took no political initiatives, and behaved like a faithful servant of Washington. A training camp for mercenaries destined for the Free Syrian Army was opened by the CIA in the Emirate. The Qatari Minister for Defence organised the buying and transfer of Ukrainian air defence systems (Pechora 2D) to the Muslim Brotherhood in Syria, via Bulgaria and Turkey. In 2015, the same Minister bought 2,000 fragmentation bombs (OFAB 250-270), again from Ukraine, for three times their real price. The idea was to fire them from Coalition aircraft on the armed groups in Syria, and to pretend that Russia was responsible, since it sometimes used the same bombs. But the affair was leaked, and the operation in progress was cancelled.

The self-indulgent spending of the Hamad Princes only lasted for two decades.

Qatar's erratic ambitions ceased with the election of Donald Trump in the United States. Moscow sold 19.5% of the largest company in the world, Rosneft, to Qatar, either directly or indirectly via Glencore. Consequently, as from that moment, the investments of the Emirate were linked to those of Russia, when until that time they had been adversaries in Syria. Simultaneously, although the Rockefellers were selling their stake in Exxon-Mobil – which more or less owns

---

[49] See "Qatar's Insidious Influence on the Brookings Institution," Investigative Project on Terrorism, Oct. 28, 2014,
https://www.investigativeproject.org/4630/ipt-exclusive-qatar-insidious-influence-on

the Emirate – its Director Rex Tillerson also left the company to become the US Secretary of State.

In May 2017, when Qatar disobeyed the order from Washington to cease funding terrorism, the Emirate was attacked by its Saudi neighbour, which at first attempted to lay siege to Qatar and prevail by starvation. Doha then turned to Turkey and received the unexpected support of Iran. With the help of the United Kingdom, Doha also managed to admit Malaysia and Sudan into this new alliance.

The instability of Turkey and Ukraine

An inheritor of the Ottoman Empire, Turkey lives with three political traditions – that of the Turko-Mongol invaders who swept in successive waves through India, the Near East and Europe; that of Islam, to which they converted; and that of the pro-Western reformer Mustafa Kemal. This inheritance is all the more oppressive because when the Ottoman Empire came to an end in the First World War, this "Sick Man of Europe" was drowning in a quicksand of problems – bureaucracy, corruption, stagnation, the complete absence of education of the masses, both an excess of authority where authority existed, and a great weakness elsewhere, the organised genocide of the Christian populations, mainly Armenian, etc.

In 2002, the Islamic Party for Justice and Development (AKP) won the legislative elections. The AKP was directed by Recep Tayyip Erdoğan, who very quickly became Prime Minister. Supervised by his US advisors, he carefully avoided doing anything about his plan for society, but concentrated on economic development. With the help of Washington, he achieved some magnificent results. Turkey showed a two-figure economic growth rate.

But Erdoğan is not really a politician *per se*. He's an ex-hooligan who left the streets for a violent militant group, the Millî Görüş. The group had been created by the Iraqi Order of the Naqshbandis, under the direction of the ex-Turkish Prime Minister, Islamist Necmettin Erbakan. For many years, Erdoğan participated in the support for the jihadists fighting in the Caucasus, who found Istanbul to be a very comfortable rear base. This secret war was organised by the CIA and financed by Saudi Arabia via the Muslim World League. It caused terrible damage in Russia. Erdoğan was arrested in 1997, and sentenced to 10 months in prison while his group was preparing a coup d'état. When he finished serving his sentence, he declared that he had been "transformed" during his detention. He announced that he was giving up violence, founded the AKP and, with a little help, won a very relative majority in the legislative elections.

His economic success awoke his deeper ambitions. In 2003, he brought into his cabinet Professor Ahmet Davutoğlu, disciple of the Greek strategist Dimitri Kitsikis. According to Kitsikis, it would be possible to create a 17th Turko-Mongol Empire, first of all by re-building diplomatic relations with the neighbouring states ("zero problem with our neighbours"), then by supporting Islam in their countries in order to unify them. This is "neo-Ottomanism".

Everything began in 2009, when Davutoğlu became Minister for Foreign Affairs. Breaking off the traditional alliance of his country with Israel and its the "Periphery Doctrine", he flattered the Arabs by taking up the cause of the Palestinians with Shimon Peres at the Davos Forum. Then, with the help of Washington, which was becoming increasingly tired of the arrogance of Prime Minister Benjamin Netanyahu, he organised the Freedom Flotilla in order to force the blockade of Gaza. Convinced that the flagship was sailing under a flag of convenience, Israel attacked in international waters. However, unknown to Israel, the cruise ship, the *Mavi Marmara*, belonged to a member state of NATO, and had changed flags during the journey.

During 2010-11, France invited Turkey to join the operations that it was preparing with the United Kingdom against Libya and Syria. Alain Juppé and Ahmet Davutoğlu concluded a secret agreement which would allow the mobilisation of the Misrata tribe in Libya and the Turkmen minority in Syria, in exchange for a solution to the Kurdish problem. This was a serious error – Libya was Turkey's major client, and a common market had just been instituted between Ankara, Teheran and Damascus. Erdoğan's entry into war against his commercial partners seriously damaged Turkey's flowering economy, until it sank into recession in 2015.

The Turkish secret services organised the pillage of 80,000 Syrian factories without raising any protest from its Western allies. The machine-tools were dismantled and transferred to Turkey, and the Erdoğan family got richer by the second. In order to send him a warning, the CIA organised the protest movement in Gezi Park, in

May and June 2013. Worried by this demonstration, the "new Sultan" cooled down.

In December 2013, Turkey participated in the demonstrations on Maidan Square in Kiev. It repatriated the Tatar jihadists – a Turkish people from the Volga – who handled the security services for the Ukrainian demonstrators in the name of "the Great Turkey". On-site, the situation was extremely confused – although the Ukrainians were demonstrating in favour of signing an agreement with the European Union, they were supervised by armed militants from Nazi groups, who were themselves supervised by Israeli officers – as had been the case in Georgia in 2003 and 2008. They denounced President Viktor Yanukovych – an ex-Soviet apparatchik – whom they accused of being pro-Russian. Senator John McCain held a meeting with them, while one of the women of 9/11, assistant to Hillary Clinton and ex-ambassador to NATO Victoria Nuland-Kagan, (who had saved Israel from a high-visibility defeat against Hezbollah), distributed sandwiches and drinks to the demonstrators. Finally, Yanukovych fled to Russia, where he was offered a chilly reception. The Nazis invaded the Rada (Parliament) which adopted, under threat, various measures for changing the régime. On 21 February 2014, the putsch was recognized by the European Union and the Russian Federation.

During a telephone conversation with the United States ambassador in Kiev, leaked by members of the Ukrainian secret services opposed to the coup d'état, Victoria Nuland-Kagan revealed that Jeffrey Feltman had a man in place at the UN to cover for the coup, and that the aim was for Washington to control the Ukraine, and … to "f*** the European Union". (sic)

From the very first days of the coup, protests against NATO's New European Order in Ukraine were brutally quashed. The ex-chief of Polish security, Jerzy Dziewulski, directed the repression of the resistance by mercenary special forces.[50]

The new Ukrainian National Security Advisor, Dmytro Yarosh, was the leader of Stepan Bandera Tryzub (Trident) and Pravy Sektor ("The Right Wing"), two organisations which claim to have their roots in Nazism. In a fake video, widely distributed by Western televisions as if it were authentic witness testimony, he played the

---

[50] See Korybko, "Sikorski and Dziewulski: The Strategy and Tactics of the Neo-Commonwealth," http://www.voltairenet.org/article184283.html

part of a poor demonstrator that the police had dragged out into the snow to be beaten and humiliated. Above all, on 8 May 2007, the anniversary of the Nazi defeat in 1945, Yarosh he created a so-called Anti-Imperialist Front in Ternopol, Western Ukraine, in order to fight against Russia. In attendance were various anti-Russian figures from Eastern Europe, along with Islamic separatists from the Caucasus. Dokka Umarov – President of the "Republic of Ichkeria" (Chechnya) and the "Emir of the Caucasus" – who had fought together with Yarosh in Chechnya, could not make it as he was listed as an international terrorist, so he had his speech read for him.

The inhabitants of Crimea rejected the coup d'état in Kiev and the new government which included the Nazis. They voted in a referendum with a majority of at 96,7% to rejoin the Federation of Russia, which welcomed them with open arms. For Moscow, it was an honourable return of its children to the motherland. Indeed, Crimea is historically Russian, since its conquest by Tsarina Catherine II during her expedition to Syria. It was only redistricted to Ukraine in 1954 by Nikita Khrushchev, for the sole purpose of facilitating administrative tasks in the digging of a navigation canal. Above all, Crimea includes the port of Sebastopol, which harbours the Russian fleet in the Black Sea. Without Crimea, this sea would have fallen under the control of Turkey, in other words, NATO. Immediately, the member states of the Atlantic Alliance reacted by levying a series of economic sanctions against Russia, whom they accused of having taken Crimea by force.

The Russian-speaking Donbass region in Eastern Ukraine also rose up against the Nazis, but for Moscow, this region is less important than Crimea. A Russian Orthodox oligarch took over the Resistance, and proclaimed two independent Republics, Donetsk and Luhansk. However, the Kremlin was not happy with the idea of a billionaire running the two states. Vladimir Putin therefore asked the benefactor to withdraw. Donetsk and Luhansk were left to build their own networks abroad, while Ukrainian shells rained down on their civilian population.

The new Ukrainian régime was soon headed by Petro Poroshenko, who rose to the title of "Chocolate King" by privatizing Ukraine's sweets industry during the 1990's. This billionaire, with Viktor Pinchuk – a friend of Hillary Clinton – had played an important role during the colour revolution of 2004. He had been President Viktor

Yushchenko's campaign director. He was the son of a Nazi extermination camp guard, and had been recruited by the NATO secret services into the Gladio network. For two years running, he nominated as his Prime Minister Arseniy Yatsenyuk, a friend of the very secretive head of the Church of Scientology, David Miscavige. Despite his denials, Yatsenyuk had apparently become one of the executives of the cult, with the rank of OT-6 (Operating Thetan Level 6).

Poroshenko and Erdoğan used the Ukrainian armament industries, inherited from the Soviet era, to equip the jihadists. Millions of tons of weapons were transported into Syria on many ships, then special trains from the MIT (Turkish secret services).

This collaboration between Nazis and jihadists was not new. It had its origins in the three Muslim divisions of the Waffen SS. The 13th division, "Handschar" was formed of Bosnians, the 21st "Skanderbeg" of Kosovars, and the 23rd "Kama" of Croatians. Most of them were members of the Naqshbandi Order. However, a majority of these combatants defected during the war against the Red Army.

Taking note of his economic shipwreck, and with some of his popular support ebbing away, Recep Tayyip Erdoğan accepted, in December 2014, a Russian proposition which Vladimir Putin came to present in person – the construction of a pipeline to export Russian gas to the European Union via Turkey.[51] In this way, Russia could avoid sanctions and the problems with gas exports via Ukraine, and Turkey would earn a bundle in transit fees. Stunned by this idea, which brought him a little fresh air, Erdoğan accepted. But it was also another grand miscalculation – nobody could be a military ally of Washington (as a NATO member) and an economic ally of Moscow at the same time.

The Alliance reacted immediately, trying to block the Russian project in the Balkans, and went so far as to attempt a coup d'état in Macedonia. Ex-officers of the Kosovo Liberation Army (UÇK), who

---

[51] This is TurkStream, currently under construction. It will be laid under the Black Sea between Russia and Turkey's European region of Thrace, near the Greek border. It replaces the SouthStream project from Russia across the Black Sea to Bulgaria, with branches through the Balkans to Austria and Italy, which was cancelled due to sanctions against Russia.

had very close ties with the US ambassador in Skopje, prepared for a sizeable armed operation, but were arrested on 9 May 2015, during a major police operation which claimed 22 dead. At the same time, Zoran Zaev's[52] Muslim Social Democrats were preparing to launch a colour revolution with the support of the embassies of Germany, Holland and the United Kingdom.

Simultaneously, NATO and the CIA financed and reorganised the Turkish opposition in order to bring about the fall of Erdoğan. Indeed, during the general elections of June 2015, the HDP, or Party of the Minorities (ethnic and social) managed to pass the 10% hurdle of registered voters and gain seats in the Grand National Assembly. Erdoğan was unable to patch together a majority to support him. He therefore dissolved the Grand Assembly and called for a new round of elections in November. This time he took no chances, and brazenly rigged both the electoral campaign and the ballot.

▶ Military conscripts, students from military schools and citizens in provisional detention were deprived of their voting rights.

▶ The opposition medias were gagged – the major dailies Hürriyet and Sabah, as well as the television channel ATV, were attacked by thugs from the party in power; journalists and Press outlets were investigated and accused of supporting terrorism or having made defamatory statements about President Erdoğan; websites were blocked; digital service providers deleted several TV channels from their offerings; three of the five national TV channels, including the public channel, were clearly favourable to the party in power; the other national TV channels, Bugün TV and Kanaltürk, were closed by the police.

▶ Saudi Arabia, donated "gifts" worth 7 billion Turkish lira to "convince" the electors to support President Erdoğan.

▶ 128 political offices of the HDP were attacked by thugs from President Erdoğan's party. Many candidates and their teams were badly beaten. More than 300 Kurdish businesses were destroyed. Several dozen HDP candidates were arrested and kept in provisional detention.

---

[52] Zaev became PM of Macedonia in 2017. He is a member of the country's large ethnic Albanian minority, and an anti-nationalist who aims for full membership in the EU and NATO.

► More than 2,000 opponents of the régime were killed, either by terror attacks, or by government repression aimed at the PKK. Several villages in the South-East of the country were partially destroyed by army tanks.

► International observers were asked to leave seven voting stations, and citizen observers accredited by the political parties were forbidden access to other polling stations.

Despite all that, the AKP only managed to get 50,81% of the votes. Inspired by the Nazi Constitution, Recep Tayyip Erdoğan announced his intention to follow that model in order to concentrate increased power into his own hands. He named as his Prime Minister one of the godfathers of the Mafia, Binali Yıldırım.

Meanwhile, the White House, for the umpteenth time, changed its position on the Kurdish question. At the end of the First World War, President Woodrow Wilson had sent experts to the Middle East to evaluate the best way of dividing up the Ottoman Empire – this was the King-Crane Commission. They confirmed the possibility of creating a Kurdistan – which was one of the war objectives of the United States in 1917 – but only on several conditions. First of all, it was planned for this new Kurdistan to occupy only a small territory within what is now Turkey (in other words, neither in Iran, nor Iraq, nor Syria). Second, it would be necessary to avoid mixing Kurds and Armenians, since the Ottomans had used Kurdish soldiers to massacre the Christians. Kurdistan was therefore created by the Treaty of Sèvres (1920). But faced with the Turkish revolt led by Mustafa Kemal, it was never actualised, and the United States gave up the idea with the Treaty of Lausanne (1923).

Washington accepted the Franco-Turkish (Juppé-Davutoğlu) project to create a Kurdistan in Syria – despite the fact that nowhere in that country was there any truly Kurdish presence – and then expel the Kurds from Turkey to this imaginary "Kurdish" homeland. They therefore supported the Syrian Kurds (who are mainly refugees from Turkey) in their fight against Damascus. However, taking into account their political and cultural differences, these Kurds refused to work with the Kurds of Iraq, and moved closer to their brothers from the Turkish PKK. By an inevitable boomerang effect, the Franco-Turkish project spun back on Turkey.

The Europeans, who had not had a Kurdish policy for many years, and who had not understood the radical change that had taken place, made two mistakes. After the battle of Ain al-Arab ("Kobane" in the Kurmandji Kurdish language), François Hollande received the co-President of the Syrian Kurds, Asya Abdullah, at the Elysée Palace. At the same time, Belgium allowed a sit-in by the Syrian Kurds in front of the offices of the European Commission. Furious at their treachery, Erdoğan ordered the attacks in Paris (13 November 2015, Bataclan Theatre) and Brussels airport (22 March 2016). They were carried out by two separate commandos, except for one member who was on both teams, Mohammed Abrini from MI6.

Seeking to develop his terrorist troops, on 1 August 2015, Erdoğan organised a Tatar World Congress in Ankara, in the presence of the Ukrainian Minister for Foreign Affairs and the Turkish Vice-President. At the congress, the creation of an International Islamic Brigade destined to take back Crimea was announced by Mustafa Dzhemilev – (Mustafa Abdülcemil Cemiloğlu in Turkish).

Mustafa Dzhemilev joined the CIA during the Cold War and was implicated in several acts of sabotage. He participated in the creation of Nazi Dmytro Yarosh's Anti-Imperialist Front. He waged a campaign so that the new "Ukrainian state would not damage Turkey's honour by recognising the Armenian genocide". In 2014, he had been awarded the Solidarność Prize, worth 1 million Euros. The award was given to him by Polish President Bronisław Komorowski, in the presence of Secretary of State John Kerry, the Ukrainian President and the Turkish Vice-Prime Minister.

The International Islamic Brigade is based in Kherson, where there was already a provisional Crimean government in exile. In order to formalise it, Vice-Prime Minister Numan Kurtulmuş led a delegation presided by Dzhemilev to meet with President Recep Tayyip Erdoğan at the White Palace.

Specialised in sabotage, the Brigade wasted no time in making a name for itself, notably by cutting off the electricity to the whole of Crimea.

Distinguishing Turkey – an indispensable ally for the United States – from its President – an unpredictable dictator – President Obama instructed the CIA to eliminate Recep Tayyip Erdoğan, just as it had poisoned President Turgut Özal in 1993.

Turkey had re-established good relations with all its neighbours in 2010, had once again managed to make enemies of them all. If bad luck runs in threes, it was now in disputes with the Europeans, the Americans and the Russians. It was now Russia's turn to express its exasperation with Turkish support for the jihadists in Syria. President Vladimir Putin openly accused Turkey during the G20 summit in Antalya. In response, on 24 November 2015, the Turkish army shot down a Russian Sukhoi-24 jet fighter which allegedly entered its airspace for 17 seconds. The two airmen ejected from the downed aircraft and landed in Syrian territory. The principal leader of the Turkmen militia, Alparslan Çelik, a member of the Grey Wolves, the Turkish neo-fascist party historically linked to the NATO secret services, gave the order to kill them both. One of the airmen was in fact killed. Furious, the Kremlin forbade all Russian businesses from continuing to trade with Turkey – a severe blow for Ankara, which suffered the loss of receipts from more than 1 million Russian tourists annually.

On 15 July 2016, a group of Kemalist soldiers, recruited by the CIA, attempted – for the third time – to assassinate Recep Tayyip Erdoğan. A commando made an assault on the hotel where he was staying during the holidays. But the plan had been leaked by Islamist soldiers who warned the secret services, and the President was evacuated in time. Perplexed, the conspirators decided risk everything and gamble on a coup d'état without any preparation. They were crushed the next morning. A vast campaign of repression fell over the country. Erdoğan decided to get rid of everyone who contested his power – first of all his old Islamist allies who were working for the CIA (Fethullah Gülen's Brotherhood), then the Kurdish combatants, and finally the Kemalist laymen who had survived the previous purges. More than 150,000 citizens were dismissed from the army and the administration, more than 50,000 were taken in for questioning and imprisoned. There were so many of them that it became necessary to liberate the ordinary prisoners in order to house them all.

As in 2014, Vladimir Putin once again held out his hand to President Erdoğan. He offered to save him and his country if he would agree to cut all links with the jihadists and accept peace with Syria. It was obviously a painfully difficult choice for Erdoğan, who came from the Islamist background himself, had accompanied its development and become its uncontested leader. He relayed his promises to Damascus and asked for time to carry out this 180 degree turn. Moscow and Teheran then organised the peace conference meetings in Astana (Kazakhstan). The Syrian government and opposition sat at the same table without speaking to one another – but the real negotiations took place between the Turks and the Syrians, who had not spoken for six years.

Recep Tayyip Erdoğan, the street hooligan, was ready to give up his dreams in order to stay in power.

He defined his new foreign policy. On 15 October 2016, he gave a speech at the inauguration of the university which bears his name (RTEÜ). He promised to honour the "national oath" sworn by the last Ottoman parliament in 1920. He claimed the territories of the North-East of Greece (Western Thrace and the islands of the Dodecanese), all of Cyprus, the North of Syria (including Idlib, Aleppo and Hassakeh), and the North of Iraq (including Mosul). Having consolidated his régime by allying himself with the nationalists of the MHP, he engaged in a new British project on the occasion of the Saudi-Qatari crisis. He sent 1,500 soldiers to Somalia and 35,000 to Qatar. He moved others to Sudan and prepared to do the same in Djibouti. Finally, he supervised the Chadian army. In January 2018, his troops invaded Northern Syria to engage the Kurdish dominated, US-backed "Syrian Democratic Forces."

Organised Migrations used as Weapons of War

The belligerent powers used population displacement throughout the war against Syria. They were putting into practice Kelly Greenhill's theories concerning "Strategic Engineered Migration as a Weapon of War". Already in 1999, the CIA had organised the displacement of more than 290,000 Kosovars from Serbia to Macedonia in just three days, before the cameras of the Western Press agencies. The point was to make the world believe that a policy of ethnic cleansing was being carried out by Slobodan Milošević's government, which would be used to justify the coming war against Yugoslavia.

At the beginning of the Syrian war, Turkey proposed to pay Syrians who sought refuge there, for however long it took to overthrow the "Alawite dictatorship". Tens of thousands of people fled the fighting, and were at first housed in refugee camps, then in towns. But Erdoğan's generosity had strings attached. He hoped to empty

Northern Syria of its population to make room for a new state, the future "Kurdistan". Then he would expel the Turkish Kurds there. Finally, he would sort through the refugees, settle the Sunnis into the areas that had been Kurdish, and send the rest back to whatever might be left of Syria. This was all right in line with the Juppé-Davutoğlu plan.

Lebanon is normally home to hundreds of thousands of Syrian migrants, most of them working in construction. With this influx, Saad Hariri with his Future Movement hoped to accomplish what his father had attempted with the Palestinians – to take in the greatest number possible of Sunni Muslims, in order to weaken Shiite influence in Lebanon. [resp. modify Lebanon's religious demographics in his favour.]

In 2012, the kingdom of Jordan tried the same thing. Today, 80% of the population is of Palestinian origin, so that the local Bedouins who exercise power are now in the extreme minority. Jordan therefore also differentiates between its new Syrian arrivals, giving preference to the Syrian Bedouins.

These three states are therefore not alarmed by the influx of population, but in fact deliberately provoke it. However, since the Syrian Arab Republic continues to resist the jihadist invasion, the situation is changing. First of all, the refugees also rally to President Bashar al-Assad, apart from those who are stationed in Jordan. Indeed, in Jordan, they are mainly parked in a gigantic camp where they are supervised by preachers from the Muslim Brotherhood. And their number is continually increasing until it has become almost unmanageable.

It was in this context that Ulrich Grillo, President of the Federation of German Industries (BDI), came up with the idea of bringing 800,000 immigrant workers to Germany, in order to develop German factories and at the same time, to sabotage the wage demands of German workers. He presented this plan at the annual meeting of the Bilderberg Group, in 2013, and then again the following year, to the Deutsche Presse-Agentur. He presented the idea not as a profit opportunity, but as an expression of European humanitarianism.

As noted by the Austrian secret services (Österreichische Abwehramt), the first agreement was concluded by the Obama administration between Turkey, the German authorities, and the

European industrial groups united around Peter Sutherland,[53] a Bilderberg administrator. The game was kick-started by NATO – for two days, they made "headline news" for the world Press with the photograph of Aylan Kurdi dead on a Turkish beach. "This child died as he and his family tried to cross the Mediterranean – we must stop this tragedy and welcome Syrian refugees into Europe".[54] The United Nations High Commissioner for Refugees (UNHCR), the Portuguese António Guterres, called for requiring all EU states to help make room for a wave of migrants – which incidentally landed him the job of Secretary General of the UN. He had just cancelled UN humanitarian aid for Syrians living in Turkey – but not for anyone else. With no means of support, they migrated to Europe *en masse*. They were joined by the Iraqi and Afghan refugees, who had been prepared for this in advance, and supervised by hundreds of humanitarian workers paid by the various associations of George Soros. Within a few days, a human tide swept across the Balkans and arrived in Berlin brandishing portraits of Chancellor Merkel. Germany, which had once expelled the Jews, was now welcoming the Syrians.

First of all supported by public opinion, this massive invasion quickly began posing serious problems for the German population. Several Bundesländer abolished the minimum wage in order to "facilitate the integration of the refugees" – a decision which was unacceptable for the workers' unions. There was widespread anger, despite attempts by Berlin to dampen the mood of its population by the extravagant publication of news items deploring xenophobic violence.

The first concrete proposal for dealing with the crisis was formulated by the Berlin think-tank European Security Initiative (ESI) in September and October 2015. The idea was to forge an agreement between the EU and Turkey to stem the flow of migrants, while at the same time organising the transfer of 500,000 more Syrian

---

[53] See Meyssan, "How the European Union is manipulating the Syrian refugees," http://www.voltairenet.org/article191568.html, May 2, 20016. Sutherland was on the Bilderberg steering committee, and honorary chairman of the Trilateral Commission, according to Wikipedia.
[54] There are indications that most of the refugees were actually economic migrants. "72 per cent of refugees and migrants arriving in Europe across the Mediterranean are men, with 13 per cent women and 15 per cent children." *The Independent* (UK) Sept. 16, 2015

refugees into the EU over the next twelve months. Turkey would agree to take back other migrants who continued to enter the EU illegally, and in exchange, Turkish citizens would no longer require visas for travel to Europe.

"This is the recognition that the Syrian crisis is indeed unique, and is creating a humanitarian crisis on a scale unlike anything Europe has known since the Second World War", trumpeted the ESI, declaring that Germany should take the initiative as a response to the military intervention of Russia in Syria.

The ESI pointed out that its plan was also intended to:

► prevent the development of the extreme right wing in Austria; the director of the think-tank, Gerald Knaus, is Austrian;

► prepare a similar operation for the 1.1 million Syrian refugees who were based in Lebanon, and who were to be sent to North America and Australia.

Apart from anything else, by proposing to send migrants back into Turkey, the ESI seemed to ignore the fact that this country was not a safe place for refugees, and that it had refused to sign the Refugee Convention of 1951.

But no matter – Turkey continued to facilitate passage to Europe until, on 17 and 18 March 2016, the European Council agreed to:

► pay Turkey 3 billion Euros annually to help it to handle its obligations, but without any mechanism for verifying the use of these funds, which, of course, would therefore be spent to continue its war against Syria;

► put an end to visa requirements for Turkish citizens entering the EU;

► speed up negotiations for Turkish membership in the Union.

The employers of German heavy industry got what they wanted – more than a million immigrants. The next problem: reuniting families, since two thirds of the refugees were young men.

During the few weeks of free transit, several European states had been playing their own tune. France, for example, whose Imprimerie Nationale had, until 2010, been printing Syrian passports, had kept the printing plates. It therefore fabricated a lot of realistic passports which it distributed, on one hand, to Lebanese citizens, and on the other, to problem immigrants from the Maghreb. France sent these people on to Germany, where they could get double the social assistance payments as in France.

For Syria, this migratory wave was a catastrophe. As is always the case in Southern countries, a part of the population dreamed of a better quality of life in Europe. Syrians joined this exodus en masse, depriving their country of the manpower it needed to defend their besieged homeland.

The plan of the US deep state against Syria

After the resignations of the head of the Arab League's observation mission, Mohammed Ahmed Mustafa al-Dabi, in early 2012, and of the negotiator for the League and the UN, Kofi Annan, in mid-2012, the United States began to follow two contradictory policies in the "Greater Middle East". On one hand, the Raven Rock Mountain "Continuity of Government" group pursued the Anglo-US plan for carving up the region under the aegis of the Muslim Brotherhood. On the other hand, the Obama administration with Secretary of State John Kerry attempted to stop the massacre and share control of the region with Russia.

Although it is currently impossible to identify with certainty those responsible for this "Continuity of Government", several personalities appear to be working with it against the White House.

From July 1, 2012 to March 28, 2018, Hillary Clinton's assistant for the Greater Middle East, Jeffrey Feltman, was Under-Secretary-General for Political Affairs at the UN. In practice, he served as the real head of the UN, since the Secretary General limits himself to delivering honeyed speeches and augmenting his own wealth, as was revealed by Inga-Britt Ahlenius, the Under-Secretary General. Tasked with producing an internal audit for the UN Office of Internal Oversight Services, she delivered a shocking report exposing Ban Ki-moon as the most corrupt man in the organisation. After which, she resigned.

Angus McKee – the MI6 agent who had conceived of the role of the Muslim Brotherhood, was named Deputy Head of Mission at the British embassy in Damascus until its closing in March 2012, after which he set up the headquarters of Her Majesty's secret services first in Beirut, then in Erbil, the capital of Iraqi Kurdistan.[55]

In 2012, Jeffrey Feltman hired Volker Perthes, director of the most powerful German think-tank, the Stiftung Wissenschaft und Politik (SWP).[56] As you may remember, in 2008, at the annual conference of the Bilderberg group, Mr. Perthes had recommended supporting the Muslim Brotherhood in order to "democratise" the Arab world. In 2010, he counselled Condoleezza Rice in her sabotage of the Iranian economy. In 2011, he published an op-ed in the New York Times mocking President al-Assad for pretending that his country was under attack. Perthes also organised the "Working Group on Economic Recovery and Development", which distributed to the member-states of the "Friends of Syria" (not!) concessions for the exploitation of Syrian gas – which had still to be captured – in exchange for their support for the overthrow of the régime. In Berlin, he organised meetings between the Syrian opposition in exile and certain Pentagon lawyers.

Feltman and Perthes drew up a document entitled "The Day After Project: Supporting a Democratic Transition in Syria", which became the programme of the Syrian "opposition".

But alongside this programme, Perthes and the Pentagon lawyers drew up a secret fifty-page document formulating the US deep state's plan, which it was Jeffrey Feltman mission to set in motion. It was composed of two recommendations, an explanatory memorandum, and nine (later eleven) appendices. This document was never published, but the Kremlin had a copy of the entire thing by the summer of 2015. It demanded the absolute and unconditional capitulation of the Syrian Arab Republic. The terms were much more drastic than those imposed at the end of the Second World War on Germany and even Japan – the two states which had been the cause of the war – while Syria was a victim of aggression. The discovery of these documents enabled Moscow to change the course of diplomatic relations.

---

[55] https://www.linkedin.com/in/angus-mckee-28b2aa11a/
[56] Meyssan, "Germany and the UN against Syria," Jan. 28, 2016, http://www.voltairenet.org/article190102.html

Since it seems to me impossible for one to understand the stakes of this war, and all that has happened since 2012, without a knowledge of these documents, here is a brief résumé:

First of all, the United Nations Security Council will supervise the negotiations between the Syrian Arab Republic and its "opposition". Then, once the Interim Agreement has been signed by both parties, a transitional régime will be set up, under the control of an International Contact Group.

The principle of this transition is simple. Once the Interim Agreement has been signed:

▶ the sovereignty of the Syrian People will be abolished;

▶ the Constitution will be repealed;

▶ the President will be dismissed (but a Vice-President will remain in charge of formal functions);

▶ the Peoples' Assembly will be dissolved;

▶ at least 120 leaders will be considered guilty and forbidden access to any political functions (this probably refers to the list of people sanctioned by the European Union);

▶ the Directorates of Military Intelligence, Political Security, and General Security will either be deprived of their commanding officers or dissolved;

▶ "political prisoners" will be freed and anti-terrorist trials will be closed down;

▶ Hezbollah and the Revolutionary Guards must withdraw.

Then, and only then, will the international community engage in the fight against terrorism.

Within a period of 2 to 3 weeks, a "Syrian Transitional Government" will be constituted, and will enjoy all political, executive, legislative and judicial powers. It will be composed of:

▶ 2/5 representatives of the Syrian Arab Republic, including members of the loyalist opposition,

▶ 2/5 representatives of the non-loyalist opposition,

▶ and 1/5 of personalities from civil society, to be chosen by the UN.

The members of this government and all other institutions:

▶ must not have belonged to any of the organisations listed as terrorists by the United Nations Security Council (that is to say, only the al-Nusra Front and Daesh).

▶ must not figure on the list of the 120 leaders ostracised.

In each institution, a minimum of 30% must be women.

Concerning the personalities chosen by the UN (which means Jeffrey Feltman himself), 2/3 of them will be proposed by the civil society, while the last third will be designated at the last moment, at random, in order to politically "re-balance" the composition of the overall "Syrian Transitional Government".

Thereafter, the "Syrian Transitional Government" will be presided over in rotation, every month, by personalities representative of the different elements composing this organisation. Decisions will be taken collectively by simple majority – meaning by the representatives of the non-loyalist opposition – except in cases concerning the minorities, which must be carried by a majority of 2/3.

The new administration should employ senior civil servants from different regions of the country, different towns and various political parties.

During the first 5 months, the "Syrian Transitional Government" will take care to eliminate the old régime, while state services (social services, electricity, water) will be managed by the administration of the Syrian Arab Republic. After this period, these senior civil servants may be fired.

The "Syrian Transitional Government" will also guarantee to re-activate the local authorities which were created by the Constitution of 2012 (although it was repealed), but which are often ineffectual.

A "Joint Military Council" will also be created, and will command both the Syrian Arab Army and the forces of the non-loyalist opposition, tasked with enforcing the cease-fire between the two parties. The composition of this Council and its functions will be determined by the "Syrian Transitional Government", in other words, by simple majority of the non-loyalist opposition.[57] Its members will

---

[57] More commonly known as jihadists or terrorists

be submitted to the same restrictions as those of the "Government". The Council will be assisted by a committee for the supervision of the cease-fire, and will report to the "Government". Since the members of the Council will not elect their President, the UN will place an international senior civil servant at its head. A UN force will contribute to the supervision of the cease-fire.

When the "Syrian Transitional Government" calls on the International Community to help it combat terrorism, it will abstain from addressing its request to the Security Council in particular, but will simply issue a general declaration.

The governments which respond to the call from the "Syrian Transitional Government" may exchange information with the Syrian Transitional Government or else directly with the "Joint Military Council". Thereafter, a Syrian National Congress will be constituted in order to designate a Committee for the Revision of the Constitution and favour a national dialogue which will serve as a basis for the work of the Committee. It will be constituted in the same proportions as the "Syrian Transitional Government". It will enjoy no power of initiative, but will discuss the texts proposed by a Commission designated by the "Government". It will enjoy no legislative power either, since this role is reserved for the "Government". (In brief, a rubber stamp parliament.)

The "Syrian Transitional Government" will rescind anti-terrorist courts – pending cases to be transferred to the ordinary courts – and will designate an Independent Commission for Transitional Justice. It will be composed of between 9 and 15 members representative of various "points of view". This Commission will propose a reform of the legal system and the procedures for judging the crimes of the Republic which will have to be approved by the "Government" or by Congress.

The regional and international actors having interests in Syria will negotiate with the "Government" the guarantees which will ensure the preservation of their interests.

At no moment do the Syrian People have anything to say about all this, since their sovereignty has been repealed. Any choices of direction have been predefined by the US "Continuity of Government".

This contemptible text needs some clarification:

► "Transition" here does not mean the passage from war to peace, but a régime change after the absolute and unconditional capitulation of the Republic.

► The designations "by mutual consent" do not mean that the candidates will be approved by both parties, but only that they do not belong either to al-Qaeda or Daesh, and that they have never been the object of US sanctions.

► The Syrian Arab Republic, which today protects more than 18 million Syrians, will have only 40% of the voices in the Government, the Congress and the Military Council. But the "non-loyalist opposition" – which, at the height of its powers, terrorised between 400,000 and 1 million Syrians – will enjoy 60% of the voices in all these instances, if we add the 20% from a civil society nominated by the UN. Since the decisions are to be finalised by simple majority, the "non-loyalist opposition" will have all the power.

► The 20% representative of the "civil society" does not designate the representatives of associations, as in French law, but the representatives of the "productive forces", that is to say, business bosses.

► Although it was decided not to reproduce the Iraqi model – management and government of the country by a private company – multinational companies would be allowed to negotiate for privileges with the government. Iraq now lives under irrevocable laws which will be valid for a century – they affect not only concessions for the exploitation of oil, but also oblige farmers to buy non-reproductive GMO seeds.

► Since the religious minorities are recognised in the new institutions, but never mentioned in the Administration, the Alawites and the Shiites may be excluded from any post of public responsibility by the Muslim Brotherhood. And even though it is unlikely that this exclusion will be applied to Christians in the near future, it would nonetheless mark the end of a six-thousand-year civilisation of tolerance and living peacefully side by side.

► The crimes committed by the "non-loyalist opposition" will never be considered as such, and never judged by regular courts, while those blamed on the 120 leaders of the Syrian Arab Republic may be tried either by a local court or an international Tribunal.

► Genuine power resides with the international Contact Group, which will supervise the work of the UN, the Syrian transitional instances, and the international Coalition, which will be tasked with fighting terrorism.

► This international Contact Group was originally intended to be the basic Group of the "Friends of Syria" (Germany, Saudi Arabia, Egypt, the United Arab Emirates, the United States, France, Italy, Jordan, Qatar, United Kingdom and Turkey).

► The international Coalition against terrorism is to be NATO, on the model of what transpired in Afghanistan and finally in Iraq. This is why the documents specify that any call for help from the transitional Government should not be addressed to the Security Council – Russia and China are thus deprived of their veto.

► In addition, since real power in Syria will fall to the Joint Military Council, it was planned to place it under the authority of a foreign personality, on the model of Kosovo. Apart from that, foreign states, particularly those of the "Contact Group", will be authorised to share their information with this foreign personality, thereby short-circuiting the "Transitional Government". This is indeed the creation of a mandate of these 11 states over Syria, as once before, when the League of Nations gave France a mandate to administer the country.

Starting in 2012, Jeffrey Feltman tried to carry out this plan, which at least spares the reader hypocritical drivel about a "revolution", or an "Arab Spring", but simply sets out what they will do after NATO defeats Syria with the weapons of proxy terrorism.

Feltman relied on the UN and Special Envoys to Syria. This was the Algerian Lakhdar Brahimi, until he was succeeded in 2014 at Feltman's request by his friend, the Italian Staffan de Mistura.[58] But Syria obtained a copy of the Feltman-Perthes "Day After" plan, and in summer 2015, Damascus asked Mistura to explain. He swore that the text was now out of date, and was made to sign a statement promising that he would no longer attempt to implement it. After this disgrace he was no longer in the loop – Kerry and Lavrov took the reins.

---

[58] Meyssan, "Two thorns in Obama's side," Sep. 1, 2015, http://www.voltairenet.org/article188577.html

The myth of international justice

The Feltman plan did not stop at annulling the sovereignty of the Syrian People – the US "Continuity of Government" hoped to crown itself with triumph, in the ancient and absolute sense of conquest. It would take the spoils of victory with a judgement comparable to those of Nuremberg and Tokyo at the end of the Second World War, and to condemn the 120 leaders who resisted.

This obsession goes far beyond anti-Syrian propaganda. It is a way of affirming its victory and crushing the enemy. Already, after the assassination of Rafic Hariri – committed under the authority of Jeffrey Feltman, then ambassador in Beirut – a special Tribunal was set up by the Secretary General of the UN and the Lebanese Prime Minister. Its purpose was to blame the crime on Presidents Emile Lahoud and Bashar al-Assad.

Although it would have been competent had it been activated by the Security Council, the brand-new International Criminal Court was nonetheless rejected, because the United States were not yet sure how to make it work for them. Moreover, the accusations against the Lebanese and Syrian Presidents had to be abandoned it was revealed that false witness statements had been used against them. However, the special Tribunal still exists. It has only two cases to its credit so far – it returned a guilty verdict against the daily newspaper *al-Akhbar* and its investigative journalist, Ibrahim al-Amin – for exposing foul play by magistrates.

The idea of creating a special Tribunal for Syria must be likened to the attempt to judge President Vladimir Putin, first of all for having defeated the Islamic Emirate of Ichkeria (Chechnya), then, more recently, for having opposed the coup d'etat in Kiev. This was why Washington fudged the evidence on the shootdown of commercial flight MH17 in Ukraine, then attempted to force through Security Council Resolution which would allow the "trial" of the crime's authors. A prosecuting Committee was intended to accuse Vladimir Putin of having given the order to shoot down the plane and kill the passengers, and an international tribunal would be set up to find him guilty. Moscow used its veto on July 29, 2015.

Against powers that resist, like Lebanon, Syria and Russia, first they decide on the guilty parties, then forage around to see if anything can be trumped up to find them guilty.

The hatred against Presidents Vladimir Putin and Bashar al-Assad should be likened to the way in which President Slobodan Milošević was assassinated in his cell in Holland, the way in which President Saddam Hussein was deprived of his right to a defence and then hanged in Iraq, and the way in which the Guide Muammar el-Gaddafi was tortured and lynched in Libya.

Over the last few years, the US "Continuity of Government" has first of all created its own jurisdiction, the special Tribunal for Iraq, via its own private company, the Coalition Provisional Authority (CPA). 36 tonnes of prosecution documents were collated by the FBI. No one has ever had the opportunity to read them, especially not the accused. Four judges were fired during the trial, accused of being too lenient, and three of President Hussein's lawyers were assassinated, one after the other. The sessions were broadcast live on television, but whenever the accused was speaking, the audio track was missing. In the absence of a fair trial, we will never know if he was actually guilty of anything. But no surprise, once the parody was over, he was condemned to death and executed.

During the aggression against Libya, the prosecutor of the International Criminal Court consumed major resources in investigations to document the "crimes of the dictator", but completely ignored what he had done for his country. In practice, the prosecutor never questioned people who claimed to be victims of the accused, but merely collected articles from the Anglo-Saxon press, most of them inspired by MI6. It was therefore exclusively on the basis of this propaganda that he demanded the arrest of the accused. Since Muammar el-Gaddafi was assassinated, he never had the benefit of a fair trial, and so we will never know if he was guilty of anything, but we will keep in mind the imaginary crimes of which prosecutor Luis Moreno Ocampo accused him.

The ICC discredited itself when Moreno Ocampo tried to help NATO by pretending, in the middle of the battle of Tripoli, that he had Saif el-Islam Gaddafi under lock and key. A dozen states refused to apply the ICC's arrest warrants. Four of them announced that they wanted to withdraw their membership, and Russia didn't want to hear any more about it.

Concerning President Bashar al-Assad and his 119 future co-accused, the US "Continuity of Government", via the "Friends of Syria", founded an agency on April Fools Day 2012, with the mission of fabricating proof of their guilt. This is the "Syria Justice and Accountability Centre" (SJAC). Registered as a NGO in Holland and the United States, it is financed by the coalition states. This NGO is in reality an excrescence of the "Office of Global Criminal Justice" (sic) of the US State Department.

Its first grand operation was to create the Caesar Files, via Qatar and the British law firm Carter-Ruck – 55,000 photographs from the Syrian Minister for Defence, documenting crimes committed by the jihadists but for which the "Office of Global Criminal Justice" blamed Damascus. Thus we were introduced to regime torturers who themselves painstakingly photographed their crimes, yet forgetting to note the identity of their victims.

In an attempt to make this accusation more or less credible, Carter-Ruck solicited three ex-international lawyers. Problem – each of them had a very murky past. The first, Sir Desmond Lorenz de Silva, was a British lawyer who had been the prosecutor during the trial of Charles Taylor, ex-President of Liberia. But he had often worked in secret for David Cameron's government, notably in the affair of the MI5 assassination of Irish leader Pat Finucane, where he covered up the identity of the policemen involved. The second expert, Sir Geoffrey Nice, was an assistant prosecutor during the trial of Slobodan Milošević. For two years, Sir Geoffrey accused him of having ordered crimes against humanity, until the ex-President of Yugoslavia was assassinated in his cell. Ten years later, the International Criminal Court admitted his innocence. The third expert was a US citizen who had preceded de Silva as prosecutor of Charles Taylor, before working for the CIA and becoming legal advisor for the Defense Intelligence Agency (DIA). From the beginning of the war, he created the Syria Accountability Project (SAP), which fed information to the Syria Justice and Accountability Centre (SJAC).

The second operation was the invention of the "human slaughter-house" in Sednaya, via Amnesty International. 13,000 anonymous people were allegedly hanged in this prison, situated near Damascus.

In the absence of eye-witnesses, and considering the incoherencies of the report, which condemns summary executions while at the same time describing a complex judicial process, this grotesque accusation is only worth mentioning at all because it is championed by a prestigious NGO, Amnesty International. However, all the founders of this organisation have lamented its loss of direction its new director since 2010. *The Observer*, which participated in its foundation, calls it a "shipwreck". I myself joined AI at the end of the 1970's. At that time, it defended imprisoned conscientious objectors, victims of the horrors of the Cold War. It chose them in a balanced way – a victim from the United States, another from the USSR. It was therefore impossible to invent cases without hurting one's own side. We spent entire evenings writing letters, especially to leaders from Latin-America and Eastern European countries, asking for the liberation of one prisoner or another.

When Salil Shetty became the director of Amnesty, he fired the association's experts and hired a bunch of publicity specialists and fundraisers, transforming the association into a brisk business affair. This allowed him to pay severance packages totalling £850,000 to the preceding director and deputy director.[59] The resulting scandal cost AI a great deal of credibility. Today, Shetty claims that human rights are now only a marginal problem in the developed countries, and that it is only the Third World that must be reformed. The 80,000 people tortured by the Bush administration, like the three million killed by the Western war of terror, apparently do not count in his eyes. And in order to collect a contribution from a US foundation, he did not hesitate to sign on – without the slightest trace of proof and against all logic – to the slander of Syria's "human slaughterhouse".

At the end of 2014, the Obama administration itself considered that the accusations against Syria were the same as those that had been presented in 2005 – sheer fiction. As a result it stopped financing the Syria Justice and Accountability Centre. However, under the impulse of Jeffrey Feltman, the SJAC's activities were to begin again, on the occasion of a meeting at the Dutch embassy, on 6 October 2016, when Germany, Belgium, Denmark, Italy, Norway, the United Kingdom, Sweden, Switzerland and of course the United States agreed to begin financing it again.

Generally speaking, international criminal law has been gradually transformed over the years. At the end of WW2, in their courts at Nuremberg and Tokyo, the Allies exposed the crimes of the

---

[59] https://en.wikipedia.org/wiki/Irene_Khan In contrast, his predecessor Irene Khan assailed the US detention camp at Guantanamo Bay as "the gulag of our time," for which she was attacked by Bush, Cheney and the corporate media. It would appear that AI was "taken out" by a putsch at the helm.

vanquished in order to better conceal their own. This was the justice of the victors... Today, the international courts work to justify – *a posteriori* – the wars waged by the Allies by condemning the vanquished, and, if necessary, by inventing the crimes of which they accuse them. This evolution corresponds to a vision of the world in which war is a crime in itself, and can only be waged under legal pretences. The Allies no longer declare war – they accuse their victims before the Human Rights Council in Geneva of real or imagined crimes, via the testimony of alleged NGO's. Then they announce that they are intervening like an international police force to save people who are genuinely or fictitiously oppressed. Finally, at the end of the war, the legal condemnation of the ex-leaders legitimises their defeat.

The implementation of the Feltman plan

Since President Obama had rejected the Feltman plan, the end of his first term was marked by a head-on internecine war. Feltman, representing the "Continuity of Government", was supported by Secretary of State Hillary Clinton and the Director of the CIA, David Petraeus, so they became the object of enquiries, and then traps. However, nothing of this leaked out during the electoral campaign.

Secretary of State Clinton fell "seriously ill" the day after the re-election of President Obama, and was unable to exercise her functions during the period of transition between Obama I and II. She resigned shortly thereafter, on Feb. 1. She had succeeded Condoleeza Rice and was succeeded by John Kerry.

The FBI proved unable to exploit General Petraeus' pedophilic abuse of his power and position overseas. Finally, he was arrested in handcuffs, the day after the vote and re-election of Barack Obama. After a plea bargain, he was only charged with having passed classified information to his mistress and biographer, Paula Broadwell (an Army Intelligence agent who had infiltrated his boudoir). He was sentenced to a fine of $100,000.

Petraeus joined the investment fund KKR, headed by Henry Kravis. This billionaire and his wife, the economist Marie-Josée Drouin, are the only couple that attend the Bilderberg Group. Working with the Turkish bank Kuveyt Turk Katilim Bankasi (KTKB), KKR began to play the role which was once played by the Pakistani bank BCCI – providing financial support for the jihadists. Petraeus began to travel, telling his listeners that "... the nigger [that is to say, President Obama] is kissing the Russians' ass" (sic), and that the jihadists were not the real problem, but Iran, and therefore it was worth while supporting al-Qaeda and Daesh. In public, he limited himself to underlining the possibility of recruiting certain individual members of these terrorist organisations to be "moderate rebels," but without ever revealing his real thoughts.[60]

Around Petraeus there were several transnational companies which were already involved in the war against Syria. For example, Lafarge-Holcim, which built the underground bunkers for the jihadists. The link was all the more clear since during the 1980's, Lafarge was defended in an Alabama pollution trial by a famous lawyer, namely Hillary Rodham-Clinton. She managed to reduce their fine by the Environmental Protection Agency to only $1.8 million. During the Presidential term of George Bush Sr., Lafarge did a favour for the CIA by illegally transporting to Iraq the weapons which would later serve in the rebellion when the international Coalition came to the support of Kuwait. From 1990 to 1992, Hillary Clinton was a member of the Lafarge board, a post which she left when her husband was elected to the White House. President Bill Clinton further reduced Lafarge's fine by two-thirds, to $600,000. These good relations continued – in 2015, the company donated $100,000 to the Clinton Foundation, and its new CEO, Eric Olsen, had his photo taken with Hillary Clinton. (She was also a member of the board of Arkansas-based Walmart while husband Bill was Arkansas governor.)

In order to dig the tunnels, the great speciality of the jihadists since the war in Afghanistan, the "Continuity of Government" relied on Caterpillar, who had acquired the Canadian tunnel-digger company, Lovat. It is clear that Caterpillar could not possibly have been unaware of the purpose of these machines, bought for use in the war against Syria. Particularly since the Obama administration had pronounced an embargo against Syria specifically targeting seismic detection equipment, which could reveal tunnel-digging activity. Caterpillar has a long military history – its tractors played an important role during the First World War, and are still used today

---

[60] See "Petraeus proposes using al-Qaïda against Syria," Sept. 10, 2015, http://www.voltairenet.org/article188653.html

by the Israeli army. It has a military production unit in the United Kingdom and serves part of the NATO armies.

The multinational companies which support the jihadists also include non-USA companies like Toyota. They have sold Daesh thousands of Hilux double cabin pick-up trucks, identical to those of the US Special Forces. Their motors are adapted to the conditions in the Middle East, protected from heat and sand-storms. Besides this, the leaders of Daesh had armoured Toyotas assembled for them in Jordan. The whole of this market was channelled through the firm's only regional outlet – the Saudi Abdul Latif Jameel. Claiming to be "astonished" by this gigantic traffic, he decided to interrupt his deliveries in Syria (sic) when Secretary of State John Kerry questioned him about it.

Finally, the Obama administration allowed the "Continuity of Government" to deal with the Greater Middle East, and turned its attention to other cases. General David Petraeus' alter ego, General John Allen, had succeeded in staying out of the clutches of the FBI. He left upon his retirement and was nominated as the President's special representative for the International anti-Daesh Coalition. The two men had no trouble supervising logistics for the jihadists. There is a mass of evidence proving the existence of this organisation – for example, US military helicopters escorting columns of jihadists, or the parachuting of weapons to the jihadists by the very Coalition which is supposed to be fighting them. After that, to be sure that nothing would change, General Allen was replaced by Brett McGurk, one of the men who had created the Islamic Emirate in Iraq, predecessor of Daesh.

The jihadists, a powerful land army

The jihadists form one of the most powerful land armies in the world. Contrary to the image we have of them as composed of multiple groups, some allied and some rival, they all in fact use the same logistics, and share the same command structure.

For example, although none of these groups claim to have large numbers of troops, the Spanish Guardia Civil in Valencia seized a cargo of 20,000 uniforms ready to be transported to Syria. They were obviously meant for several different groups – organised by *katiba*, which means "company", or between one hundred and two hundred and fifty men. According to the needs of the moment, these companies were assigned a particular cause – moderate or extremist. They continually changed their insignia, but always received a distinctive name and logo.

In all probability, the common military command has changed. It was moved to Turkey, where, in 2013, it ended up at the new NATO Command of Land Forces (LandCom) in Izmir.

The jihadists who had at first all been members of al-Qaeda, which was at that time dispersed into a number of small groups, were once again reunited – either with the Assembly for the Liberation of the Levant, for the troops tasked with overthrowing the Syrian Arab Republic, or as part of Daesh, for those tasked with cutting the Silk Road.

They all received real time information, either from NATO AWAC aircraft or from US satellites, about the movements of the Syrian Arab Army. They could therefore escape whenever necessary. However, until the arrival of the Russian army, the Syrians had no airborne or space-based intelligence with which to follow the movements of the jihadists. Today they have such equipment, as well as Iranian drones.

When the NATO communication briefcases were seized by the Syrians, they were taken to the army technical centre to be analysed. The Israeli Air Force then bombed the centre, in coordination with a ground attack launched by the jihadists. The attackers were beaten back, but the briefcases were destroyed.

The jihadists are able to move much faster than other land armies, since they do not transport their heavy weapons with them. Instead, heavy equipment is waiting for them when they arrive. In this way, Daesh was able to conquer one third of Iraq in only a few days. Its combatants had crossed the desert in thousands of Toyota double cabin Hilux vehicles, which had been delivered to them in Raqqa by the Turkish secret services. When they arrived in Mosul, they found the weapons that the United States had left there for them, often still packaged, including tanks and Manpads.

As well as their shared staff in Izmir, the jihadists also had operation centres at their disposition, not only in Iraq and Syria, but also in Lebanon and Jordan. So, when the Syrian Arab Army liberated Aleppo, in December 2016, it discovered a NATO bunker used by foreign superior officers (some Saudis, and liaison officers from the USA, Israel, Jordan, Morocco, Qatar and Turkey).

The jihadists have only a land army – no aviation, no navy. However, they could if they wanted – they have a large number of tanks. When they took Mosul, they had with them helicopter and jet pilots who flew for one day only. The United States immediately forbade them this extension of their forces, as they had forbidden the Lebanese army to possess a credible air force. Simply because with aviation, Daesh could have gone its own way and escaped the control of its creators.

This land army is the cheapest fighting force in the world. Its soldiers accept a ridiculously small salary, no more than a few hundred dollars – with no wounded to care for, no psychological problems to treat, no veterans waiting for retirement pay, no families to be compensated in case of death in combat.

Behind the staff in Izmir and the local operations rooms, there exists somewhere a supreme command which defines the objectives. It is probably situated close to the US "Continuity of Government" complex inside Raven Rock Mountain. In any case, the jihadists are no more than an epiphenomenon, a secondary symptom. They have collided with the fundamental logic of both Russia and China.

Operation "Timber Sycamore"

As from 2012, General David Petraeus, then Director of the CIA, set up a series of channels to supply weapons to the jihadists. This was called Operation Timber Sycamore.

First we learned that Bulgaria had sold $500 million worth of Soviet-type weaponry to Saudi Arabia, intended for the Muslim World League. Then that Croatia, with the help of Turkey, Jordan and Qatar, had delivered 230 tonnes of weapons to the jihadists. And then further, that Ukraine and Japan had sold enough equipment to Daesh to fill two special trains.

However, when General Petraeus was arrested and forced to resign from the CIA, the operation continued, this time under the supervision of the Pentagon. Three naval routes were established to reach the Syrian battlegrounds, the first from the US base at Livorno in Italy, the other two from Romania and Bulgaria.

General Petraeus, who joined the private finance company KKR, then organised the greatest arms traffic in History. At least 16 states participated (Afghanistan, Germany, Saudi Arabia, Azerbaidjan, Bulgaria, the United Arab Emirates, Hungary, Israel, Pakistan, Poland, Romania, Serbia, Slovakia, the Czech Republic, Turkey and the United Kingdom). And since the system functioned very efficiently, secondary deliveries were organised for the profit of South Africa and the Congo.

28,000 tonnes of weapons were transported by Silk Way Airlines, Azerbaidjan's public cargo company. In order to do so, they obtained diplomatic immunity for at least 350 flights, despite the fact that the states they visited to pick up their merchandise were informed of the nature of the cargo – authorisations which violate the civil principle of diplomatic status as well as international air laws for civilian flights. An operation of this colossal size, handling huge quantities of weapons and involving so many heads of state, would not have been possible without the help of the Under (or Uber) Secretary General of the United Nations, Jeffrey Feltman.

Supervising this traffic, Israel supplies Azerbaidjan with all sorts of false certificates which enable them to buy from NATO and transport the most sensitive materials.

The manipulation of the Kurdish question

The Kurds are nomads who have only recently become sedentary. They are clans, speaking different languages, who journey along the Euphrates. Some of them supplied mercenaries to the Ottomans to help with the massacre of Christians, and others to the French to help crush the Arab nationals. In 1917, the United States promised to assemble them as a single people and to give them a State in what is now Turkey, and France made the same promise in 1921.

During the Cold War, the Kurds divided into two distinct populations – in Iraq, the allies of Israel and the United States, led by the Barzani family, spoke Kurmandji – in Turkey, the allies of the Soviet Union, led by Abdullah Öcalan, spoke Sorani.

During the present conflict, the Turkish Kurds who settled in Syria in the 1980's attempted to profit from the confusion to create a new State, Rojava, while the Iraqi Kurds tried to transform the zone where they had found refuge under Anglo-US protection during "Desert Storm" into a "Kurdistan".

By doing so, they echoed the erratic attitude of the PLO which, unable to recover Palestine, attempted to create a new State, successively in Jordan, Lebanon and Tunisia.

The United States abandoned the idea of creating a Kurdistan in Turkey a long time ago. They never made any attempt to establish such a state elsewhere, but often supported the claims of the Kurds without believing in them. France, on the other hand, whenever the situation looks favourable, still attempts to reboot the Kurdistan project, anywhere in the Middle East, in order to create a colonial trading post for itself.

In September 2017, the Regional Government of Iraqi Kurdistan organised a referendum for independence. At that time, it enjoyed the sympathy of almost all the Arabo-Muslim world. For the Barzanis, it was the opportunity to create a sovereign and independent State, and to gain approval for the conquest of the region of Kirkuk which they had undertaken with the aid of Daesh. Barzani claimed to be supported by 60 States, but none of them dared to confirm this publicly, despite numerous visits by foreign representatives.

President Massoud Barzani was detested by his own people. He clung to power by preventing new elections under the pretext of war, but revealed his hypocrisy when he organised a referendum. He presented himself as the saviour of the "Kurdish People", despite having allowed the massacre of the Yazidi Kurds by Daesh. Many Kurds therefore abstained from voting.

On the evening of the ballot, a huge celebration was organised in Erbil. When Massoud Barzani announced the victory of the "Yes" vote, thousands of Kurdish and Israeli flags were unfurled before the eyes of the astounded Arab audience. The Turkish Press revealed that the magazine *Kurds-Israel* had published the existence of a secret agreement between Erbil and Tel-Aviv. 200,000 Israelis were soon to be transferred to the new, independent Kurdistan. Missiles were to be installed, pointed at Iran and Syria.

Instantly, Iraq, Iran and Turkey ordered Erbil to give up its independence. The Press published maps for a Turko-Iranian invasion. But Iraq attacked first and freed Kirkuk. The Kurdish settlers scattered without a fight. In Erbil, Massoud Barzani was overthrown.

On the same model, the Syrian Kurds supervised by the anti-Daesh Coalition created a self-administered zone, Rojava. These Marxist-Leninists swallowed whole the anarchist theories of Murray Bookchin (a US theorist of the extreme left, believed to be an agent of the CIA in Latin America). At first, they enjoyed the support of France and Turkey. But Ankara turned against them when it became aware of their persistently close ties with Turkey's nemesis, the PKK (the Kurdish Workers' Party that has fought a guerrilla war with Ankara for over 30 years). President Erdogan agreed to support Rojava only on the condition that they publicly abandon PKK leader Abdullah Öcalan, and give up the idea of extending their territory to the Mediterranean (whence they could supply the Kurdish terrorist organisations in Turkey).

Finally, events turned nasty when Brett McGurk, one of the co-founders of the Islamic Emirate in Iraq (in other words, Daesh), decided to recycle between 10,000 and 15,000 jihadists into a security force at the frontier with the combatants of Rojava. Turkey, which believed that this new army was designed to overthrow President Erdogan, decided to kill two birds with one stone. On 20 January 2018, it invaded Afrin, Syria, in order to crush both the Syrian Kurds and the jihadists. Contrary to official declarations, the operation had been secretly prepared with Russia. The director of the Turkish secret services, Hakan Fidan, had discussed the subject exhaustively in Moscow for two days. The Russian military staff denounced the Turkish invasion --and withdrew its troops from the area in order to leave the road clear.

Russia's intervention

Russia's foreign policy was defined by Tsars Catherine II and Nicolas II. It was intended to create an Orthodox region and secure the access to warm waters – not for reasons of conquest, but in respect of an International Law which was at that time under development.

Russia never accepted the fall of the Holy Roman Empire in the Orient and the rise of the Ottoman Empire. That is why Catherine the Great attempted to create an Orthodox Empire with Constantinople – currently Istanbul – as its capital. During the Russo-Turkish war, she was able to annex Crimea (1783) and the northern littoral of the Black Sea, making it an Orthodox Sea. This success led her to deploy a fleet in the Mediterranean and, for a short time, occupy Beirut. She declared Greater Syria was "the key to the House of Russia".

The Russo-Ottoman wars followed one after another without interruption, with Russia penetrating always a little deeper into Ottoman territory. In 1853, the Sultan forged an alliance with the United Kingdom and France to take back Crimea from Russia. They succeeded. However, Russia would not admit defeat. At the beginning of the First World War, Russia negotiated with the United Kingdom and France to determine the shape of the world after the conflict. These were the Sykes-Picot-Sazonov agreements. They planned for the transfer of Constantinople to Russia and control of the Black Sea.

The revolution of October 1917 interrupted this project. Lenin, who was financed by the same sponsors as Mustafa Kemal Atatürk, opposed it. The secret Sykes-Picot-Sazonov agreements were published by Pravda, and the USSR backed off. It is in any case most improbable that London and Paris would have allowed the Bolsheviks to profit from Russia's agreements, since they had withdrawn from the world war.

This is the project that Vladimir Putin re-activated, but within the legal framework of Nicolas II. The Tsar had convened The Hague Peace Conferences in 1898-1899 with a view to preserving the peace, disarming the great Empires and, ultimately, preventing the First World War. He was unable to do so, faced with the opposition of the United Kingdom and the German Empire, who were spoiling for a fight. However, with the help of the President of the French Radical Party, Léon Bourgeois, Russia sketched out the basis for international public law and international humanitarian law. The October Revolution prevented Russia from pursuing this goal, but another French Radical, Aristide Briand, promoted the League of Nations, the ancestor of the United Nations. Léon Bourgeois, followed by Aristide Briand, both received the Nobel Prize for Peace. As for the Tsar, through his peace conferences, he established the Permanent Court of Arbitration in The Hague, which today serves as the internal tribunal of the UN.

It was precisely in this line of thought that in 2005, I organised the Axis for Peace Conference in Brussels, with the notable participation of the Russian ex-Joint Chief of Staff, General Leonid Ivashov.

During the Cold War, the USSR attempted to find an ally in the Greater Middle East with whom to re-animate the dream of Catherine the Great. It therefore forged an alliance with Egypt – but President Nasser was assassinated and then his successor, Anwar el-Sadat, expelled anyone who cooperated with the Soviets. Russia then tried for an alliance with Ba'athist Iraq, but Saddam Hussein was an agent of the CIA. In the end, it was with Syria that a true alliance was possible, thanks to Hafez al-Assad.

Once in power, Bashar al-Assad tried to move closer to Russia. But Russia had not yet recovered from the dissolution of the USSR and the pillage of its economy. It was only in 2012 that Moscow felt ready to accept the challenge. The Kremlin and the White House were negotiating a new distribution of the Greater Middle East. The United States wanted to withdraw their troops from the region in order to operate their "pivot" towards the Far East. They were ready to leave Russia a wide margin for manœuvre, on the condition that it would guarantee the safety of Israel. This was not a problem for Russia, since a million ex-Soviets had emigrated and obtained Israeli nationality. The regional agreement was signed in Geneva on 30 June, and included the resolution of the Syrian question.

In the months before Geneva I, General Hassan Turkmani negotiated with his counterparts the deployment of a stabilisation force from the Collective Security Treaty Organization (CSTO). In this way, soldiers from countries with a Muslim majority allied with Russia could help the Syrian Arab Army to hold the whole of its territory.

Reproducing the coalition of the Crimean War, France, the United Kingdom and Turkey opposed the Geneva I agreement. Supported by a faction of the Obama administration which was affiliated with the "Continuity of Government", they launched a new war against Syria by bringing in jihadists from all over the world. The Republic resisted as far as possible, but the superiority in numbers and equipment of the Islamist mercenaries forced it to fall back to the towns. General Hassan Turkmani had been assassinated, and Moscow seemed to have forgotten its promise. The Syrian Arab Army waited for the Russian forces who did not come. And yet

Moscow opposed Washington with determination at the Security Council, and prevented the implementation of the Feltman plan.

There was a good reason for this long silence – Moscow was preparing new weapons which would perhaps change the course of History. When his arsenal was ready, Vladimir Putin announced the deployment of Russian forces in Syria. He shelled the installations that Lafarge and Caterpillar had built, and destroyed the bunkers and the tunnels with penetrating "bunker-buster" bombs. It was a huge job, and demanded six months instead of the three which were originally planned.

The US "Continuity of Government", mostly composed of followers of Leon Trotsky and disciples of Leo Strauss, know nothing of History. Blind to national culture, and therefore understanding nothing about international relations, this clique persuaded itself that Russia had intervened in Syria because of solidarity between "dictators," Putin and Assad. The "CoG" believed it could overthrow them and establish a world government. US wrong-headedness about Russia is equalled only by their incomprehension of China.

The intervention of China

More than any other country, China conceives of its foreign policy only in the very long term. In 2013, after six centuries of absence from the international scene, it elected Xi Jinping as its President, with the mission to re-open the historic "Silk Road" and to build another across Europe. In China, the President is elected by the National People's Congress (NPC) upon nomination by the presidium of the NPC. The presidium chooses its man and begins to prepare him years in advance. Xi has thus been preparing for his mission since 2008. The President is usually also Secretary General of the Communist Party and Commander in Chief of the PLA.

During antiquity, a network of markets grew up across Central Asia, linking the Chinese capital Xi'an to the Mediterranean – the Silk Road. Contrary to its name, which was only dreamed up in the 19th century, this network of markets handled a variety of products, such as spices, cotton, paper, and what we call today gunpowder (although they were as yet no guns). It was also the channel for many intellectual and artistic exchanges. The merchants linked one market to the next, and only rarely travelled the whole length of the route. Many different peoples were involved, and one commercial language imposed itself – Persian. Eventually, an intense chain of commerce linked China to the Roman Empire, and Oriental merchandise became available throughout the Mediterranean. This axis of communication suffered from the fall of the Roman Empire in the Orient, and fell progressively into decline, although the Venetian Marco Polo revived it during the 13th century.

The Ming dynasty envisioned a re-opening of the "Silk Road". In the 15th century, the emperor asked Admiral Zheng He, the "great eunuch of the three gems", to build a navy of 70 ships and 30,000 sailors. He made the pilgrimage to Mecca, sailed up the Red Sea as far as Egypt and down the African coastline as far as Mozambique. For internal political reasons, his notes were burned at his death. The Emperor destroyed the fleet and China withdrew into itself until the time of Deng Xiaoping.

Starting in 2009, the presidium of the National Peoples' Congress, which had chosen the future President Xi Jinping, launched a campaign to awaken the Chinese people's ancient spirit of international influence. The national television produced a fabulous series in 59 episodes about the historical period of Admiral Zheng He, while the blockbuster movie, Dragon Blade, reminded its viewers that at one time, along this route, the Empires were not necessarily enemies.

Historically, this route crosses what is today Iran, Iraq and Greater Syria. The western end passed through Palmyra, then Damascus, and then divided into two branches, one leading to Tyre (currently Lebanon), the other towards Antioch (currently Turkey).[61]

In 2011, during her speech in Chennai (Madras), Secretary of State Hillary Clinton spoke in support of the new Silk Road, but the United States quickly changed their minds when President Xi took power. They decided instead to develop Daesh and award it a territory comprising parts of Iraq and Syria, thus creating a new state which blocks the route.[62] This proposal was made public, with

---

[61] Now called Antakya, it is the capital of Hatay province, which Turkey wrested from Syria in 1938 through intrigue, by promising to help France against Germany.
[62] For a map of Wright's "new state of Sunnistan," see ISIS IS U.S. from Progressive Press, 2016, p. 243

supporting maps, by Robin Wright in the New York Times, on 13 September 2013 – almost a year before the events.

Historic relations between China and Syria have left few traces. But a pagoda may still be seen in the mosaics on a wall of the Grand Mosque of Damascus.

From the Chinese point of view, the Silk Road could cross Syria just as well as Egypt or Saudi Arabia.

In 2015, Westerners were astounded by the Pharaonic efforts of Cairo to double the size of the Suez Canal, while Egypt was not even capable of feeding its population. It soon became apparent that this project, which makes little or no sense in terms of current world commerce, has more to do with China's plans for the medium term.

A vast industrial zone has been opened at the mouth of the Canal, about 120 kilometres (75 miles) from Cairo. Unprecedented invest–ments are planned, offering work to 40,000 Egyptians. The Chinese have invested in over 100 Egyptian quarries, so that stone has become a major item in Egypt's exports to China.[63] Apart from this, China is participating in the construction of a new Egyptian capital.

China is also Saudi Arabia's biggest customer, importing over $20 billion worth of Saudi oil per year. However, the Chinese and the Saudis are rivals in Pakistan, and are fighting a bitter war in the Xinjiang province. For at least a decade, via the Saudi secret services, the United States have been recruiting Chinese jihadists during their pilgrimage to Mecca. These men are often Uyghurs, and are later influenced by the Turkish services to commit terrorist attacks in the name of the Islamic state, first of all in the western regions of China, but more recently all over the country.

In January 2016, King Salman and President Xi inaugurated the refinery of Yasref-Yanbu, on the Red Sea coast of Saudi Arabia. This is the first refinery ever built by Sinopec in a foreign country, and is worth $10 billion. Five eighths (62.5%) of the refinery is owned by Aramco, and 37.5% by China Petroleum. This gigantic plant was built in two years, while the US International anti-Daesh

---

[63] China Daily, "Broad prospect for China-Egypt economic and trade cooperation,"
http://www.chinadaily.com.cn/world/2016xivisitmiddleeast/2016-01/22/content_23204973.htm

Coalition were busy bombing and destroying earlier Chinese investments in Iraq. In any future partition of Arabia, the refinery should find itself in the state with the holy cities of Mecca and Medina.

In any case, faced with the Arab Springs, China has joined its voice to Russia's at the Security Council. It has used its veto six times, which makes Syria, even more than the China Sea, the main subject of friction between Beijing and NATO.

In August 2016, Admiral Guan Youfei (the man responsible for the new Chinese department of International Military Cooperation) went to Damascus in the context of introductory meetings with all the countries in the region. For the moment, according to the signed agreement, the Chinese Army has only agreed to train Syrian health services personnel for the military. However, everyone understands that this agreement hides another, because for the last four years half of Syria's military medical staff has been trained in China. Although we do not know what has really been decided, the existence of this agreement marks a change of strategy.

In any case, architects and engineers from the Chinese Army Corps of Engineers are currently drawing up the plans for a new military port in Tartus.

Meanwhile, President Xi Jinping is working on a new Silk Road across Siberia to Duisburg in Germany – this was the reason for his visit to Germany in March 2014. However, this second route must pass either through Ukraine – currently at war – or Belarus.

Since February 2015, Belarusian President Alexandre Lukashenko has been courted by NATO, which, until recently, qualified him as a "dictator".

Refusing to take sides in the Ukrainian conflict, he instructed his Justice Department to give prison sentences to volunteers who leave to fight on either side. He also refused to take a position in the conflict between Russia and Turkey and the problem between Armenia and Azerbaidjan.

The European Union has discreetly lifted the sanctions it had imposed on Belarus, and a Belarus/EU work group has been created. Although diplomatic relations with Washington still have not been re-established, a delegation from the Pentagon was received in Minsk, April 2016.

Then President Lukashenko went to Istanbul in April to participate in the summit of the Organisation of Islamic Cooperation (OIC). He enjoyed friendly communications with his opposite numbers from Pakistan, Qatar and Turkey.

Historically, Belarus and Ukraine were centers of arms production in the USSR. Currently, the Belarusian weapons factories are 90% the property of Russia. In 2015, arms exports suddenly increased by 31%. According to the Russian Press, Belarus had sold arms to Qatar which were destined for the jihadists operating in Syria. President Lukashenko recently announced that, contrary to what had been planned, he had no intention of handing back the remaining parts of the arms industry to Russia.

In October 2014, in order to build the two Silk Roads, China created the Asian Infrastructure Investment Bank (AIIB), with an incredible capital of $100 billion. 50 states have agreed to participate, notably the United Kingdom, which brought other European states along with it – but not the United States, who were in total opposition. According to the ex-United States Secretary of the Treasury, Larry Summers, "this bank has already cost the United States its place as the guarantor of the world's economic system".

And quite the opposite of what had been expected, Beijing did not begin a monetary war – the AIIB is presently treating all its operations in dollars.

While Russia has become the world's first conventional military power, China has become the world's most important investor. The United States are falling behind. Everywhere the policies of the deep US state destroy without rebuilding. Many regions of the Greater Middle East are no more than expanses of ruins. And although the populations resist with rare courage, and cling to assistance from the Russians and the Chinese, the solution can only come from inside the Atlantist camp.

The Damascene spirit

Although the Russians and the Chinese understand – and applaud – the reactions of the Syrian Arab Republic to the aggression it is being forced to suffer, the Western powers, who continue to pursue their strategy of total war, seem bewildered. For example, they consider it a victory to have led Damascus to participate in the Geneva negotiations secretly piloted by Jeffrey Feltman. And they ask themselves why President Bashar al-Assad continues to send his delegations to meetings whose aim is to throw him out and destroy his country.

Civilisations are only mortal. Humanity has known brilliant ones, of which only ruins now remain. As for the city-kingdom of Damascus, it is the oldest inhabited city in the world. It has often been attacked and partially destroyed, but it is still there. No one has ever been able to lay it to waste.

To survive over the millennia, the Damascenes created a particular civilisation which shone throughout the region. According to the times, they have governed vast empires, stretching from Spain to the Chinese frontier, or only small territories, like today. They may gain or lose influence, but they are still there.

This Damascene spirit, resonant today in great cities like Aleppo, Latakia or Deir ez-Zor, is founded on the absence of the fear of death, and the respect of others, including our own most ferocious enemies. It has expressed itself through two universal religions, Christianity and Islam, which were not founded in Jerusalem, nor Mecca, but in Damascus.

Syrian society is divided into the regions – mostly urban – which share this spirit, and the others – mostly rural – which reject it. And it is in part on this sociological division that war has prospered. The traveller who discovers Damascus, and strolls through the cafés or public parks, is first of all struck by the harmony which reigns within family gatherings. Unlike in the West, the Œdipus complex and generational crises are absent. The relations between grand-parents, parents and children are not based on authority, but on respect. Everyone knows instinctively what he or she must concede to ensure that the family stays united.

Over the millennia, the Damascenes have never sought victory. Instead, they have tried to show their enemies that they cannot be enslaved. Then they assimilated their invaders. This tactic demands courage from everyone, because it takes a long time to complete, and until then, society suffers heavy losses.

For example, when the Umayyad dynasty settled in Syria, the Dasmascenes welcomed their army and allowed them to exercise power. But they also insisted that the city should be divided in two parts, one of them autonomously administered by the city's Christian inhabitants. The church of Saint John the Baptist became the Great Mosque, but was used simultaneously by Christians and Muslims. A century later, for reasons of convenience, the Muslims alone used the building, and the Christians had a church of their own. With time, the Muslims not only accepted co-existence with the Christians, but the two religions mutually supported one another – it was not a question of converting others, but rather helping them on their journey. In this way, for centuries, Christian monks sang the Muslim call to prayer, and Muslim imams rang Christian bells. Even today, Christians and Muslims pray together on a daily basis in the presence of the relics of John the Baptist. From confrontation there came cooperation, and ever since, Muslims have defended this "living together" even more than the Christians.

The Syrian Arab Republic agreed to participate in the negotiations of Geneva II, III and IV, despite the fact that they were organised by Jeffrey Feltman, the man who has demanded the total and unconditional capitulation of Syria. The so-called "opposition" delegations change all the time. They are mostly Syrians with no following in their own country, but are mere mouthpieces for the foreign powers sponsoring the war. At Geneva IV, another group joined in – from Cairo, representing the law-abiding internal opposition and presided over … by the ex-spokesman for the Syrian government, Jihad Makdissi. This group supports the Republic while disputing the decisions of its government.

The "external opposition" incessantly demands the implementation of the Feltman plan, while the "internal opposition" and UN ambassador Bashar Ja'afari propose to work together to form a new government. The aggressors can continue this war as long as they receive money, men, and weapons from abroad. But after six years of fighting, it looks as though Syria will never surrender, even when it is exhausted. So for the moment, there appear to be only two solutions – either exterminate all the Syrians, or deal with them.

The "internal opposition" and ambassador Bashar Ja'afari are ready for any compromise, on the condition that the "external opposition" accepts the secular character of the institutions. This means, in practice, that it must let go of the idea of placing the Muslim Brotherhood and their Western allies in power. The negotiations get bogged down as soon as the participants approach the question of the next Constitution – the "internal opposition" and UN Ambassador Bashar Ja'afari go as far as to offer some Ministries to the jihadists, if the "external opposition" will renounce its clause requiring that the President can only be a Muslim, and agrees not to partition the country.

It is this state of mind to which Christ referred, and preferred over the Code of Hammurabi – "You have learned 'an eye for an eye, and a tooth for a tooth'. But I say to you "do not resist". If someone hits you on the right cheek, offer him the other. If someone wants to bear witness against you and take your jacket, give him your coat as well...."

This is why Syria has not declared "total war". The Republic has never enforced enlistment in its armies, but has always looked after its schools and public gardens. Conscription is mandatory, but there are many ways of avoiding it. What is important is not the war of a few, but the resistance of the whole society.

Syria is the only state to have a Minister for Reconciliation, not after, but during the war. President al-Assad offered amnesty to more than 1,300 villages whose combatants rallied behind the Republic.

This technique has begun to bear fruit, insofar as the Kurdish YPG has finally admitted that it would be safer under the protection of the Syrian Republic than in an independent state. It has therefore given back to Damascus some territories liberated from Daesh.

The aggression by NATO and its allies should not end in the victory of the Syrian Arab Republic over the West and the Gulf, but by a compromise – some jihadists will accept it, and others will refuse. The former will blend into the government and will marry Syrian women. They will progressively fit into the social fabric, and in twenty years, one will not be able to tell where they came from. Those who refuse will leave the country – if Russia allows them to go – and will go and fight further away, as pawns of the Muslim Brotherhood, on behalf of certain Anglo-Saxon powers.

Epilogue:
The Trump Insurrection

Stunned by the attacks of 11 September, Americans did not react immediately to the coup d'etat. It took three years for tongues to loosen and the "Truth Movement" to form. Once it got going, the "Continuity of Government" side-tracked it into any number of dead-ends and technical disputes (how were the Twin Towers destroyed? What happened to the plane that was supposed to have hit the Pentagon? etc.). That democracy was at stake was forgotten.

Nor did they react when they realised that millions had died in the Greater Middle East. For them, there is no doubt that Washington is a vipers' nest, and the deep state is a monster which grinds distant peoples into the dust.

However, two things were to drag them from their torpor – first of all, the return of their children, who had gone off to fight terrorism. They had dreamed of serving their Homeland and offering their help to populations crushed under the yoke of dictators. And yet they came home silent and depressed. Quite clearly, the reality over there had no connection with what they had been told.

Then there were the closed factories, cities abandoned and turned into ghost towns, decaying infrastructure, homes foreclosed, and finally, poverty. At first it was only the sad stories of individuals, which might be due to laziness or bad luck, but now it became a mass phenomenon. Little by little, people began to realise that the state was too occupied with régime change and distant wars to pay any attention to them. They understood that their lives would not improve unless they fought the deep state.

During the electoral campaign of 2016, an outsider, the real estate promoter Donald Trump, who had distanced himself from the Bushist version of 9/11, denounced the seizure of power by a very small group, who backed Hillary Clinton's candidacy. He called for service to the People, in other words the restoration of the Republic, and warned against the terrible clash brewing within the country. At first written off as a crank, he eliminated his sixteen competitors from the Republican party, one by one, got the nomination, and then won the presidency.

Shocked by this victory which had never seemed possible, Hillary Clinton's sponsors mobilised their acolytes all over the world, but especially those in NATO, the European Union and the UN, in order to discredit him. They organised the major media on a global scale to decry him as a homophobe, a misogynist and a racist who was out to destroy democracy.

This campaign was orchestrated by David Brock, the agit-prop (agitation & propaganda) specialist, whom the deep state had already used against Bill Clinton (Troopergate, Whitewater and the Lewinsky affair) to force him into going to war against Yugoslavia. Now he was working for Hillary. "The right-wing assassin has become a left-wing assassin".

At the head of an empire of mass manipulation, within a few weeks Brock had set up a system designed to discredit Donald Trump. He used four organisations:

▶ "Media Matters" was tasked with uncovering the errors of the new President.

▶ The "American Bridge 21st Century" PAC collected more than 2,000 hours of videos of Donald Trump taken over the years, and more than 18,000 hours of his cabinet members. It has access to sophisticated technologies which were created for the Department of Defense – and were allegedly off-market – enabling the search for contradictions between their targets' earlier declarations and their current positions. It should soon be extending its work to the President's 1,200 collaborateurs.

▶ "Citizens for Responsibility and Ethics in Washington" – CREW[64] – is a firm of high-level lawyers charged with tracking anything that might be used to create a scandal within the Trump administration.

▶ "Shareblue" is the showcase for an electronic army which already has its hooks into 162 million internet users in the United States. It is tasked with spreading pre-established themes, according to which –

---

[64] "CREW uses aggressive legal action, in-depth research, and bold communications," according to the outfit's self-description at https://www.citizensforethics.org/who-we-are/

• Trump is authoritarian and a thief.

• Trump is under the influence of Vladimir Putin.

• Trump has a weak and irate personality, he is manic-depressive.

• Trump was not elected by the majority of US citizens, and is therefore illegitimate.

• His Vice-President, Mike Pence, is a fascist.

• Trump is a billionaire who will continually be scraping into conflicts between his personal interests and those of the nation.

• Trump is a puppet of the Koch brothers, the notorious financiers of the extreme right wing.

• Trump is a white supremacist and a threat to minorities.

• The anti-Trump opposition just keeps on growing outside of Washington.

• To save democracy, we need to support the Democratic legislators who attack Trump, and demolish those who cooperate with him.

• Same thing with the journalists.

• Overthrowing Trump will take time, so don't give up the fight.

Shareblue produces newsletters and 30-second video clips. It relies on two other groups – a documentary video company, "The American Independent", and a statistics unit "Benchmark Politics".

During the transition, the budget of these groups was only $35 million. It has since risen to $100 million.

Paradoxically, the fact of seeing the international media, which have always relayed the White House point of view, now attacking the President of the United States of America before he has had time to do anything at all, is enough to sow confusion.

It is particularly surprising to witness such a charge by the deep state. When we look at the consequences of the hanging of President Saddam Hussein and the lynching of the Guide Muammar el-Gaddafi in their respective countries, we might well be concerned about the consequences of an impeachment of President Trump on US society. Remember that no US President has ever been impeached successfully. David Brock's message is relayed by an international media alliance, founded on the last few years' experience in the world of propaganda. It was built around the five or six TV channels which spread the myth of Bin Laden and the fable of the Arab

Springs (al-Jazeera, BBC, CNN, France 24, Sky News, but apparently not al-Arabiya). The Alliance was negotiated by a mysterious NGO called "First Draft" about which we know nothing, and which does not even have a Wikipedia page – it is facilitated by the services of Google Media Lab.

Over the last forty years, we have been witnessing a progressive consolidation of the media into certain international corporate trusts. Currently, 14 groups share the majority of the Western Press. This Alliance is strengthening the links between them, although they already enjoy a dominant position. This "Alliance" is no doubt a form of "illicit collusion" – not one for fixing prices, but for fixing minds – the imposition of an already dominant viewpoint.

Over the last six years, most of the members of this Alliance have painted a one-sided picture of the wars and the Arab Springs. And yet there was no previous agreement between them, or at least we had never heard of such an agreement. So now the time had come to consolidate this system for the proliferation of propaganda by using it not only to report the news from the Greater Middle East, but also news from the USA, France and Germany. Until now the Western Press had been pluralist, with the exception of certain topics in foreign policy. But from now on, it was to be monolithic.

In the United States, France and Germany, Google and First Draft assembled the local and international media to check the veracity of certain arguments – in theory, a good idea. The initiative was preceded by a vast campaign of denunciation of Fake News, in other words, erroneous conclusions, as if these were more numerous today than yesterday, and were only proffered by civilians, not journalists.

Besides the fact that we do not know who is hiding behind First Draft, and what political interests may have persuaded a commercial company specialised in computer science to finance this initiative, the results achieved have little to do with a return to objectivity.

First of all because the supposed errors are of no particular public interest or relevance, but are cherry-picked to vilify individuals the media Alliance has targeted. One might be tempted to welcome all fact-checking as getting us a little closer to the truth, but the bias is built in. The intention is to indoctrinate the citizenry that the media are honest, while the people they are condemning are liars. The aim is not a better understanding of the world, but crushing the opposition.

Next, because an unwritten rule of this media Alliance is that only allegations from sources outside the Alliance should be checked. The members agree not to use any critical faculty in the mutual appreciation of each other's work. They agree to reinforce the idea that the world is divided in two – "we" who tell the truth, and "the others" who are liars. Whether deliberate or not, this approach is damaging for the principle of pluralism, a precondition for democracy – it opens the way to a totalitarian, top-down society.

Finally, because the allegations that are supposedly shown to be "false" are never considered as mistakes, but always as intentional lies. The point is to blacken the "others" with Machiavellian intentions. This approach undermines the presumption of innocence.

Moreover, citizens no longer react when the media Alliance itself broadcasts falsehoods. Thus, in the United States, they fell for the tale that the Russian secret services really did have a compromising dossier on Donald Trump and were blackmailing him. Or that Putin had interfered with the US electoral process, by hacking the e-mail of John Podesta, Hillary Clinton's campaign director – although Wikileaks itself insisted that the documents it published definitely did not come via Russia. Or else, in France, this Alliance invented the idea that it is possible to employ fictitious parliamentary assistants – a claim which had already been considered by the public prosecutor's office, but rejected by the court – and went on to accuse François Fillon of doing just that. Or again, during the election campaign, they spread a false rumor that Emmanuel Macron's Internet site had been hacked by the Russian secret services.

The coalition initiative was accompanied by sermons about our entry into the post-Truth era – supposedly by using the Internet, certain poorly-educated citizens may have inadvertently misunderstood and scrambled the narratives, damaging all sorts of people and Institutions. Luckily, the modern clergy, in other words professional journalists, are able to spot their errors and restore the Truth – a self-serving advertisement for a Ministry of Truth, deflecting attention from centuries of deep contemplation – from Plato philosophising about Truth to George Orwell stigmatising propaganda.

This media Alliance was officially created in the United States in 2015, during the Presidential primary campaign, then extended to Europe for the major elections of 2017: the French Presidential campaign in April-May, the UK general election in June, and the German Federal elections in September.

The same US and French media attacked two candidates for the French Presidential election – François Fillon and Marine Le Pen. The basic problem of the media Alliance is further complicated by the false impression that these targets are victims of a French conspiracy, whereas in fact, the orders are coming from a US entity (First Draft/ Cross Check). The French have noticed that their media are rigged, but wrongly believe in a home-grown conspiracy against the right wing.

That Nicolas Sarkozy's Prime Minister, François Fillon, should come under fire is a surprise. After all, his government waged the wars against the Ivory Coast, Libya and Syria. However, Fillon did oppose the war against Libya – though to no avail – and managed to disengage France from Syria with the aid of his Minister for Defence, Gérard Longuet, and his Minister of the Interior, Claude Guéant.

In any case, for the first time, a West-European electoral campaign was played out on the model of a colour revolution. No one spoke of politics, but exclusively about the struggle against corruption. Senior civil servants and major CEO's put all their weight behind Emmanuel Macron, who promised hope and change, to eliminate the old political class – marketed as an "outsider", although he earned his spurs as an investment banker with the Rothschild group. The synthetic candidate composed his campaign team of the young people who used to gather around Dominique Strauss-Kahn, eleven years earlier. Despite some problems with his personality, the French chose this thirty-year old poster-boy. The spell will soon wear off.

During Watergate, the media claimed the moral high ground of a "Fourth Estate", after the Executive, the Legislative, and the Judiciary, but arguably with greater power and immunity. They claimed that the Press was exercising a function of checks and balances over the government, in the name of the People. Yet President Nixon was charged with an offense no more serious than that of President Obama – spying on his opponent. We know today that the Watergate source, "Deep Throat", far from being an idealistic "whistle-blower", was in reality the Director of the FBI, Mark Felt. The background of the affair was a battle between the White House and the Deep State within the administration, in which the electorate was manipulated by both sides at once.

The idea of a "Fourth Estate" presumes that we grant the same legitimacy to the 14 unelected corporate media trusts as to the People. This would be to accept the usurpation of democracy by an oligarchy.

To conserve the reality of Power and ruin President Trump, the "Continuity of Government" has decided to apply the "Wolfowitz doctrine" inside its own country. After the chaos generated by the hanging of Saddam Hussein and the lynching of Muammar Gaddafi, it seems to want to destroy the United States, France and Germany in the same way, by frontally attacking President Trump and the possible French President and German Chancellor.

Donald Trump may have all the faults for which he is lambasted – he's a blowhard, an upstart who used to host a TV reality show – so what? That has nothing to do with his patriotism, nor his capacities. As soon as he moved into the White House, he discreetly took up the reins of a power that his two predecessors had never fully exercised.

The unanimity of the attacks against President Trump by the Western medias makes it all the more difficult to analyse his actions, so much has the information on this subject been deliberately twisted. But in any case, concerning his challenge to the "Wolfowitz doctrine" and the usurpation of power which resulted, numerous initiatives were begun during his first month in office.

Before he even entered the White House, Donald Trump entrusted General Michael Flynn with the mission of unmasking the members of the "Continuity of Government", only a few of whom were known.

In the minutes following his inauguration, he fired all of America's ambassadors overseas, whether they were working with States or international organisations, and also immediately terminated the functions of all the political representatives in the Pentagon.

In the days that followed, his priority was building a security team – Secretary for Defense, Secretary for Homeland Security and National Security Advisor. Contrary to usual practice, they are all ex-army men – a *sine qua non* condition for retrieving the power usurped by the "Continuity of Government". They are all part of the same group who have opposed the deep state since 2003 – Generals James Mattis, John Kelly, Michael Flynn and Herbert Raymond McMaster.

H. R. McMaster is a high-level intellectual. He took charge of the analysis of new Russian strategies and weapons after their deployment in Syria. Extracts from his reports were used by David Brock to make people believe in a profound hostility against Russia ... trying to show Trump as betraying his own constituency.

Reforming the National Security Council, Donald Trump removed the permanent seats of the Director of the CIA and the head of the Joint Chiefs of Staff, which is to say the two senior civil servants charged with expanding the American Empire.

This action means no more nor less than putting an end to imperialism. Without delay, the CIA responded by refusing security clearance for six members of the Presidential cabinet, then accused four others of having violated the Logan Act. The Agency used this pretext to force General Flynn to resign.

The Logan Act is a lethal weapon of the US ruling class. In 1798, a Congressman from Pennsylvania, the Quaker George Logan, intervened in the quasi-war that US President John Adams was waging against France. The United States were refusing to pay their debt to Paris on the pretext that it was owed to King Louis XVI, who had been overthrown by the Revolution. On his own initiative, Logan travelled to France and negotiated peace. On his return, he found he had been denounced by the anti-Jeffersonian Federalists, who had passed a statute informally known as the "Logan Act", forbidding individual citizens to interfere in any conflict between the United States and a foreign power. This law has never – absolutely never – been enforced.

The Logan Act is wheeled out every time that the deep state feels threatened. This was the case, for example, during the war against Nicaragua. Or again, in 2007, when the Minority Leader of the House of Representatives, Nancy Pelosi, attempted to negotiate with Damascus in order to avoid war. This time, General Flynn was accused of having confirmed to the Russian ambassador, during the transition, that President-elect Trump meant what he said in his speeches and would in put them into action.

But this did not mean that the Trump administration was ready to toe the line. However, General Flynn's exit looked as though it could block the reform of the Intelligence agencies that he had promised to implement. During the Bush and Obama administrations, the agencies had abandoned the traditional distinction between agents on the ground and analysts working in the operational centres, such as we see in the TV series "24". These centres excel in the immediate management of current information. They are capable of locating individuals anywhere in the world, and if necessary, eliminating them. In reality, we are not dealing with Intelligence, but crimes. Whereas the CIA is outstanding at trashing régimes which displease the White House, and has at its disposition a number of secret prisons, it is no longer capable of anticipating political evolution, and even less, military evolution in one region or another.

Now, taking centre-stage, the feminist associations – frightened by the anti-Trump accusations in the Press, solicited by the Brock organisation, and sponsored by George Soros from overseas – organised a huge pre-emptive demonstration against Donald Trump on the second day of his Presidency. He responded by signing a decree which blocked Federal subsidies for these associations if they continued to accept sponsorship from overseas. The Press concluded that the President was attacking the right to abortion. Brock is already preparing a new demonstration for 22 April, this time in favour of scientists.

Applying his own programme, Donald Trump signed a decree limiting immigration. In this text, he made it clear that in order to prevent the entry of jihadists, he would be suspending visas for a three-month period, for people from countries in which his administration is unable to verify their identity. Although he suspended visas for only 7 countries out of the 57 member-states of the Organisation of Islamic Cooperation, CREW concluded that he is Islamophobic. Then he was accused of having established his suspension list to favour Saudi Arabia (a Muslim state about which the United States knows everything) to the detriment of Syria (a secular state where the United States no longer have an embassy and consequently cannot check anything). The Attorney General of the state of Washington, Bob Ferguson, was able to suspend the application of the decree, but the Supreme Court re-instated it.

The accusation of Islamophobia is all the more central for the "Continuity of Government" because Donald Trump – like French politicians François Fillon and Marine Le Pen – makes no secret of his desire to get rid of the Muslim Brotherhood.

In the wings, as a show of good faith, the Trump administration transmitted information to the Russian army concerning the location of jihadist underground bunkers in Deir ez-Zor. They were immediately destroyed with bunker-buster bombs. The new Secretary for Defense, General James Mattis, went to NATO, partly to calm down his worried allies, but also to suspend AWACS flights over Syria. At the same time, the new Director of the CIA, Mike Pompeo, froze all Agency support for the jihadists.

The deep state responded by launching an attack by Peshmergas from Iraqi Kurdistan against the Syrian Kurds who were fighting Daesh.

Donald Trump is developing new channels of communication with Moscow and Beijing. He chose Rex Tillerson as Secretary of State. The ex-Director of ExxonMobil, Tillerson has conceived a new form of partnership with his Russian counterparts. Gazprom, then Rosneft, authorised the United States to go and work in Russia on the condition that the Russians will also be able to go and work with the Americans. So the Russians have invested one third of the cost of ExxonMobil operations in the Gulf of Mexico, while the multinational played its part in the discovery of a gigantic field of hydrocarbons in the Kara Sea.

It is this shared success that saw Rex Tillerson receive the Order of Friendship medal from the hands of President Vladimir Putin. He is a close friend of Igor Sechin, Putin's right-hand man.

At the head of ExxonMobil, Tillerson took a stand against the Rockefeller family, founders of the company. Finally, he was able to impose his point of view, and the Rockefellers began selling their shares with a view to leaving the company.

According to the Rockefellers, oil and gas are depletable resources which will soon be exhausted (a theory which was popularised in the 1970's by the Club of Rome). Their use expels carbon particles into the atmosphere and thus provokes global warming (a theory promoted in the 2000's by the IPCC "Intergovernmental Panel on Climate Change", and Al Gore). Perhaps the moment had come to investigate renewable sources of energy. But on the contrary, according to Rex Tillerson, there is no proof that hydrocarbons are a form of composted biological waste. New reserves are continually being discovered at increasing depths, and in areas where there is no source-rock. There is also no proof that hydrocarbons are going to run out in the centuries to come. Still according to Tillerson, there is no proof that the carbon expelled into the atmosphere by human activity has any effect on the evolution of the climate. In this debate, and in the absence of conclusive arguments, each of the two camps has financed an intense lobbying campaign to convince political decision-makers.

In fact, the two camps defend positions which are diametrically opposed in terms of foreign policy. This is why the struggle between the Rockefellers and Tillerson most certainly had an impact on international politics. So, in 2005, the former advised Qatar – whose revenue comes almost exclusively from ExxonMobil – to support the Muslim Brotherhood, and then, in 2011, to invest in the war against Syria. But Tillerson considered that while clandestine war may be good for imperial politics, it doesn't really do much for business. Since the defeat of the Rockefellers, Qatar has increasingly withdrawn from the conflict and dedicated its expenses to the preparation of the Football World Cup.

In any case, for the moment, the Trump administration has taken no decision concerning Russia, apart from lifting the sanctions levied in reaction to presumed Russian interference in the Presidential electoral campaign, allegedly detected by the CIA.

In order to block this policy, the friends of Hillary Clinton and Victoria Nuland-Kagan have relaunched the war against Donbass. The heavy losses incurred since the beginning of the conflict had caused the Ukrainian army to retreat, and place paramilitary Nazi militia in the front line. The fighting inflicted serious civilian casualties on the inhabitants of the new Popular Republic.

In order to resolve the Ukrainian conflict, Donald Trump is looking for a way to get rid of President Petro Poroshenko. To this effect, he received at the White House the head of the Ukrainian opposition, Yulia Tymoshenko, even before he accepted a telephone call from Poroshenko.

At first, President Trump shocked China by accepting a telephone call from the President of Taiwan before President Xi, despite the principle of the "One China" policy. He then apologised to Xi and warmly wished him a "Happy New Year of the Rooster".

At the same time, he offered him a magnificent present by cancelling the Trans-Pacific Treaty. This agreement, which had not yet been ratified, was designed – like all of the globalisation measures over the last fifteen years – to exclude China from any power of decision.

Trump has opened up a channel for negotiations with the major commercial and financial authorities of China, via the members of the strategic and political Forum that he created at the White House. Blackstone is the name of the company of the Forum's President, Stephen Schwarzman. Since 2007, a 9.3% share in it has been owned by the sovereign wealth fund of the Popular Republic, China Investment Corp., which is the world's largest repository of foreign exchange reserves. The fund's Director at that time, Lou Jiwei, is today the Chinese Minister of Finances.

Schwarzman is part of the Advisory Council of the School of Economy and Management of the University of Tsinghua. This Council, placed under the presidency of ex-Prime Minister Zhu Rongji, unites the most important Chinese and Western personalities. Amongst these are – Mary Barra from General Motors; Jamie Dimon from JPMorgan Chase; Doug McMillon from Wal-Mart Stores; Elon Musk from Tesla Motors; and Indra K. Nooyi from PepsiCo – who also sit on the new Strategic and Political Forum of the White House.

Finally, the clean-up of the international institutions has also begun. The new US ambassador to the UN, Nikki Haley, has demanded an audit of the 16 "peace-keeping missions". She has made it known that she intends to close down any of these missions which is proving inefficient. As regards the Charter of the United Nations Organisation, this is in the case with all of them. The founders of the UN never foresaw this kind of military deployment (which today totals more than 100,000 men). The UN was created to prevent or resolve inter-state conflicts, not to intervene in intra-state problems. When two parties conclude a cease-fire, the Organisation may deploy observers to make sure that the agreement is respected. However, "peace-keeping operations" are aimed at imposing a solution chosen by the Security Council and refused by one of the parties in the conflict – so in reality, this is simply a continuation of colonialism.

In practice, the presence of these forces does little more than prolong war, while their absence changes nothing at all. For example, the troops of the FINUL deployed at the Israelo-Lebanese frontier (but only on Lebanese territory) can not prevent either a military action by Israel nor a military action by the Lebanese Resistance, as we have already seen several times. They serve only to spy on the Lebanese for the benefit of the Israelis, thereby prolonging the conflict. Similarly, the troops of the FNUOD, deployed at the line of demarcation of the

Golan Heights, were chased away by al-Qaeda – which changed absolutely nothing concerning the Israelo-Syrian conflict. Putting an end to this system is returning to the spirit and the letter of the Charter, giving up colonial privileges, and pacifying the world.

After five months of internecine war against the 98% of senior civil servants who voted for Hillary Clinton, President Trump, CIA director Mike Pompeo[65] and National Security advisor H. R. McMaster finally managed to shut down all the support programmes for jihadists, everywhere in the world.

Donald Trump then gave an important speech in Riyadh on 21 May 2017, before representatives of almost all the member states of the Organisation of Islamic Cooperation. He urged them to cease all contact with the jihadists immediately and to expel them from their territories.

Saudi Arabia agreed to do without the Muslim Brotherhood and the Order of the Naqshbandis in return for the promise of US military protection, which costs $110 billion. Prince Mohammed ben Nayef was relieved of his duties, while Prince Mohammed ben Salman became the new crown Prince. Immediately, Saudi Arabia, Bahrain, Egypt and the Arab Emirates broke off relations with Qatar, which persisted in supporting the Brotherhood. A new fracture line then appeared in the Greater Middle East – on one side, those states which agreed to no longer impose religion on their citizens, and on the other, the partisans of political Islam (Iran, Qatar, Turkey).

On 25 May, President Trump travelled to Brussels, the new headquarters of NATO, which he had declared "obsolete". While the protocol had originally planned for the inauguration of a vestige of the Berlin Wall, he asked for the addition of a vestige of the Twin Towers of New York. He changed his speech, and congratulated NATO for having defeated the Soviet Union (which is untrue, but flattered the Allied military). Then he noted that the Alliance had applied article 5 of its statutes (the duty to defend an attacked ally) only once in its history, on 11 September 2001. That said, he forced a 90° turn on the members – from now on, the aim of NATO would no longer be to compete with Russia, but also to fight terrorism.

---

[65] In April, 2018, Pompeo succeeded Tillerson as Secretary of State, and McMaster resigned as National Security advisor. They were succeeded by Porter Goss and John Bolton, respectively.

Finally, on 26 May, at the G7 summit in Taormina, he obtained an agreement from his partners, not against the Muslim Brotherhood and terrorism in general, but at least that they cease supporting Daesh.

However, this progress in the Greater Middle East did not prevent the ex-heads of the Strategy for Global Democracy from pursuing their own agenda in Latin America. Around Elliott Abrams, they were plotting a "Latin Spring" in the North-West of the South American continent and the Caribbean. This programme began in Venezuela with a number of deaths during demonstrations, a call for insurrection by the police and the army, and even the creation of a parallel justice system. Just as in the Arab world, neither the Maduro government nor its legitimate opposition understood what was being hatched. They persisted in interpreting these events as a political conflict, and did not imagine that the US deep state was preparing to eliminate them both and to destroy their country.

As I finish the writing of this book, the Herculean confrontation between the forces of war and the forces of peace has only just begun. The conflict, which had earlier been limited to the Greater Middle East, has now spread to the whole of the Western world, even though the West may not yet know it. Already, Vladimir Putin and Mahmud Ahmadinejad have expressed their hopes that Donald Trump will be able to beat the System, and encourage him to go for it. Nothing has yet allowed us to anticipate whether the businessman will be able to display the qualities of a statesman, or to guess whether he will be able to master the deep US state and cooperate with his present adversaries. Whatever happens, the conflagration will continue in the years to come until the power usurped by the "Continuity of Government" has been dismantled, until the Western world has been freed of its imperialist fantasy, and until international peace has been restored.

August, 2018

Bibliography

Official Documents

ɪn military operations, Research paper, Parliament of Australia, ɪ, 2017.

in a zone of conflicts within conflicts, Research paper, Parliament of ɔber 14th, 2016.

ɑliphate and Australia, Research paper, Parliament of Australia, July

esponses to the Syrian uprising: March 2011-June 2012, Research
ent of Australia, July13th, 2012.

ɪ
L.   *'Jnited Nations Security Council Resolution (UNSCR) 1973*, Research
paɟ   nt of Australia, March 24th, 2011.

Fra

*Rappɔ   ɪoyens mis en œuvre par l'État pour lutter contre le terrorisme
depuis .   ʳ 2015*, Georges Fenech & Sébasten Pietrasanta, Commission
d'enquêt   ɪlée nationale, Juillet 2016.

Rapport   ion sur le Liban, Axel Poniatowski & Benoît Hamon, Mission
d'informa   mblée nationale, Juin 2016.

Rapport d   on sur les moyens de Daech, Kader Arif & Jean-Frédéric
Poisson, M   information, Assemblée nationale, Juin 2016.

Rapport d'ɪɲ   ion sur la Libye, Nicole Ameline, Philippe Baumel, Jean
Glavany, Mission d'information, Assemblée nationale, Novembre 2015.

Question(s) d'Orient(s), Les Carnets du CAPS, Centre d'analyse, de prévision et de
stratégie, Ministère des Affaires étrangères, Eté 2015.

Filières "djihadistes": pour une réponse globale et sans faiblesse, Jean-Pierre
Sueur, Commission d'enquête, Sénat, Avril 2015.

Rapport d'information sur le Proche-Orient, Jean-Luc Reitzer & Odile Saugues,
Mission d'information, Assemblée nationale, Mars 2015.

Rapport d'information sur les révolutions arabes, Jacques Myard & Jean Glavany,
Mission d'information, Assemblée nationale, Novembre 2013.

Germany

*Fundamental Attitudes of the Russian Political Elite: Law, Truth, Public Welfare
and Violence*, Susan Stewart, Stiftung Wissenschaft und Politik, June 2017.

Syria's Sectarian Quandary, Khaled Yacoub Oweis, Stiftung Wissenschaft und
Politik, April 2017.

*Syria's Uneasy Bedfellows: Perpetuation of Conflict Serves Radicals, Prospect for
Compromise Increases Moderation*, Khaled Yacoub Oweis, Heiko Wimmen,
Stiftung Wissenschaft und Politik, December 2016.

Syria after the Russian Intervention, Khaled Yacoub Oweis, Stiftung Wissenschaft und Politik, March 2016.

The Return of the Kurdish Question, Günter Seufert, Stiftung Wissenschaft und Politik, August 2015.

Sieges and Ceasefires in Syria's Civil War, Khaled Yacoub Oweis, Stiftung Wissenschaft und Politik, May 2015.

Erdoğan's "New Turkey", Günter Seufert, Stiftung Wissenschaft und Politik, October 2014.

The New "Lions of Syria", Guido Steinberg, Stiftung Wissenschaft und Politik, April 2014.

Divisive Rule: Sectarianism and Power Maintenance in the Arab Spring: Bahrain, Iraq, Lebanon and Syria, Heiko Wimmen, Stiftung Wissenschaft und Politik, March 2014.

Syrian Muslim Brotherhood Still a Crucial Actor, Petra Becker, Stiftung Wissenschaft und Politik, October 2013.

Syria's Business Elite, Samer Abboud, Stiftung Wissenschaft und Politik, August 2013.

Losing the Syrian Grassroots: Local Governance Structures Urgently Need Support, Doreen Khoury, Stiftung Wissenschaft und Politik, February 2013.

Civil War in Syria, Muriel Asseburg, Heiko Wimmen, Stiftung Wissenschaft und Politik, December 2012.

The Day After Project: Supporting a democratic transition in Syria, The Day After, 2012.

Crisis in Syria: Possibilities and Limits of Military Intervention, Markus Kaim, Stiftung Wissenschaft und Politik, March 2012.

The Violent Power Struggle in Syria, Muriel Asseburg, Heiko Wimmen, Stiftung Wissenschaft und Politik, March 2012.

United Kingdom

The Middle East: Time for New Realism and *Government Response*, Foreign Affairs Committee, House of Commons, May 2017.

'Political Islam', and the Muslim Brotherhood Review and *Government Response*, Foreign Affairs Committee, House of Commons, November 2016.

Libya: Examination of intervention and collapse and the UK's future policy options and *Government Response*, Foreign Affairs Committee, House of Commons, September 2016.

The UK's role in the war against ISIL following the Cessation of Hostilities in Syria, and *Government Response*, Foreign Affairs Committee, House of Commons, March 2016.

The extension of offensive British military operations to Syria, and *Government Response*, Foreign Affairs Committee, House of Commons, November 2015.

British foreign policy and the 'Arab Spring': follow-up, and *Government Response*, Foreign Affairs Committee, House of Commons, March 2015.

UK Government policy on the Kurdistan Region of Iraq, and *Government Response*, Foreign Affairs Committee, House of Commons, January 2015.

Iran, the Nuclear Negotiations and Relations with the UK, Ben Smith, Research Papers, House of Commons, December 2014.

ISIS: The Military Response in Iraq and Syria, Louisa Brooke-Holland & Claire Mills, Research Papers, UK House of Commons, October 2014.

Islamic State of Iraq and the Levant (ISIS) and the Takeover of Mosul, Ben Smith, Louisa Brook-Holland, Rob Page, Research Papers, House of Commons, June 2014.

Election Against a Background of Violence in Syria, Ben Smith, Research Papers, House of Commons, June 2014.

The UK's response to extremism and instability in North and West Africa, and *Government Response*, Foreign Affairs Committee, House of Commons, March 2014.

The Deal with Iran, Idir Ouahes, Ben Smith, Research Papers, House of Commons, December 2013.

The UK's relations with Saudi Arabia and Bahrain and *Government Response*, Foreign Affairs Committee, House of Commons, November 2013.

US Government and Congress Response to Syria, Vaughne Miller, Research Papers, House of Commons, September 2013.

The Kurds: New Perspectives?, Ben Smith, Research Papers, House of Commons, August 2013.

Sanctions on Syria: Existing EU/UK Measures, Ben Smith, Research Papers, House of Commons, August 2013.

Intervention in Syria, Ben Smith, Research Papers, House of Commons, August 2013.

Syria: The Legality of Arming the Rebels after the Lifting of the EU Arms Embargo, Ben Smith, Arabella Lang, Research Papers, House of Commons, June 2013.

Military Forces in Syria and the Rise of the Jihadis, Ben Smith, Research Papers, House of Commons, April 2013.

British foreign policy and the "Arab Spring" and *Government Response*, Foreign Affairs Committee, House of Commons, July 2012.

In Brief: Arab Uprisings 2011, *Arab Uprisings: An Update*, Ben Smith, Research Papers, House of Commons, June 2011 & August 2012.

Syria: No End in Sight?, Ben Smith, Research Papers, House of Commons, August 2012.

Military Operations in Libya, Claire Taylor, Research Papers, House of Commons, October 2011.

Unrest Spreads to Syria, Ben Smith, Research Papers, House of Commons, June 2011.

UK Relations with Libya, Ben Smith, Research Papers, House of Commons, March 2011.

Qatar 2011, Ben Smith, Research Papers, House of Commons, January 2011.

The British-Syrian Relationship On the Psychiatrist's Couch, Nicholas Beecroft, Defence Academy of the United Kingdom, 2005.

United Nations

Letters from the United States to Security Council Committee established pursuant to Resolution 1970 (2011) concerning the Libyan Arab Jamahiriya. Ref.: S/AC.52/2011/NOTE.93 and S/AC.52/2011/COMM.153

Russian Intelligence Reports Dealing with ISIS. Ref. S/2016/94, S/2016/143 and S/2016/224 (Turkey answer), S/2016/262 and S/2016/337 (Turkey answer), S/2016/298 and S/2016/425 (Turkey answer), S/2016/457.

Committee from the Security Council Reports Dealing with ISIS S/2015/976, S/2016/92, S/2016/501, S/2016/830.

"Draft Geneva Communique Implementation Framework", "Confidence Building Measures", "Essential Principles", "Representativeness and Inclusivity", "The Preparatory Phase", "The Transitional Governing Body", "The Joint Military Council and Ceasefire Bodies", "The Invitation to the International Community to Help Combat Terrorist Organizations", "The Syrian National Council and Legislative Powers during the Transition", "Transitional Justice", "Local Governance", "Preservation and Reform of State Institutions", "Explanatory Memorandum", "Key Principles revealed during Consultations with Syrian Stake-holders", "Thematic Groups", United Nations Department of Political Affairs (DPA), 2012-2014 (unpublished).

United States of America

Syria After the Missile Strikes: Policy Options, Hearing before the Committee on Foreign Affairs, House of Representatives, April 27, 2017.

Defeating Terrorism in Syria: A New Way Forward, Hearing before the Committee on Foreign Affairs, House of Representatives, February 14, 2017.

The Future of Counter-Terrorism Strategy, Hearing before the Committee on Foreign Affairs, House of Representatives, December 1, 2016.

Regional Impact of the Syria Conflict: Syria, Turkey and Iraq, Hearing before the Committee on Foreign Affairs, Senate, September 29, 2016.

From Iraq and Syria to Libya and Beyond: The Evolving ISIL Threat, Hearing before the Committee on Foreign Affairs, House of Representatives, February 10, 2016.

U.S. Policy After Russia's Escalation in Syria, Hearing before the Committee on Foreign Affairs, House of Representatives, November 4, 2015.

US Counterterrorism Efforts in Syria: A Winning Strategy?, Hearing before the Committee on Foreign Affairs, House of Representatives, September 29, 2015.

The Iran, North Korea, and Syria Nonproliferation Act: State Department's Non-Compliance, Hearing before the Committee on Foreign Affairs, House of Representatives, June 17, 2015.

The regional impact of U.S. policy toward Iraq and Syria, Hearing before the Committee on Foreign Affairs, House of Representatives, April 30, 2015.

The fight against ISIS: building the coalition and ensuring military effectiveness, Hearing before the Committee on Foreign Affairs, Senate, February 25, 2015.

Authorization For The Use of Military Force Against ISIL, Hearing before the Committee on Foreign Affairs, Senate, December 9, 2014.

Qatar: Background and US Relations, Christopher M. Blanchard, Congressional Research Service, November 2014.

United States Strategy To Defeat The Islamic State In Iraq and the Levant, Hearing before the Committee on Foreign Affairs, Senate, September 17, 2014.

Armed Conflict in Syria: Overview and US Response, Christopher M. Blanchard, Carla E. Humud, Mary Beth D. Nikitin, Congressional Research Service, September 2014.

Turkey: Background and US Relations, Jim Zanotti, Congressional Research Service, August 2014.

Iran Sanctions, Kenneth Katzman, Congressional Research Service, August 2014.

Iraq Crisis and US Policy, Kenneth Katzman, Carla E Humud, Christopher M Blanchard, Rhoda Margesson, Alex Tiersky, Congressional Research Service, July 2014.

Egypt: Background and US Relations, Jeremy M. Sharp, Congressional Research Service, June 2014.

Iran: US Concerns and Policy Responses, Kenneth Katzman, Congressional Research Service, June 2014.

Syria Spillover: The Growing Threat of Terrorism and Sectarianism in the Middle East and Ukraine Update, Hearing before the Committee on Foreign Affairs, Senate, March 6, 2014.

Lebanon: Background and US Policy, Christopher M. Blanchard, Congressional Research Service, February 2014.

Terrorist Groups in Syria, Hearing before the Committee on Foreign Affairs, House of Representatives, November 20, 2013.

Syria, Hearing before the Committee on Foreign Affairs, Senate, October 31, 2013.

Syria's Chemical Weapons: Issues for Congress, Mary Beth D. Nikitin, Paul K. Kerr, Andrew Feickert, Congressional Research Service, September 2013.

Armed Conflict in Syria: US and International Response, Jeremy M. Sharp, Christopher M. Blanchard, Congressional Research Service, September 2013.

Syria: weighing the Obama administration's response, Hearing before the Committee on Foreign Affairs, House of Representatives, September 4, 2013.

Possible US Intervention in Syria: Issues for Congress, Jeremy M. Sharp, Christopher M. Blanchard, Congressional Research Service, September 2013.

Crisis in Egypt, Hearing before the Committee on Foreign Affairs, Senate, July 25, 2013.

Religious minorities in Syria: caught in the middle, Hearing before the Committee on Foreign Affairs, House of Representatives, June 25, 2013.

A crisis mismanaged: Obama's failed Syria policy, Hearing before the Committee on Foreign Affairs, House of Representatives, June 5, 2013.

The United States and Europe: Responding to Change in the Middle East and North Africa, Kristin Archick, Derek E. Mix, Congressional Research Service, June 2013.

Syria's Chemical Weapons, Mary Beth Nikitin, Andrew Feickert, Paul K. Kerr, Congressional Research Service, May 2013.

Breaking the Iran, North Korea and Syria nexus, Hearing before the Committee on Foreign Affairs, House of Representatives, April 11, 2013.

Crisis in Syria: the US response, Hearing before the Committee on Foreign Affairs, House of Representatives, March 20, 2013.

Next Steps in Syria, Hearing before the Committee on Foreign Affairs, Senate, August 1, 2012.

Assessing the situation in Libya, Hearing before the Committee on Foreign Affairs, Senate, May 12, 2012.

Syria: Unrest and US Policy, Jeremy M. Sharp & Christopher M. Blanchard, Congressional Research Service, May 2012.

Syria: US Policy Options, Hearing before the Committee on Foreign Affairs, Senate, April 19, 2012.

Syria: the crisis and its implications, Hearing before the Committee on Foreign Affairs, Senate, March 1, 2012.

Egypt at a crossroads, Hearing before the Committee on Foreign Affairs, House of Representatives, February 16, 2012.

Reflections on the revolution in Egypt (2 parts), Hearing before the Committee on Foreign Affairs, House of Representatives, February 15 & June 20, 2012.

Political Transition in Tunisia, Alexis Arieff, Congressional Research Service, December 2011.

Confronting Damascus: US Policy toward the evolving situation in Syria (2 parts), Hearing before the Committee on Foreign Affairs, House of Representatives, December 14, 2011 & April 25, 2012.

Persian Gulf, Loren Yager, Congressional Research Service, November 2011.

US Policy in Syria, Hearing before the Committee on Foreign Affairs, Senate, November 9, 2011.

Libya: Unrest and US Policy, Christopher M. Blanchard, Congressional Research Service, September 2011.

Iran and Syria: Next Steps (2 parts), Hearing before the Committee on Foreign Affairs, House of Representatives, June 23 & October 14, 2011.

Shifting Sands: Political Transitions in the Middle-East (2 parts), Hearing before the Committee on Foreign Affairs, House of Representatives, April 13 & May 5, 2011.

Perspectives on the crisis in Libya, Hearing before the Committee on Foreign Affairs, Senate, April 6, 2011.

Operation Odyssey Dawn (Libya), Jeremiah Gertler, Congressional Research Service, March 2011.

Assessing the situation in Libya, Hearing before the Committee on Foreign Affairs, Senate, March 31, 2011.

Libya: Defining US National Security Interests, Hearing before the Committee on Foreign Affairs, House of Representatives, March 31, 2011.

Libya: Background and US Relations, Christopher M Blanchard, Jim Zanotti, Congressional Research Service, February 2011.

Tunisia: Recent Developments and Policy Issues, Alexis Arieff, Congressional Research Service, January 2011.

Handbook for the Egyptian Revolution, Albert Einstein Institution, 2011.

Hezbollah: Background and Issues for Congress, Casey L. Addis & Christopher M. Blanchard, Congressional Research Service, October 2010.

US Security Assistance to Lebanon, Casey L. Addis, Congressional Research Service, September 2010.

The Iraq Study Group Report, James A. Baker, III, Lee H. Hamilton, Lawrence S. Eagleburger, Vernon E. Jordan, Jr., Edwin Meese III, Sandra Day O'Connor, Leon E. Panetta, William J. Perry, Charles S. Robb, Alan K. Simpson, December 2006.

Disarming Libya: Weapons of Mass Destruction, Sharon A Squassoni, Congressional Research Service, September 2006.

Themes

Arab Spring

The International Politics of the Arab Spring: Popular Unrest and Foreign Policy, Robert Mason, Palgrave Macmillan, 2014.

Routledge Handbook of the Arab Spring: Rethinking Democratization, Larbi Sadiki, Routledge, 2014.

Arab Spring, Libyan Winter, Vijay Prashad, AK Press, 2012.

Arms Trafficking

United States Budgetary Costs of Post-9/11 Wars Through FY2018: A Summary of the $5.6 Trillion in Costs for the US Wars in Iraq, Syria, Afghanistan and Pakistan, and Post-9/11 Veterans Care and Homeland Security, Neta C. Crawford, Brown University, November 2017.

"Heikle Fracht aus Ramstein", "Millionen Schuss Munition für Kalaschnikows", Frederik Obermaier & Paul-Anton Krüger, *Süddeutsche Zeitung*, 12. & 20. September 2017.

"350 diplomatic flights carry weapons for terrorists", Dilyana Gaytandzhieva, *Trud*, July 2, 2017.

"US arms shipment to Syrian rebels detailed", Jeremy Binnie & Neil Gibson, *Jane's*, April 7th, 2016.

"Where will the Ukrainian bombs explode?", by Andrey Fomin, *Oriental Review*, December 2015.

"War Gains: Bulgarian Arms Add Fuel to Middle East Conflicts", Maria Petkova, *Balkan Investigative Reporting Network*, December 21, 2015.

"Qatar and Ukraine come to deliver Pechora-2D to ISIS", by Andrey Fomin, *Oriental Review*, November 2015.

"TAJNA LETOVA JORDANSKIH AVIONA S PLESA Sirijski pobunjenici dobivaju oružje preko Zagreba !", Krešimir Žabec, *Jutarnji list*, 23 veljača 2013. "TRANSFER HRVATSKOG ORUŽJA POBUNJENICIMA U SIRIJI Sve je dogovoreno prošlog ljeta u Washingtonu !", Krešimir Žabec, *Jutarnji list*, 26 veljača 2013. "VIDEO: JUTARNJI OTKRIVA U 4 mjeseca za Siriju sa zagrebačkog aerodroma Pleso otišlo 75 aviona sa 3000 tona oružja !", Krešimir Žabec, *Jutarnji list*, 7 ožujak 2013. "PUT KROZ ASADOVU SIRIJU Nevjerojatna priča o državi sravnjenoj sa zemljom i njezinim uništenim ljudima: 'Živote su nam ukrali, snove ubili...'", Antonija Handabaka, *Jutarnji list*, 9 ožujak 2013.

Chemical Weapons

Possible Implications of Faulty US Technical Intelligence in the Damascus Nerve Agent Attack of August 21, 2013, Richard Lloyd & Theodore A. Postol, MIT, January 14, 2014.

About the Nerve Agent Attack in Khan Shaykhun, Syria (April13, 2017), Theodore Postol, MIT, April 13, 2017.

Muslim Brotherhood and Jihadist Groups

The Master Plan: ISIS, Al-Qaeda, and the Jihadi Strategy for Final Victory, Brian H. Fishman, Yale University Press, 2016.

ISIS is US: The Shocking Truth Behind the Army of Terror, John-Paul Leonard, G. Washingtons's Blog, Wayne Madsen, Progressive Press, 2015.

The Muslim Brotherhood – The Organization and Policies of a Global Islamist Movement, Barry Rubin & Co, Palgrave Macmillan, 2015.

Foreign Fighters in Syria, Richard Barrett, The Soufan Group, 2014.

The Islamic State, Richard Barrett, The Soufan Group, 2014.

The Muslim Brotherhood: From Opposition to Power, Alison Pargeter, Saqi, 2013.

The Inevitable Caliphate?: A History of the Struggle for Global Islamic Union, 1924 to the Present, Reza Pankhurst, Oxford University Press, 2013.

Classified Woman. The Sibel Edmonds Story: A Memoir ; *The Lone Gladio*, Sibel Edmonds.

A Mosque in Munich: Nazis, the CIA, and the Rise of the Muslim Brotherhood in the West, Ian Johnson, Houghton Mifflin Harcourt, 2010.

Architect of Global Jihad: The Life of Al Qaeda Strategist Abu Mus'ab Al-Suri, Brynjar Lia, Columbia University Press, 2009.

The Management of Savagery: The Most Critical Stage Through Which the Umma Will Pass, Abu Bakr Naji, 2005. English version translated by William McCants, Harvard University, 2006.

Wie der Dschihad nach Europa kam, Jürgen Elsässer, Niederoesterr Pressehaus, 2005.

Al-Qaida's Jihad in Europe: The Afghan-Bosnian Network, Evan Kohlmann, Berg, 2004.

Political Islam

Revival of Political Islam in the Aftermath of the Arab Uprisings: Implications for the Region and Beyond, Mohammed El-Katiri, Strategic Studies Institute of the US Army War College (SSI), July 2014.

Islamism and Security in Bosnia-Herzegovina, Leslie S. Lebl, Strategic Studies Institute of the US Army War College (SSI), May 2014.

Reforming the Muslim Brotherhood, Ed Husain, Council on Foreign Relations, October 2013.

Arab Spring, Turkish "Summer"? The Trajectory of a Pro-Western "Moderate Islam", Kees van der Pijl, Norwegian Peacebuilding Resource Centre, November 2012.

A Tyranny of the Majority?, Moataz El Fegiery, FRIDE, October 2012.

Political Islam: A Critical Reader, Frédéric Volpi, Routledge, 2011.

Political Islam and European Foreign Policy, Samir Amghar, Talal Atrissi, Senem Aydin, Amel Boubekeur, Ruşen Çakir, Salah Eddine Jorshi, Salam Kawakibi, Emad el-Din Shahin, Robert Springborg, Nathalie Tocci, Centre for European Policy Studies, 2007.

Terrorism

• Journals

CTC Sentinel (ten issues per year), Combating Terrorism Center, United States Military Academy West Point.

Counter Terrorist Trends and Analysis, S. Rajaratnam School of International Studies.

Journal of Terrorism Research (three issues per year), Handa Centre for the Study of Terrorism and Political Violence, University of St Andrews.

Perspectives on Terrorism (six issues by year), Terrorist Research Initiative, University of Leiden.

• Reports

Antiquities Destruction and Illicit Sales as Sources of ISIS Funding and Propaganda, W. Andrew Terrill, Letort Papers, Strategic Studies Institute of the US Army War College (SSI), April 2017.

The Al-Qaeda Organization and the Islamic State Organization: History, Doctrine, Modus Operandi, and U.S. Policy to Degrade and Defeat Terrorism Conducted in the Name of Sunni Islam, Paul Kamolnick, Strategic Studies Institute of the US Army War College (SSI), February 2017.

Then and Now: Comparing the Flow of Foreign Fighters to AQI and the Islamic State, Brian Dodwell & Daniel Milton & Don Rassler, Combating Terrorism Center, December 2016.

From Cradle to Grave: The Lifecycle of Foreign Fighters in Iraq and Syria, Arie Perliger & Daniel Milton, Combating Terrorism Center, November 2016.

Financial Futures of the Islamic State of Iraq and the Levant. Findings from a RAND Corporation Workshop, Colin P. Clarke, Kimberly Jackson, Patrick B. Johnston, Eric Robinson, Howard J. Shatz, Rand Corporation, June 2016.

The Caliphate's Global Workforce: An Inside Look at the Islamic State's Foreign Fighter Paper Trail, Brian Dodwell & Daniel Milton & Don Rassler, Combating Terrorism Center, April 2016.

Competing Visions for Syria and Iraq: The Myths of an Anti-ISIS Grand Coalition, Frederick W Kagan, Kimberly Kagan, Jennifer Cafarella, Harleen Gambhir, Christopher Kozak Hugo Spaulding, Katherine Zimmerman, Institute for the Study of War, January 2016.

Foundations of the Islamic State. Management, Money, and Terror in Iraq, 2005–2010, Patrick B. Johnston, Jacob N. Shapiro, Howard J. Shatz, Benjamin Bahney, Danielle F. Jung, Patrick Ryan, Jonathan Wallace, Rand Corporation, 2016.

The French War on Al Qa'ida in Africa, Christopher S. Chivvis, Cambridge University Press, 2016.

The Islamic State We Knew. Insights Before the Resurgence and Their Implications, Howard J. Shatz, Erin-Elizabeth Johnson, Rand Corporation, September 2015.

There and Back: Trajectories of North African Foreign Fighters in Syria, Hasnaa El-Jamali & Laurent Vinatier, Small Arms Survey, July 2015.

Syria Calling: Radicalisation in Central Asia, International Crisis Group, January 2015.

Eurojihad. Patterns of Islamist Radicalization and Terrorism in Europe, Angel Rabasa, Cheryl Benard, Cambridge University Press, January 2015.

Managing a Transnational Insurgency: The Islamic State of Iraq's "Paper Trail," 2005-2010, Danielle F Jung, Pat Ryan, Jacob N Shapiro, Jon Wallace, Combating Terrorism Center, December 2014.

The Group That Calls Itself a State: Understanding the Evolution and Challenges of the Islamic State, Muhammad al-'Ubaydi, Nelly Lahoud, Daniel Milton, Bryan Price, Combating Terrorism Center, December 2014.

The Inseparable Twins: Diaspora Shishan and Chechen Muwahhidun & Jihadis in al-Sham, John R. Haines, Foreign Policy Research Institute, November 2014.

The Resurgence of al-Qaeda in Syria and Iraq, Azeem Ibrahim, Strategic Studies Institute of the US Army War College (SSI), May 2014.

Jihadi Discourse in the Wake of the Arab Spring, Nelly Lahoud, Muhammad al-'Ubaydi, Combating Terrorism Center, December 2013.

Routledge Handbook of Political Islam, Shahram Akbarzadeh, Routledge, 2012.

Al-Qa'ida's Foreign Fighters in Iraq: A First Look at the Sinjar Records, Joseph Felter, Brian Fishman, Combating Terrorism Center, December 2007.

Jihadi After Action Report: Syria, Stephen Ulph, Combating Terrorism Center, November 2006.

UK support to jihad

Secret Affairs: Britain's Collusion With Radical Islam, Mark Curtis, Profile Books, 2011.

When progressives threat with reactionaries. The British State flirtation with radical Islamism, Martin Bright, Policy Exchange, 2004.

Warfare

Defence Industries in Arab States: Players and Strategies, Florence Gaub & Zoe Stanley-Lockman, European Union Institute for Security Studies, March 2017.

The Remote Warfare Digest, Chris Abbott, Steve Hathorn, Scott Hickie, Oxford Research Group, November 2016.

Countries

Egypt

Can Egypt Lead the Arab World Again? Assessing Opportunities and Challenges for U.S. Policy, Gregory Aftandilian, Strategic Studies Institute of the US Army War College (SSI), May 2017.

Arab Fall: How the Muslim Brotherhood Won and Lost Egypt in 891 Days, Eric Trager, Georgetown University Press, 2016.

The International Dimensions of Democratization in Egypt: The Limits of Externally-Induced Change, Gamal M. Selim, Springer, 2015.

Assessing Egyptian Public Support for Security Crackdowns in the Sinai, Gregory Aftandilian, Strategic Studies Institute of the US Army War College (SSI), February 2015.

Egypt's New Regime and the Future of the US- Egyptian Strategic Relationship, Gregory Aftandilian, Strategic Studies Institute of the US Army War College (SSI), April 2013.

Egypt's Islamist President: What Lies Ahead?, Anthony Bubalo, Lowy Institute for International Policy, July 2012.

Who's Who in the New Egypt?, Jacob Høigilt, Norwegian Peacebuilding Resource Centre, February 2011.

The Egyptian Muslim Brotherhood: Islamist Participation in a Closing Political Environment, Amr Hamzawy & Nathan J. Brown, Carnegie Endowment for International Peace, May 2010.

The Muslim Brothers in Egypt: The driving force behind a Muslim dictatorship, Julien Duval-Leroy, Research Institute for European and American Studies, October 2007.

Iran

Iran and its Path-Dependent Military Doctrine, Air University, 2016.

Saudi Arabia and Iran: Friends or Foes?, Banafsheh Keynoush, Palgrave Macmillan, 2016.

From Frozen Ties to Strategic Engagement: US-Iran Relationship in 2030, Roman Muzalevsky, SSI, Strategic Studies Institute of the US Army War College (SSI), May 2015.

Prospects for Iran's New Direction, Letort Papers, Strategic Studies Institute of the US Army War College (SSI), February 2015.

Assessing the European Union's Sanctions Policy: Iran as a Case Study, Dina Esfandiary, Stockholm International Peace Research Institute, December 2013.

Iran and the Arab Spring: Between Expectations and Disillusion, Henner Fürtig, German Institute of Global and Area Studies, November 2013.

The Rising Power of Iran in the Middle East, Evangelos Venetis, Hellenic Foundation for Defence and Foreign Policy, July 2011.

Iraq

Limited Accountability: A Transparency Audit of the Anti-ISIL Coalition, Oxford Research Group, December 2016.

Israel and Iraqi Kurds in a Transforming Middle East, Aldo Liga, Istituto Affari Internazionali, December 2016.

Kurdistan's Politicized Society Confronts a Sultanistic System, Kawa Hassan, Carnegie Endowment for International Peace, August 2015.

Iraq's Shia Warlords and Their Militias: Political and Security Challenges and Options, Norman Cigar, Strategic Studies Institute of the US Army War College (SSI), June 2015.

Iran's Role in Iraq. Room for Cooperation?, Alireza Nader, Rand Corporation, June 2015.

Arming Iraq's Kurds: Fighting IS, Inviting Conflict, International Crisis Group, May 2015.

Strike from the Air: The First 100 Days of the Campaign against ISIL, Patricia Dias, Tobias Feakin, Ken Gleiman, Peter Jennings, Daniel Nichola, Simone Roworth, Benjamin Schreer, Mark Thomson, Australian Strategic Policy Institute, December 2014.

Turkey-Kurdish Regional Government Relations after the US Withdrawal from Iraq, Bill Park, Strategic Studies Institute of the US Army War College (SSI), March 2014.

GCC Relations with Post-War Iraq, Andrea Plebani, Ashraf Mohammed Kishk, Fatin Shabbar, Metodi Hadji Janev, Abderraouf El Ouazzani Taibi, Sanju Gupta, Degang Sun, Yacoob Abba Omar, Safa Mubgar, Gulf Research Center, 2014.

The Future of Kurdistan, Jacques Neriah, Jerusalem Center for Public Affairs, August 2012.

Israel

• Journals

Strategic Assessment (four issues per year), Institute for National Security Studies.

Cyber, Intelligence, and Security former *Military and Strategic Affairs* (three issues per year), Institute for National Security Studies.

• Report

Israel's Interests and Options in Syria, Larry Hanauer, Rand Corporation, 2016.

Turkish-Israeli Rapprochement with NATO, Hasan Aygun, The NATO Defense College, June 2016.

Lebanon

Lebanon Poised at the Brink, Tine Gade, Norwegian Institute of International Affairs, October 2016.

Syrian Jihadists Signal Intent For Lebanon, Jennifer Cafarella, Institute for the Study of War, March 2015.

From War to Deterrence? Israel-Hezbollah Conflict since 2006, Jean-Loup Samaan, Strategic Studies Institute of the US Army War College (SSI), May 2014.

"Un député libanais dirige le trafic d'armes vers la Syrie", *New Orient News*, 4 décembre 2012.

Can Lebanon Survive the Syrian Crisis?, Paul Salem, Carnegie Endowment for International Peace, December 2012.

"Кто убил Рафика Харири", Тьерри Мейсан, *Однако*, 29 ноября 2010.

Towards Lebanese National Reconciliation, Geneva Centre for the Democratic Control of Armed Forces, 2009.

Libya

After the Fall: Views from the Ground of International Military Intervention in Post-Gadhafi Libya, Remote Control Project, July 2017.

The Origins and Evolution of ISIS in Libya, Atlantic Council, June 2017.

Libya in the Arab Spring: From Revolution to Insecurity, Ramazan Erdağ, Palgrave Macmillan, 2017.

The 2011 Libyan Uprisings and the Struggle for the post-Qadhafi Future, Jason Pack, Palgrave Macmillan, 2015.

The North Atlantic Treaty Organization and Libya: Reviewing Operation UNIFIED PROTECTOR, Florence Gaub, Letort Papers, Strategic Studies Institute of the US Army War College (SSI), June 2013.

The NATO Intervention in Libya: Lessons Learned From the Campaign, Kjell Engelbrekt & Marcus Mohlin & Charlotte Wagnsson, Routledge, 2013.

"Sarkozy manovra la rivolta libica", Franco Bechis, *Libero*, 23 marzo 2011.

"Entretien du Lt-gal Charles Bouchard", *Radio Canada*, 31 octobre 2011 à 17h32.

"CIA recruits 1,500 from Mazar-e-Sharif to fight in Libya", Azhar Masood, *The Nation* (Pakistan), August 31, 2011.

Libya's Foreign Policy, George Joffe & Emanuela Paoletti, German Marshall Fund of The United States (GMF), 2010.

US-Libyan Relations: An Analytic Compendium of US Policies, Laws and Regulations, Kenneth Katzman, Atlantic Council of the United States, 2003.

US-Libyan Relations: Toward Cautious Reengagement, Chester A Crocker & Richard C Nelson, Atlantic Council of the United States, April 2003.

Middle-East

Ambiguous Endings: Middle East Regional Security in the Wake of the Arab Uprisings and the Syrian Civil War, Helle Malmvig, Danish Institute for International Studies, August 2013.

NATO

• Journal

PfP Consortium Quarterly Journal (three issues per year).

Qatar

Qatar's Diplomatic Incursions into the Horn of Africa, Berouk Mesfin, Institute for Security Studies, November 2016.

Qatar and the Recalibration of Power in the Gulf, Lina Khatib, Carnegie Endowment for International Peace, September 2014.

Qatar and the Arab Spring, Kristian Coates Ulrichsen, Oxford University Press, 2014.

"Qatar, Tunisia sign two key military pacts", Qatar News Agency ; et "Tunisie-Qatar: signature d'un mémorandum de coopération militaire", *Agence Tunis Afrique Presse*, 20 novembre 2012.

Russia

• Journal

Russian Analytical Digest (12 issues per year).

• Reports

Spirituality as a Political Instrument: The Church, the Kremlin, and the Creation of the Russian World, Veera Laine & Iiris Saarelainen, Finnish Institute of International Affairs, September 2017.

Russia Military Power: Building a Military to Support Great Power Aspirations, US Defense Intelligence Agency, July 2017.

The Turning Point for Russian Foreign Policy, Keir Giles, Letort Papers, Strategic Studies Institute (SSI), May 2017.

The North Caucasus Insurgency and Syria: An Exported Jihad, International Crisis Group, March 2016.

"Russisches Syrien-Abenteuer: Das Ende der alten Weltordnung", Matthias Schepp, *Der Spiegel*, 10. Oktober 2015.

"Cu ce arme ultrasecrete a cîstigat Putin suprematia în razboiul radioelectronic din Siria?", Valentin Vasilescu, *Ziarul de gardă*, 12 octobre 2015

"KALIBRating the foe: strategic implications of the Russian cruise missiles' launch", Vladimir Kozin, *Oriental Review*, 14 October 2015.

Homo Jihadicus: Islam in the Former USSR and the Phenomenon of the Post-Soviet Militants in Syria and Iraq, Maciej Falkowski & Józef Lang, Centre for Eastern Studies, September 2015.

Russia and the Arab Spring, Alexey Malashenko, Carnegie Endowment for International Peace, October 2013.

The Mythical Alliance: Russia's Syria Policy, Dmitri Trenin, Carnegie Endowment for International Peace, February 2013.

Saudi Arabia

A Saudi-Led Military Alliance to Fight Terrorism. Welcome Muscle in the Fight Against Terrorism, Desert Mirage, or Bad Idea?, Brian Michael Jenkins, Rand Corporation, April 2016.

In Search of Stability: Saudi Arabia and the Arab Spring, Gulf Research Center, July 2014.

Saudi Arabia's Nuclear Thinking and the Pakistani Connection, Reshmi Kazi, Institute for Defence Studies and Analyses, January 2014.

Syria

• Journal

Regional Analyses of the Syrian Conflict, ACAPS (since December 2012 until June 2015).

• Reports

A Peace Plan for Syria IV. A Bottom-Up Approach, Linking Reconstruction Assistance to Local Government Formation, James Dobbins, Philip Gordon, Jeffrey Martini, Rand Corporation, November 2017.

Putin's Syrian Gambit: Sharper Elbows, Bigger Footprint, Stickier Wicket, John W. Parker, Strategic Perspectives, Institute for National Strategic Studies, National Defense University, July 2017

Future of Syria, F. Gaub, S. Kawakibi, J.Quero, E.Soler, E.Woertz, (Editors – M. Akgün, S.Tiryaki), European Institute of the Mediterranean, April 2017.

Preventing State Collapse in Syria, Andrew Parasiliti, Kathleen Reedy, Becca Wasser, Rand Corporation, January 2017.

Countering War Propaganda: of the dirty war on Syria: A selection of social media infographics, 2012-2017, Tim Anderson, Amazon, 2017.

Washington's Long War on Syria, Stephen Gowans, Baraka Books, 2017.

Who's Who in Syria's Civil War, Zachary Laub, Council on Foreign Relations, December 2016.

From the Bottom, Up: A Strategy for US Military Support to Syria's Armed Opposition, Nicholas A. Heras, Center for a New American Security, May 2016.

Distract, Deceive, Destroy: Putin at War in Syria, Maksymilian Czuperski, John Herbst, Eliot Higgins, Frederic Hof, Ben Nimmo, The Atlantic Council, April 2016.

Syrian Armed Opposition Powerbrokers, Jennifer Cafarella & Genevieve Casagrande, Institute for the Study of War, March 2016.

UN Mediation in the Syrian Crisis: From Kofi Annan to Lakhdar Brahimi, Raymond Hinnebusch, I. William Zartman, Elizabeth Parker-Magyar, Omar Imady, International Peace Institute, March 2016.

The Kremlin's Actions in Syria: Origins Timing, and Prospects, Frederic C Hof, Vladislav Inozemtsev, Adam Garfinkle, Dennis Ross, The Atlantic Council, February 2016.

Inside Syria: What Local Actors are Doing for Peace, Metwaly Abo Naser, Sara Hellmüller, Leila Hilal, Ryme Katkhouda, Yosra Nagui, Swiss Peace, January 2016.

The Battle for Syria: International Rivalry in the New Middle East, Christopher Phillips, Yale University Press, 2016.

The Collapse of Iraq and Syria: The End of the Colonial Construct in the Greater Levant, Roby C. Barrett, Joint Special Operations University, 2016.

Syrian Opposition Guide, Jennifer Cafarella & Genevieve Casagrande, Institute for the Study of War, October 2015.

International Community's Position on Syrian President Bashar al-Assad, Institute for the Study of War, September 2015.

The Balance-Sheet of Conflict: Criminal Revenues and Warlords in Syria, Omar Abdulaziz Hallaj, Norwegian Peacebuilding Resource Centre, May 2015.

The Role of Ideology in Syrian-US Relations – Conflict and Cooperation, J. K. Gani, Palgrave Macmillan, 2015.

Jabhat al-Nusra in Syria: An Islamic Emirates for al-Qaeda, Jennifer Cafarella, Institute for the Study of War, December 2014.

Support for Syria's Civil Society –Misguided and Ineffective, Petra Becker, Stiftung Wissenschaft und Politik, October 2014.

Alternative Futures for Syria. Regional Implications and Challenges for the United States, Andrew Liepman, Brian Nichiporuk, Jason Killmeyer, Rand Corporation, October 2014.

"Cold War and Ayatollah Residues: Syria as a Chessboard for Russia, Iran, and the United States", Matthew D. Crosston, *Strategic Studies Quaterly*, Winter 2014.

Implications of the 2011-13 Syrian Uprising for the Middle Eastern Regional Security Complex, Fred H. Lawson, Center for International and Regional Studies, 2014.

Anything But Politics: The State of Syria's Political Opposition, International Crisis Group, October 2013.

The Chemical Attacks on East Ghouta to Justify Military Right to Protect Intervention in Syria, Mother Agnès-Mariam of the Cross, Institut international pour la Paix, la Justice et les Droits de l'homme, September 2013.

Obstacles to a Resolution of the Syrian Conflict, David W. Lesch, Frida Nome, George Saghir, William Ury, Matthew Waldman, Norwegian Institute of International Affairs, September 2013.

Arms for Syria?, Saferworld, July 2013.

Syria's Uprising, Steven Heydemann, FRIDE, May 2013.

The Syrian Opposition's Leadership Problem, Yezid Sayigh, April 2013.

Power Sharing in Syria, Stephan Rosiny, German Institute of Global and Area Studies, May 2013.

Syria: From Rebellion to All-Out War, Christian-P Hanelt, Kristin Helberg, Bertelsmann Foundation, February 2013.

Establishing a 'Military Transition Council' in Syria, Abdulaziz O Sager, Gulf Research Center, February 2013.

Tentative Jihad: Syria's Fundamentalist Opposition, International Crisis Group, October 2012.

Asad Under Fire: Five Scenarios for the Future of Syria, Melissa G Dalton, Center for a New American Security, September 2012.

Addressing the Syrian Crisis Stalemate, Randolph Cobankiat, Research Institute for European and American Studies, September 2012.

Master Narratives Country Report Syria, Open Source Center, Central Intelligence Agency, June 2012.

Subverting Syria, Tony Carlucci & Nile Bowie, 2012.

The Syrian Revolution: Will the Presumed Social Unity be Challenged in the Post-Assad Period?, Naomí Ramírez Díaz, British Society for Middle Eastern Studies, 2012.

Sanctioning Assad's Syria, Rune Friberg Lyme, Danish Institute for International Studies, 2012.

The Syria Uprising: Implications for Israel, Eyal Zisser, Jerusalem Center for Public Affairs, August 2011.

Power and Policy in Syria: Intelligence Services, Foreign Relations and Democracy in the Modern Middle East, Radwan Ziadeh, I. B. Tauris, 2011.

The EU Association Agreement with Syria, Marie Skov Madsen, Transatlantic Institute, 2009.

The Secret and Unofficial Talks between Israel and Syria, Can Yirik, Global Political Trends Center, August 2008.

America's Role in Israel-Syria Talks, Marshall Breger, Nathan Brown, Thomas A Dine, Frederic C Hof, Scott Lasensky, Samuel Lewis, Robert Malley, Robert Pelletreau, Steven L Spiegel, Edward S Walker, Israel Policy Forum, July 2008.

Dealing with Damascus, Mona Yacoubian & Scott Lasensky, Council on Foreign Relations, June 2008.

Political Islam in Syria, Salam Kawakibi, Centre for European Policy Studies, June 2007.

Restarting Israeli-Syrian Negotiations, International Crisis Group, April 2007.

Washington and Damascus, Moshe Ma'oz, United States Institute of Peace, April 2005.

Syria Under Bashar (I): Foreign Policy Challenges (II): Domestic Policy Challenges, International Crisis Group, February 2004.

Setting the Stage for Peace in Syria: The Case for a Syrian National Stabilization Force, Frederic C. Hof & Bassma Kodmani & Jeffrey White, The Atlantic Council, April 2015.

There and Back: Trajectories of North African Foreign Fighters in Syria, Hasnaa El Jamali & Laurent Vinatier, Small Arms Survey, July 2015.

Tunisia

A Quiet Revolution: The Tunisian Military After Ben Ali, Sharan Grewal, Carnegie Endowment for International Peace, February 2016.

Market for Jihad: Radicalization in Tunisia, Georges Fahmi & Hamza Meddeb, Carnegie Endowment for International Peace, October 2015.

Between the Syrian Stalemate and the Egyptian Coup: In Search of a "Reset" for Turkish Foreign Policy in the Middle East, Ioannis N. Grigoriadis, Hellenic Foundation for European and Foreign Policy, January 2014.

The Cycle of Conflict in Post-Revolutionary Tunisia, 2011-2014, Andrea Carboni, Robert S. Strauss Center for International Security and Law.

Turkey

An Independent Actor: Turkish Foreign and Energy Policy toward Russia, Iran, and Iraq, Aaron Stein, The Atlantic Council, June 2017.

"Whistleblower exposes how NATO's leading ally is arming and funding ISIS", Nafeez Ahmed, *Insurge-Intelligence*, September 16, 2016.

The Kurdish Peace Process in Turkey, Mesut Yeğen, Istanbul Policy Center, 2015.

Ukraine

Balkan Foreign Fighters: From Syria to Ukraine, Jelena Beslin, Marija Ignjatijevic, European Union Institute for Security Studies, June 2017.

The Hour of Truth: The Conflict in Ukraine–Implications for Europe's Energy Security and the Lessons for the U.S. Army, Ariel Cohen & Ivan Benovic, Strategic Studies Institute of the US Army War College (SSI), 2015.

The White Book on Violations of Human Rights and the Rule of Law in Ukraine, Ministry of Foreign Affairs of the Russian Federation, 5 mai 2014.

Российский союз инженеров: реконструкция атаки на "Боинг" (Analysis of the reasons for the crash of flight MH1), Анатольевич Андриевский, *Однако*, September 2014.

"Малайзийский "Боинг" сбил украинский летчик – капитан Волошин" (Vladislav Voloshin: "The Plane Was In the Wrong Place at the Wrong Time") Дмитрий Стешин, Николай Varsegov, Владимир Сунгоркин, *Комсомо́льская пра́вда*, December 25, 2014

Update: Recent Essays

The geopolitical situation in the Middle East, the US, and Europe has been evolving rapidly. Following their failure to destroy Syria in the same way as Libya, the Deep State and its Empire regroup to counterattack, with a foot-dragging President Trump hanging on to the tiger by the tail. The story of fake wars and big lies is not over yet, not by a long shot.

Here we offer up-to-the-minute analyses by Thierry Meyssan. As well as the founder and editor of the Voltaire Network (Réseau Voltaire), he is the most prolific contributor, with over 5,000 articles at his author page, https://www.voltairenet.org/auteur29.html?lang=en .

The 116th US Congress is preparing a new war against Syria

Jan. 31, 2019. We were wrong to think that the Syrians were out of danger after their victory over the jihadists. They are not. Israel and the United States have not abandoned their war objective of the destruction of state structures. They are preparing a new war, this time financial, in order to prevent the reconstruction of the country and condemn the Syrian people to rot in the ruins…

This strategy clearly aims at pursuing the same objective as that of President Barack Obama and Secretary of State Hillary Clinton during the seven years of war against Syria - not by military means, since Russia is present, but by financial means. It is still not a question of overthrowing President Bashar el-Assad (which was only the war objective of Saudi Arabia), nor the Syrian Arab Republic (the war objective of certain old colonial powers), but to weaken the Syrian state to the extreme in application of the Rumsfeld-Cebrowski doctrine.

What Senator James Risch and Representative Eliot Engel [heads of the respective Foreign Affairs Committees] are preparing against Syria has already been implemented by the European Union… it was Engel who tabled the *Syria Accountability and Lebanese Sovereignty Restoration Act* in 2003, the US declaration of war against Syria.

At the opening of the new session and even before they were elected as heads of the Committees, on 3 January 2019, Risch and Engel each presented to their respective assemblies a bill (S.1 and H.R. 31) including an almost identical passage aimed at preventing the reconstruction of Syria. The two men are pretending to believe that the photographs from the Caesar Report show bodies tortured by "Bashar's régime" (in other words the Syrian Arab Republic) and not by the jihadists (alias the "moderate rebels"). They therefore agree to punish the Syrian People for having supported those labeled as "torturers" against the real torturers [1]66.

By doing so, they are pursuing the strategy implemented by Jeffrey Feltman when he was US ambassador to Lebanon. In 2005, he created a "Special Tribunal" to try President Bashar el-Assad, who was guilty, according to Feltman and certain false witnesses, of having commandeered the assassination of Rafic Hariri. Yesterday, el-Assad was an "assassin", today he's a "torturer"....

Since 2001, the United States Treasury has become a political power working in tandem with the Pentagon. This administration has availed itself of astounding powers, notably by creating a jurisprudence which allows it to extra-territorialise US laws under the pretence that certain international transactions have been made in dollars. It is not a law, but an interpretation which today is accepted by US courts. Simultaneously, the Treasury has set up financial tools which enable it to sanction persons, companies and states with a severity that has never been equaled. The most frightening example is the series of sanctions progressively enacted against Iran since 2005...

Contrary to what it claims, when the Treasury sanctions a state, it does not condemn either the state or its leaders, but deprives its population of all economic contact with the West... These sanctions can be of extreme cruelty, like those implemented against the Houthis in Yemen, which maintained conditions of murderous famine... Illegal in international law, they are acts of war comparable to the sieges of the Middle Ages[5]67. Today, the US Treasury is applying political sanctions against Belarus, Burundi, North Korea, Cuba, Iran, Libya, Nicaragua, the Central African Republic, the Democratic Republic of the Congo, Russia, Sudan, Syria, Venezuela and Zimbabwe, to which we must add the Donetsk People's Republic Ukraine), Hezbollah (Iran), the Houthis (Yemen), and many others.

At http://www.voltairenet.org/article204951.html

Has Donald Trump been forced to give up?

Jan. 29, 2019 https://www.voltairenet.org/article204928.html

Has President Donald Trump abandoned the idea of transforming US politics? Has he bowed to the ex-ruling class of his country? Over the last two months, his administration seems to have restructured AfriCom, CentCom and SouthCom. The first military command of the Pentagon has

---

66 "Carter-Ruck's accusations against Syria", Voltaire Network, 24 Jan. 2014, "Washington and Paris reboot the propaganda machine against "the Bashar régime", Thierry Meyssan, Voltaire Network (Meyssan, VN), 11 Oct. 2016.
67 "When you want to sanction States, you call them 'terrorists'", Meyssan, VN/Mint Press News, 27 Nov 2018.

apparently been authorised to join battle against Chinese projects on the African continent; the second has been engaged to divide the Greater Middle East between Arabs and Persians; and the third to destroy the State structures of the Caribbean Basin. These new missions are accompanied by a return of the neo-conservatives.

Since the mid-term elections on 6 November 2018, President Trump has been under extreme pressure. Federal administrations have been closed since 22 December (the shutdown), because of parliamentary opposition to a budget proposition which included the financing for a Wall at the Mexican frontier. The crisis only came to an end 35 days later, on 25 January 2019, when President Trump provisionally bowed to the demands of the Democratic Party. According to S&P Global Ratings, the shutdown will have cost more than 6 billion dollars, which is more expensive than the Wall it was supposed to economise.[1]68

During this period, the Trump administration multiplied signs that it was renouncing its foreign and Defense policies, and rallying with US imperialism…

These elements tend to attest to the fact that the Republican Party and the Trump administration are radically changing their policy and returning – with the exception of the refusal to allow terrorist organisations to administer states – to the Democrat Party policies of President Barack Obama and Hillary Clinton: military imperialism in the service of transnational giants.

This renunciation seems to be implemented by the main sponsors of the Republican Party. Thus, the Koch brothers have recently announced that they will not be supporting the reelection of Donald Trump

Metamorphosis

Jan 8, 2019 https://www.voltairenet.org/article204471.html

Syria was transformed into a battleground for nations from all over the world. It was where the United States and Russia faced off. On 20 December 2018, Washington decided to withdraw without compensation.

This date will be remembered in the history of the world as the most important since 26 December 1991 (dissolution of the USSR). For 27 years, the world was unipolar. The United States were then the world's major economic and military power, and the sole masters of events.

Three years ago, overtaken by China, they lost their economic primacy. Next they lost to Russia their status as the primary conventional military power.

---

68 "US economy lost at least $6 billion to government shutdown: S&P", Reuters, Jan. 26, 2019.

They have now lost that of the first nuclear military power, faced with Russian hypersonic weapons.

President Trump and General Mattis have kept their promise to abandon US support for the jihadists, as well as the promise to withdraw their troops from combat zones in both Syria and Afghanistan. However, for Mattis, the end of the anti-Daesh Coalition uniting 73 nations around the United States prefigures the dissolution of NATO. As a soldier, he cannot accept the risk of being deprived of alliances. On the other hand, President Trump states that the decline of the United States does not allow them to wage war, whatever it might be. According to him, it is impossible for the USA to continue to command the allied forces, and urgent to stabilise the US economy.

The United States prepare a war between Latin-American states

December 18, 2018 https://www.voltairenet.org/article204400.html

Little by little, the partisans of the Cebrowski doctrine are advancing their pawns. If forced to cease creating wars in the Greater Middle East, they'll just turn around and inflame the Caribbean Basin. Above all, the Pentagon is planning to assassinate an elected head of state, ruin his country, and undermine the unity of Latin-America…

The first chapter of this plan consisted of dislocating the "Greater Middle East". The second stage was intended to perform the same task in the "Caribbean Basin". The plan was designed to destroy some twenty coastal and insular States…

When he arrived at the White House, President Donald Trump opposed the Cebrowski plan. However, two years later, he has so far only been able to prevent the Pentagon and NATO from handing over States to the terrorist groups they employ (the "Caliphate"), but not to stop manipulating terrorism. Concerning the Greater Middle East, he has managed to diminish the tension, but the wars still continue there at lower intensity. Concerning the Caribbean Basin, he restrained the Pentagon, forbidding them to launch direct military operations…

Working from several previous analyses, we concluded that the destabilisation of Venezuela - beginning with the guarimbas movement, continued by the attempted coup d'etat of February 2015 (Operation Jericho),[2][69] then by attacks on the national currency and the organisation of emigration - would end with military operations[3][70] led from Brazil, Colombia and Guyana. Multinational manoeuvres of troop transport were

---

[69] "Obama failed his coup in Venezuela," Meyssan, VN, 24 Feb. 2015.
[70] "General Jacinto Perez Arcay considers the invasion of Venezuela 'inevitable'", VN, 12 June 2019

organised by the United States and their allies in August 2017.[4][71] This was made possible by the election of pro-Israeli President Jair Bolsonaro, who will come to power in Brasilia on 1 January 2019...

A group of 734 mercenaries is currently being trained in Tona (Colombia) in order to perpetrate a false flag attack, allegedly by Venezuela, against Colombia – thereby justifying a Colombian war against Venezuela. The war would be under the command of Colonel Oswaldo Valentín García Palomo, who is today in hiding after the attempted assassination by drone of President Maduro during the anniversary of the National Guard on 4 August 2018. These mercenaries are supported by Special Forces stationed on US military bases in Tolemaida (Colombia) and Eglin (Florida). The US plan is to take over, from the beginning of the conflict, the three Venezuelan Libertador military bases of Palo Negro, Puerto Cabello and Barcelona...

Everything is therefore happening as if we were watching a remake of the events which bloodied the Greater Middle East after the attacks of 11 September 2001. The main point is not the military actions, but the appearance of disorder that the events present...It will soon become possible to destroy these states without anyone complaining... on 1 November 2018, Security Advisor John Bolton declared in Miami that Cuba, Nicaragua and Venezuela formed a "troïka of tyranny".

The United States refusal to fight for the transnational financiers

Dec. 25, 2018 https://www.voltairenet.org/article204453.html

The US withdrawal from Syria and Afghanistan, as well as the resignation of General Mattis, attest to the upheaval that is shaking the current world order. The United States are no longer the leaders, either on the economic or the military stage. They refuse to keep fighting for the sole interests of the transnational financiers. The alliances that they used to lead will begin to unravel, but without their erstwhile allies admitting the powerful ascension of Russia and China...

As soon as he entered the White House, Donald Trump was careful to surround himself with three senior military officers with enough authority to reposition the armed forces. Michael Flynn, John Kelly and especially James Mattis, have since left or are in the process of leaving. All three men are great soldiers who together had opposed their hierarchy during Obama's presidency.[1][72] They did not accept the strategy implemented by ambassador John Negroponte for the creation of terrorist groups tasked with stirring up a

---

71 "Large-scale manoeuvres encircling Venezuela," Manlio Dinucci, *Il Manifesto* (Italy) , VN, 23 Aug. 2017.

72 *Cobra II: The Inside Story of the Invasion and Occupation of Iraq*, Michael Gordon & Bernard Trainor, Atlantic Books, 2006.

civil war in Iraq.[2]73 All three stood with President Trump to annul Washington's support for the jihadists. Nonetheless, each of them had his own vision of the role of the United States in the world, and ended up clashing with the President.

The storm whipped up by the mid-term elections has arrived[3]74. The time has come to rethink international relations.

Syria

When in April, as he had promised, Donald Trump mentioned US withdrawal from Syria, the Pentagon persuaded him to stay. Not that a few thousand men could turn the tide of war, but because their presence acted as a counterweight to the Russian influence and a backup for Israel.

However, the transfer of Russian weapons of defence to the Syrian Arab Army, particularly the S-300 missiles and ultra-sophisticated radars coordinated by the automated command and control system Polyana D4M1, changed the balance of forces.[4]75 From that moment on, US military presence became counter-productive – any ground attack by pro-US mercenaries could no longer be supported by US aviation without the risk of losing aircraft.

By withdrawing now, the Pentagon avoids the test of power and the humiliation of an inevitable defeat. Indeed, Russia has successively refused to give the United States and Israel the security codes for the missiles delivered to Syria. This means that after years of Western arrogance, Moscow has declined the sharing of control of Syria that it had accepted during the first Geneva Conference in 2012, and that Washington had violated a few weeks later.

Apart from this, Moscow recognised a long time ago that the US presence is illegal in International Law, and that Syria can legitimately act in self-defence.

The Western project for the creation of a colonial state in the North-East of Syria which would be attributed to the Kurds will not happen. Indeed, fewer and fewer Kurds give it their support, considering that this conquest would be comparable to the unilateral proclamation of a state – Israel – by Jewish militia, in 1948.

---

73 *ISIS is US: The Shocking Truth Behind the Army of Terror*, George Washington's Blog, Wayne Madsen, John-Paul Leonard, Syrian Girl Partisan, Progressive Press, 2016.
74 "International relations: the calm before the storm?", Meyssan, VN, 9 Oct. 2018.
75 "Why is the United States suddenly withdrawing from Syria?", Valentin Vasilescu, VN, 21 Dec. 2018.

As we have often explained, Kurdistan would only be legitimate within the boundaries which were recognised by the Conference of Sèvres in 1920, in what is now Turkey, and nowhere else.[5]76 Yet only a few weeks ago, the United States and France were still considering the possibility of creating a pseudo-Kurdistan on Arab land, and having it administered under a UN mandate by the French ex-Minister for Foreign Affairs, Bernard Kouchner.[6]77

Who is Emmanuel Macron indebted to?

Dec. 11, 2018 https://www.voltairenet.org/article204303.html

French President Macron … owes his electoral campaign mostly to Henry Kravis, the boss of one of the world's largest financial companies, and to NATO – a considerable debt which weighs heavily today on the solution to the Yellow Vests crisis.

In December 2014, Henry Kravis created his own Intelligence agency, the KKR Global Institute. He nominated at its head the ex-Director of the CIA, General David Petraeus. With the Kravis couple's private funds (the KKR investment funds), and without referring to Congress, Petraeus pursued operation "Timber Sycamore" which had been initiated by President Barack Obama. This was the largest weapons traffic in History, implicating at least 17 states and representing many thousands of tons of weapons worth several billion dollars.[7]78 Kravis and Petraeus became the main suppliers for Daesh[8]79 …

When the Yellow Vests crisis began in France,[12]80 it quickly became evident that this was a profound problem which could only be resolved by addressing the question of global finance, which President Macron can not do. During his electoral campaign, he surprised sponsors at a dinner in New York by making accusations against the financialisation of the economy. It was no more than electoral rhetoric. He was taken to task by the Mr. and Mrs. Kravis – financialisation is the system that enables them to operate the "leveraged buy-outs", which have made them what they are.

How the West devours its children

Dec. 4, 2018 https://www.voltairenet.org/article204208.html

---

76 "The Kurdistan projects", Meyssan, VN, 5 Sept. 2016.
77 "Bernard Kouchner enters Syria illegally", VN, 14 Dec. 2018.
78 "Billions of dollars' worth of arms against Syria", Meyssan, VN, 18 July 2017.
79 "Seize the transnational corporations to rebuild Syria?", Meyssan, VN, 14 Aug. 2018.
80 "How the West eats its children", Meyssan, VN, 4 Dec. 2018.

For Thierry Meyssan, by taking to the streets, the French have become the first Western population to take personal risks to oppose financial globalisation. Although they do not realise it, and still imagine that their problems are exclusively national, their enemy is the same force that crushed the region of the African Great Lakes and a part of the Greater Middle East.

By allowing capitalism to run wild, President Bush Sr. hoped to extend prosperity to the world. But capitalism is not a political project, it is simply a system for creating profit. The logic of the US multinationals was to increase their profits by outsourcing production to China, where workers are the lowest paid in the world.

Those who were prepared to measure the cost of this advance for the West were few and far between. New middle classes began to appear in the third world, and although they were, of course, far less wealthy than those in the West, they enabled new, mainly Asian states, to play a rôle on the world stage. But simultaneously, Western middle classes began to disappear,[4][81] meaning that it became impossible for the democratic institutions they built to survive. Above all, the populations of entire regions were to be entirely crushed, starting with those of the African Great Lakes. This first regional war caused 6 million deaths, in Angola, Burundi, Namibia, Uganda, the Democratic Republic of Congo, Rwanda and Zimbabwe, and was met with general incomprehension and indifference. The aim was to continue to seize the natural resources of these countries, but to pay less and less for them, which meant dealing with gangs rather than with the States who had to feed their populations…

Today, the rate of incarceration in China is four times lower than in the United States, while their purchasing power is slightly higher. Objectively therefore, with all its faults, China has become a freer and more prosperous country than the United States.

This process was foreseeable from the beginning, and its execution has been discussed for a long time. Thus, on 1 September 1987, a forty-year-old American published a contrarian opinion piece in the New York Times, the Washington Post and the Boston Globe. He warned his compatriots about the rôle that President Bush Sr. was planning to allocate to the United States – to assume and finance out of their own pockets the responsibility for the developing "New World Order". People read it and laughed. The author of these texts was real estate promoter, Donald Trump…

The application of the economic model to international relations

One month after the attacks of 11 September 2001, US Secretary of Defense Donald Rumsfeld nominated his friend Admiral Arthur Cebrowski as

---

[81] *Global Inequality. A New Approach for the Age of Globalization*, Branko Milanovic, Harvard University Press, 2016

Director of the new Office of Force Transformation. He was tasked with changing the culture of the entire US military in order to enable it to respond to a complete change in its mission.

There was no longer question of using US armies to defend principles or interests, but to use them for a reorganisation of the world by dividing it into two parts – on one side the states integrated into the globalised economy, and on the other, the rest.[5][82] The Pentagon would no longer fight wars in order to steal natural resources, but to control access to those resources by the globalised nations. A division directly inspired by the process of globalisation which had already trashed half of the Western populations. This time, it was half of the world's population which was to be excluded.[6][83]

The reorganisation of the world began in the political zone known as the "Greater Middle East", that is to say stretching from Afghanistan to Morocco, with the exception of Israel, Lebanon and Jordan. This brought about the alleged epidemic of civil wars in Afghanistan, Iraq, Sudan, Libya, Syria and Yemen, which has already caused several million deaths.

The revolt of the Western populations

The revolt of the Western middle and working classes against the globalised upper class began two years ago.

Aware of the Western recession as compared with Asia, the people of the United Kingdom were the first to attempt to save its life-style by leaving the European Union and turning to China and the Commonwealth (referendum of 23 June 2016).[8][84] Unfortunately, the leaders of the United Kingdom were unable to conclude the agreement they hoped for with China and experienced great difficulty in reactivating their links with the Commonwealth.

Then, witnessing the collapse of their civil industries, a part of the United States voted, on 8 November 2016, for the only Presidential candidate who was opposed to the New World Order, Donald Trump. He spoke of a return to the "American dream". Unfortunately for his voters, although Donald Trump began to question the rules of globalised commerce, he had no team with him apart from his family, and was only able to modify, but not change, the military strategy of his country. Almost all of the general officers had adopted the Rumsfeld-Cebrowski ideology, and could no longer imagine themselves in any other role than defenders of financial globalisation.

---

[82] "The US military project for the world", Meyssan, VN, 22 Aug. 2017.

[83] It is obvious that the wars of Bush Jr. and Obama were never intended to extend democracy. First of all because by definition, democracy can only come from the People, not imposed by bombs. And then because the United States was already a plutocracy.

[84] "The new British Foreign Policy", Meyssan, VN, 4 July 2016.

Aware of the collapse of their national industry, and certain that they would be betrayed by their upper class, the Italians voted, on 4 March 2018, for an anti-system party composed of the Northern League and the 5-star Movement. These parties built an alliance in order to implement social policies. Unfortunately, they were rejected by the European Union.[9][85]

In France, tens of thousands of SME's (small and medium-sized enterprises), subcontractors of industry, had gone bankrupt over the last ten years, but their compulsory tax deductions, already among the highest in the world, increased by 30 % over the same period.

Several hundreds of thousands of French people suddenly took to the streets to demonstrate against abusive financial measures. Unfortunately for them, the French upper classes have been contaminated by the very idea that was rejected by the Americans people, and therefore did their best to adapt their policies to the popular revolt, but not to change its basic causes.

If we look at each of these four countries separately, we will find four different explanations for what is happening there. But if we analyse the situation as a single phenomenon affecting different cultures, we will discover the same mechanisms across the board. In these four countries, consecutive with the end of capitalism, the middle classes disappeared more or less rapidly, and with them the political system that they incarnated - Democracy.

So either the Western leaders abandon the financial system they have developed and return to the productive capitalism of the Cold War, or they will have to invent a different organisation that no-one has so far been able to imagine. Failing that, the West, which has directed the world for five centuries, will sink into a long period of internal chaos.

The Syrians were the first non-globalised people capable of surviving and resisting the destruction of Rumsfeld-Cebrowski's dystopia. The French were the first globalised people to rise up against the destruction of the West, even if they are not aware that they are fighting the same unique enemy of all of humanity...

Only the states which are able to re-affirm their sovereignty can hope to recover.

---

[85] Replacing the European Common Market, which was originally a system for cooperation between states, the European Union, as defined by the Treaty of Maastricht, is a supranational entity under the protection of NATO, and thus can override national decisions.